ALL ABOUT BOND FUNDS

A Complete Guide for Today's Investors

Werner Renberg

John Wiley & Sons, Inc.

New York • Chichester • Brisbane • Toronto • Singapore

To Dalia

Library of Congress Cataloging-in-Publication Data:

Renberg, Werner.
  All about bond funds: a complete guide for today's investors / Werner Renberg.
    p. cm.
  Includes index.
  ISBN 0-471-31195-2 (paper)
  1. Bond funds.   I. Title.
  HG4651.R458 1995
  332.63'27—dc20   94-40818

Printed in the United States of America

10 9 8 7 6 5 4 3 2 1

Contents

Illustrations

Acknowledgments

There are many people whose inspiration, assistance, or support I would like to acknowledge.

I would like first to express my appreciation to the large number of readers of my syndicated newspaper column whose letters reflect the challenge that many feel when seeking a suitable bond fund—or the tension that they feel when watching their fund(s) during market turbulence. Whether writing to ask advice before purchasing a fund or after a disappointing experience with an unsuitable fund that they had chosen or been sold, they convinced me of the need for this book.

Next I would like to acknowledge the cooperation of the many in the fund business, related service companies, and the federal government who took the time to discuss fund policies, fund and bond market performance, and fund regulation and legislation (both existing and proposed). I also greatly appreciate the cheerfulness with which they readily made available information whenever requested.

I am especially grateful to Lipper Analytical Services, which generously supplied the wealth of performance data that you'll find throughout the book; the U.S. Securities and Exchange Commission's Division of Investment Management, and the Investment Company Institute.

Individuals to whom I wish particularly to record my gratitude are: Alliance, Linda Finnerty, Elysa Gonzalez; American Funds, John Lawrence; Benham, Tom Rondell; Colonial, Robert Coburn; Dodge & Cox, W. Timothy

Ryan; Dreyfus, Patrice M. Kozlowski; Eaton Vance, Dick Brown; Federated, Dean Genge, J. T. Tuskan; Fidelity, Jeannette Akers, Teri M. Kilduff, Robyn S. Tice; Franklin, Holly Gibson; John Hancock, Renee Lynch; IDS, Michael Kennedy; Investment Company Institute, John P. Collins, L. Erick Kanter, Keith D. Lawson, Anne M. Schafer, Craig S. Tyle; Kemper, Eileen Davis, Steve Radis; Keystone, John M. McAllister; Lehman Brothers, Steven D. Berkley; Lexington, Lawrence Kantor; Lipper Analytical Services, Vincenzo Alomia, A. Michael Lipper, Jon Teall; Massachusetts Financial Services, John F. Reilly; Merrill Lynch, Gregg Durett, Peg Galbraith, Catherine Keary; Moody's Investors Service, John Lonski; Nicholas, Thomas J. Saeger; Oppenheimer, Bruce C. Dunbar; PIMCO, Jeff Sargent; PaineWebber, Susan L. Thomson; Pioneer, Jacqueline Collins, Anne W. Patenaude; Piper, Kimberly Kaul; T. Rowe Price, Rowena Itchon, Steven E. Norwitz; Prudential, Erin A. Lutz; Putnam, Janet E. Tosi; Salomon Brothers, Lori Laureano, Carol Sabia, Betsy Tompkins; Charles Schwab, Tom Taggart; Scudder, Darlene Bashir, Duff C. Ferguson, Karen Igler, Mary Ellen Wiedenbeck; Securities Data Co., Sandra J. Foight, Sharon J. Foight; Smith Barney, Sally Cates; Standard & Poor's, Jon M. Diat; USAA, Richard Erickson; United Funds, Ed Mason; U.S. Department of the Treasury, Peter Hollenbach; U.S. Securities and Exchange Commission, Barry Barbash, Kenneth Berman, Matthew Chambers, Gene Gohlke, John D. Heine, Robert Plaze; Vanguard, Ian A. MacKinnon, Brian S. Mattes, John S. Woerth; Wellington Management Co., Chrysa Da Costa, Beth K. Wahle; Wells Fargo, Daphne Larkin; Sam P. Allen, William T. Blase, and Paul Schofield. A special word of thanks goes to Anita Diamant, my literary agent and longtime friend, for her wise counsel.

Last, but certainly not least, I want to thank my family—my wife, Dalia; our son and daughter-in-law, Dan and Roz; our son, Gil, and my brother, Ken—for giving me their support and for tolerating the inconvenience they were caused by my work on this book.

Introduction

"Interest rates are rising. Get out of bond funds." "Interest rates are falling. Get into bond funds." "Stock funds perform the best. Forget bond funds."

Sound familiar? No doubt you have heard such comments from time to time and become bewildered when comparing bond funds with stock funds, money market funds, certificates of deposit (CDs), or other investment vehicles. You may have been especially bewildered in 1994, when bond prices—including those of safe U.S. Treasury securities—suffered their sharpest drop in years.

If you were already invested in a bond fund in 1994, you may have wondered whether you had done the right thing—and, if so, whether you had chosen one that is right for you. You may be wondering now what to consider—and how to proceed—if you want to find a different or a second one.

If you are now considering your first purchase of shares in a bond fund, you may wonder whether it would be the right thing to do in light of what happened in 1994—and, if so, how you go about choosing one that would be right for you.

In either case, this book is for you, whether you are making—and prepared to live with the results of—your own investment decisions or are more comfortable using a professional to advise you.

If you prefer to save the costs that you incur when you depend on a broker, bank, financial planner, insurance agent, or other dealer or adviser, this book will aid you in making your own selection of a suitable bond fund to help you to meet your long-range financial needs.

If you are willing to pay for advice—as much as 5% of your investment—while absorbing annual fees of 1% or more, you still should reassure yourself that a recommended fund is, and remains, suitable for someone in your situation. This book will help you to know enough to judge the appropriateness of a dealer's or adviser's recommendation—and to monitor the fund that you invest in during the years that you own it, as you should.

So that you will be clear about the scope of this book, you should be aware of the definitions of its three most common terms, as they are employed in these pages.

"Mutual funds," called open-end management investment companies in the Investment Company Act of 1940 under which the U.S. Securities and Exchange Commission regulates them, are corporations or business trusts that enable you to pool your money with other investors in professionally managed portfolios of government and/or corporate securities. They may issue unlimited numbers of shares, representing equal interests in such portfolios, and must stand ready to redeem your shares at any time.

Thus they differ from closed-end funds (or management investment companies), which may own similar portfolios but have fixed numbers of outstanding shares that are publicly traded. (In other words, when you buy a closed-end fund's shares, you buy already issued shares from another investor, not newly issued shares from the fund itself.)

I use the term "bond funds" as a catchall for mutual funds that are exclusively or primarily invested in bonds. "Bond funds" is a more specific term than "fixed income funds," which also applies to mutual funds that may be primarily invested in preferred stocks, or "income funds," which can include mutual funds that are invested in common stocks paying above-average dividends (and maybe in preferreds, too).

I use the term "bonds" as a catchall for the large variety of debt obligations—IOUs—that are (1) issued by a variety of U.S. and foreign governments and corporations and (2) scheduled to mature anywhere from 1 to 30 years or more from the day they're issued. (Those maturing in less than a year are known as money market instruments; money market funds are concentrated in them while bond and equity funds use small portions of them as cash reserves.)

With certain exceptions, bonds pay interest in fixed amounts on specified days twice a year from issuance to maturity, but their prices fluctuate over time—a lot or a little, depending on several factors, as you will see—and, therefore, their annual yields fluctuate, too. (You compute a bond's yield by dividing its yearly interest payments by its current price.)

While debt obligations may often be more properly known as debentures, notes, mortgage-backed securities, or something else, I loosely apply the term "bonds" to them all (except where the text requires precision) to keep things simple.

Of all that has been said about bond funds, two old sayings are perhaps the most noteworthy—and the most important for you to think about:

1. "Bond funds are sold, not bought."
2. "Yield sells."

Data calculated and reported by the Investment Company Institute, the fund industry's principal trade association, show that a high percentage of bond fund shares is owned by investors who bought them from brokers or other members of a sales force—and, thus, incurred sales charges—instead of buying them directly from funds that impose no charges or "loads."

If you're among them, have you acted rationally? A sales charge of 5%, which you may find acceptable when you buy a superior equity fund that you would not have found by yourself, offsets more than the first year's dividends of a taxable bond fund that yields 5%. After income tax—even at the lowest rate—you would be still worse off.

Even a 3% sales charge, a so-called "low load" that would offset more than one-half of a pretax 5% yield, is unnecessary when you can buy fine funds without paying any charge at all. This book will show you how to find suitable "no-load" funds (and how to regard load funds that are available to you on a no-load basis in your company's savings or retirement plan).

Although it is common for fund sales forces and investors to focus on bond funds' yields—especially when comparing funds with bank, savings & loan, or credit union accounts or CDs whose yields are constant because their principal and interest rates are constant—it is not enough and can be misleading.

The portfolio manager of a bond fund—especially one whose sponsor believes that it's easier to sell to you if its yield seems high to you—may reach for a higher yield by following investment practices that involve greater risks than you can afford. Such practices could expose you to greater erosion of principal than you would—and should—expect.

While a fund's yield, properly calculated, is not unimportant, total return is a more important measure of its performance and a more meaningful yardstick for comparing it with the performance of other funds.

Defined simply as the rate at which the value of an investment grows—assuming the reinvestment of income and capital gains distributions—total return is the one measure for you to focus on, whether you are searching for a fund on your own or weighing the advice that an investment adviser or salesperson has given you. This book will discuss both yields and total returns.

Monthly or quarterly income payments, to be sure, may be a major reason for investing in a bond fund but not the only reason. As I'll illustrate, you also may wish to consider a bond fund to reduce the risk level of a growth-oriented portfolio consisting of equity funds (and individual stocks, if any).

Except for periods when interest rates decline, whose beginnings can never be precisely forecast and whose endings always come too soon, you don't invest in a bond fund for capital appreciation and inflation protection. You look to equity funds (and/or individual stocks) for that.

Although no one knows where interest rates will be at any given time in the future—a reality that doesn't inhibit those who make or quote forecasts—it is reasonably certain that bond funds offer less opportunity for significant appreciation at rates that have prevailed in the mid-1990s than they did in the 1980s, when rates were twice as high.

At the same time, of course, there is the possibility of major capital losses in bonds—and, thus, in bond funds—if interest rates should rise substantially, as they did in 1994. This could occur again if inflation really becomes severe once more—an always present danger but one that, happily, seemed remote as this book went to press.

Since you have to take care of your future financial needs without knowing what inflation and interest rates—and other variables—the future will bring, you do the best you can under the circumstances.

This means determining your probable future financial needs—for a comfortable retirement, supplemental preretirement income, college education, down payment for a house, and/or other objective(s)—the amounts of money that you can put to work in a lump sum and/or at regular intervals, and the degree of investment risk that you are able and willing to assume, if necessary. (As you may suspect, a "suitable" fund is one that won't invest in longer maturities or lower credit quality than you can tolerate. It's also one that you plan to own long enough to ride out short-term fluctuations.)

As you contemplate the different savings and investment vehicles that are available to you—and, indeed, may already have committed money to—bond funds may emerge as one of the options that appear to make sense. This book will help to clarify whether any bond fund would be appropriate and, if so, how to proceed with fund selection and monitoring.

Chapter 1 reviews the extraordinary growth and development of bond funds from a tiny financial services sector, overshadowed by equity funds, into the major factor that they became in a relatively short time.

To help you to understand their differences, Chapter 2 describes the various types of securities in which bond funds are invested to achieve their investment objectives. It touches on both their potential for income and relative safety.

Chapter 3 describes the different types of bond funds that are available to you and the major aspects of investment policies and practices that their managers pursue, including the risks that are associated with them.

Chapters 4, 5, and 6 describe how bond funds have performed and why they have performed as they have. Chapter 4 gives you some overall comments, as well as pointers about what to look for as you study bond funds' performance data. Chapter 5 shows you how the leading funds in each category of taxable bond funds have performed in recent years—and discusses why. Chapter 6 does the same for each category of tax-exempt bond funds.

Among other things, you will see the varying impact on performance of high versus low annual fund expenses and of higher versus lower risk levels that characterize fund portfolios.

Past performance doesn't guarantee future results—whether good or bad. But if you understand why a fund performed as it did in the context of past bond market conditions, you should be better able to reckon how it might perform under similar conditions in the future.

Chapter 7 gives you pointers to consider in deciding whether any bond fund would serve your requirements.

If the answer is "yes," Chapter 8 will show you how to select one or more bond funds that would probably be suitable for you.

Chapter 9 goes into the mechanics of the investment process, including what you need to know to get started, and offers suggestions for managing your investments, including what you need to know to monitor your bond fund(s) to help you to determine if it (they) perform(s) as expected or if switching is in order.

Following these chapters, you will find a glossary of terms and an appendix of the phone numbers of fund complexes offering bond funds that have been in operation at least five years.

I've also provided the addresses of the SEC, in case you have a complaint about a fund, and of the National Association of Securities Dealers, in case you have a complaint about the sales practices of the firm or individual who sold you fund shares. I hope you never need to use either one.

Werner Renberg
Chappaqua, New York

CHAPTER 1

The Rise of Bond Funds

Bond funds, which constitute about one-third of the mutual fund business, are, for the most part, very young.

In 1958, as many as 34 years after the equity fund Massachusetts Investors Trust (MIT) became the first mutual fund to offer shares to the public, no more than 13 of 189 mutual funds registered with the Securities and Exchange Commission (SEC) were identified as bond and preferred stock funds.* (No separate data were reported for bond funds alone.)

When the Investment Company Institute (ICI) established a category for bond funds for statistical purposes in 1975, it counted only 35 corporate bond funds among 104 "bond and income funds," a broad grouping that includes funds that also may be significantly invested in government bonds, preferred, and high-dividend common stocks. The bond and income funds were a small fraction of the total of 390 mutual funds then in operation. Their total net assets of $9.8 billion were less than one-third of those of equity funds.

By 1985, however, there were 492 bond and income funds, and their assets totaled $134.8 billion—greater than those of equity funds and equivalent to the assets that the ICI had calculated for the entire industry only five years earlier.

By the end of 1992, there were 1,629 bond and income funds. Their net assets—owned in 23.4 million accounts—totaled $577.3 billion, overtaking

*"A Study of Mutual Funds," Wharton School of Finance and Commerce, University of Pennsylvania, 1962—the first comprehensive, SEC-commissioned study of the industry since one preceding passage of the Investment Company Act of 1940.

1

money market mutual funds' $546.2 billion to make them the industry's dominant sector. Equity funds were third in net assets at $522.8 billion.

After maintaining their lead in 1993—gaining $183.8 billion in assets as a favorable bond market attracted another 6.3 million accounts and inspired the creation of another 394 rivals—bond and income funds were overtaken by equity funds in 1994. The year's fall in the bond market, a drop in share sales, and an increase in redemptions pulled down bond and income fund assets to $685.7 billion from $761.1 billion at the end of 1993. Strong sales of equity fund shares in the face of a disappointing stock market, on the other hand, led to an increase in their assets from $749.0 billion at the end of 1993 to $867.4 billion at the end of 1994.

As you can see in Table 1.1, the phenomenal growth of assets that bond and income funds recorded in the 20 years ended in 1994 was due primarily to net sales of shares—that is, to investors, in the aggregate, buying more shares (including their reinvestment of dividends and capital gains distributions) than they redeemed. Until the 1990s, capital appreciation, in the aggregate, was not a major contributor.

While many factors combined to generate the sudden, vigorous growth of bond funds in the 1980s and its continuation in the 1990s, several stand out:

1. The introduction of millions of people to mutual funds—and mutual fund families—through investment in money market mutual funds and their apparent satisfaction with the performance, services, and convenience provided by mutual fund organizations, which led them to try bond (and equity) funds for longer-term investments. Especially striking has been the widespread acceptance of the concept of doing business with people you never see, by toll-free telephone calls and mail, at (no-load) fund complexes in distant cities.

2. The recognition by many that they must rely more on themselves (and less on employers or government) to provide for their expected long-term financial needs and, subsequently, their growing awareness of the potential role that bond (and equity) funds can play in their plans in addition to—or instead of—individual securities.

3. The appeal of high interest rates—higher than yields offered by federally insured savings accounts or CDs—and the subsequent expectation of appreciation as rates declined over a long stretch.

4. The extraordinary growth in the volume and variety of debt securities issued by governments and corporations.

5. Changes in the Internal Revenue Code, including (a) provisions that enabled municipal bond funds to pay federally tax-exempt dividends to their shareholders and (b) increases in federal income tax rates that persuaded growing numbers of investors to buy them.

Table 1.1 How Bond and Income Funds Have Grown through Net Share Sales and Capital Appreciation, 1975–1994 (in billions)

Year	Sales*	Redemptions*	Net Sales (Redemptions)	Capital Appreciation (Depreciation)	End-of-Year Net Assets
1975	$1.0	$(0.7)	$0.3	$1.7	$9.8
1976	1.9	(1.4)	0.5	3.0	13.3
1977	3.8	(1.8)	2.0	(0.3)	15.0
1978	4.0	(2.6)	1.4	(0.4)	16.0
1979	3.9	(2.8)	1.1	(0.5)	16.5
1980	4.6	(3.0)	1.6	(0.7)	17.4
1981	4.0	(2.7)	1.2	(1.8)	16.8
1982	7.7	(2.7)	5.0	4.5	26.3
1983	18.2	(5.7)	12.4	1.0	39.7
1984	30.5	(14.5)	16.0	(1.7)	54.0
1985	93.5	(23.2)	70.4	10.4	134.8
1986	179.9	(61.3)	118.6	9.2	262.6
1987	150.7	(125.9)	24.8	(14.3)	273.1
1988	90.5	(84.7)	5.8	(1.4)	277.5
1989	96.1	(79.7)	16.4	10.9	304.8
1990	103.3	(80.6)	22.7	(4.8)	322.7
1991	174.6	(90.6)	84.1	34.6	441.4
1992	271.5	(156.4)	115.0	20.9	577.3
1993	346.9	(207.4)	139.6	44.2	761.1
1994	267.9	(285.2)	(17.2)	(58.2)	685.7

*Includes exchanges into and out of funds within fund families.
Note: Sales include reinvested dividend distributions. Totals may not add due to rounding.
Source: Investment Company Institute

6. More opportunities to invest in mutual funds through tax-deferred retirement plans, including annual or lump-sum contributions to individual retirement accounts (IRAs) and regular contributions—often partially matched by employers—to defined contributions plans offered by companies under Section 401(k) of the tax code. (A step in the opposite direction: the 1986 elimination, by President Ronald

Reagan and Congress, of deductibility for annual IRA contributions for many employees covered by pension plans.)

7. Increases in the number and types of financial institutions that sponsor or sell mutual funds and compete intensely for investors' money through vigorous promotion and financial incentives to sales people, securities dealers, and others in the distribution chain.

8. Increased attention given to mutual funds by print and electronic media, as manifested in the numbers of personal finance books, the space given in newspapers and magazines, the time devoted on television and radio, and the proliferation of financial newsletters specializing in funds.

Given the widespread ownership of bond funds in the mid-1990s, it may be hard to understand why it took such funds so long to become a major sector in financial services and attract a large following.

Well, why *was* this so?

The Early Years: Little Interest in Bonds

When the first few open-end investment companies were conceived following MIT's debut in 1924, common stocks were the rage. Those who wanted to share in the nation's growth bought them with enthusiasm, both directly and indirectly through investment vehicles known collectively as investment trusts, most of which were the closed-end variety. As waves of buying drove share prices higher, people became dazzled by their "paper profits" and bought more shares.

For many, these were the first purchases of securities since they bought Liberty Bonds to help the government to finance military outlays for World War I. Those purchases had been largely motivated by patriotism, not the desire to achieve investment goals through the deliberate purchase of specific bonds. They did not lead to a large demand for debt securities generally.

While many were enticed by visions of huge capital gains to be made in stocks, the prospects of income from high- or medium-quality corporate bonds, yielding from around 4.5% to 7% or so, appealed to only a relatively few conservative individuals and to institutions. U.S. government bonds evoked even less interest. They were yielding less than 4% and, anyway, their supply was contracting as surpluses enabled the Treasury to reduce the federal debt.

Those who had looked to stocks for current income, of course, had a different view of bond yields. Take, for example, the new Norfolk Investment Corporation, predecessor of today's Scudder Income Fund (and the first no-load mutual fund). Norfolk wanted to pay its shareholders a dividend of around

4%, but, as stock prices soared, had increasing difficulty finding desirable stocks with adequate yields.

". . . were it not for the high return derived from fixed-income-bearing securities," President F. Haven Clark said in his December 31, 1928, report to shareholders on the fund's first half year, "the present dividend would hardly have been earned."

The problem Clark referred to—of finding stock yields below bond yields—is a familiar one for those who wish to invest for current income but prefer to use high-dividend-paying stocks as the primary means toward that objective.

Given that stocks are generally riskier than bonds and that, therefore, high-grade stocks are riskier than high-grade bonds, it should follow that they would offer higher yields to compensate. In the mid-1920s, that had been the case (Table 1.2). But stock market speculation inverted this relationship toward the end of the decade; in 1929, when stocks hit their cyclical peak, average yields of triple-A bonds were 4.83%—more than 1% higher than stocks' 3.48%.

As the stock-buying frenzy continued, feeding on proclamations such as Irving Fisher's of mid-October 1929 that stock prices "have reached what looks like a permanently higher plateau," some investors became cautious.

In his 1929 annual report, Clark would report to his shareholders that his fund had become one-half invested in bonds and call money (loans to brokers) prior to the Great Crash. "Until October 1929," he wrote, "the bonds and call money held in this fund appeared to be purely negative investments and even a drag on its progress. Since that time, however, the advantage of stabilizing types of securities is more evident." Having served their purpose, a large portion of the bonds were sold to enable the fund to pick up stocks at bargain prices.

A similar strategy was followed by Walter L. Morgan, a young Philadelphia investment adviser who founded Wellington Management Company and had recently started a mutual fund, Industrial and Power Securities Company, predecessor of today's Vanguard/Wellington Fund.

About 75% invested in stocks when it began operations on July 1, 1929, the fund halved its stock holdings by the end of the year. By then, most of its assets were in cash and cash equivalents (37%), bonds (9%), and preferred stocks (16%), enabling Morgan to report to shareholders that the fund was off 8% from the year's peak in comparison with 60% for other investment trusts.

The Birth of Balanced Funds

". . . we came to a conservative and common sense conclusion in an era of speculation: that the prices stocks commanded were just 'not in the wood';

Table 1.2   Comparison of Bond and Stock Yields, 1924–1973

Year	Bond Yields	Stock Yields
1924	5.00%	5.87%
1925	4.88	5.19
1926	4.73	5.32
1927	4.57	4.77
1928	4.55	3.98
1929	4.83	3.48
1930	4.55	4.26
1931	4.58	5.58
1932	5.01	6.69
1933	4.49	4.05
1934	4.00	3.72
1935	3.60	3.82
1936	3.24	3.44
1937	3.26	4.86
1938	3.19	5.18
1939	3.01	4.05
1940	2.84	5.59
1941	2.77	6.82
1942	2.83	7.24
1943	2.73	4.93
1944	2.72	4.86
1945	2.62	4.17
1946	2.53	3.85
1947	2.61	4.93
1948	2.82	5.54
1949	2.66	6.59
1950	2.62	6.57
1951	2.86	6.13
1952	2.96	5.80
1953	3.20	5.80
1954	2.90	4.95
1955	3.06	4.08
1956	3.36	4.09
1957	3.89	4.35
1958	3.79	3.97
1959	4.38	3.23

Table 1.2 *Continued*

Year	Bond Yields	Stock Yields
1960	4.41	3.47
1961	4.35	2.98
1962	4.33	3.37
1963	4.26	3.17
1964	4.40	3.01
1965	4.49	3.00
1966	5.13	3.40
1967	5.51	3.20
1968	6.18	3.07
1969	7.03	3.24
1970	8.04	3.83
1971	7.39	3.14
1972	7.21	2.84
1973	7.44	3.06

Sources: Aaa corporate bond yields, Moody's Investors Service; common stock yields, 1924–33, Cowles Commission; 1934–73, Standard & Poor's Corporation

. . . (that) we should have 'an anchor to windward' in the form of a large position in fixed-income securities such as bonds and preferred stocks," he wrote in a 1964 book.* "By this conservative investment decision, what came to be known as the 'balanced fund' concept was born."

"Not many were buying bonds then," Morgan recalled when I interviewed him a few years ago, "but balance worked, and it still works. When National City Bank and others were selling at sixty times earnings, it just didn't make sense to have everything in stocks. It still doesn't."

The balanced fund concept spread gradually as stocks continued their plunge to the low of 1932, lifting the year's average stock yield to 6.69%. From Boston, where the forerunner of today's EV Traditional Investors Fund was established, to San Francisco, where new investment advisory firms started what are now American Balanced Fund and Dodge & Cox Balanced Fund, the aim of holding cash equivalents, bonds, and/or preferred stocks was essentially the same: to provide shareholders some protection against the risks inherent in common stocks.

For general equity mutual funds, it was, of course, difficult to find silver linings in the gray clouds—in part because of concerns about corporations' ability to sustain dividend payments.

Although hard hit, they generally survived in better shape, however, than the large number of closed-end funds, which had flourished in the 1920s.

Main Street Comes to Wall Street (Random House)

Many, having been highly leveraged, failed; after they paid off debt incurred to buy stocks, little or nothing was left for shareholders when stock prices slumped. Since closed-end funds' shares had been selling at prices above their net asset value (NAV), they dropped more than prices of mutual funds, which sell at NAV or NAV plus a sales charge; they fell from premiums above NAV to discounts below.

With the Depression approaching its trough in 1932—unemployment was close to 25% of the labor force and consumer prices were *falling*—eight series were introduced by Keystone Custodian Funds offering investors portfolios that were divided into classes of bonds and stocks from which they could choose to meet individual investment goals: "High-grade Bonds," "Business Men's Bonds," "Convertible Bonds," "Semi-speculative Bonds," "Speculative Bonds," "Liberty-Bonds—Common Stocks," "Common Stocks," and "Low-Priced Stocks."

The investment vehicles offered in the Keystone Plan were 10-year fixed-investment trusts in which investors bought certificates of participation. They were not mutual funds, but, like mutual funds, they could be redeemed at any time. For each of the series, fixed lists of securities were chosen; the money invested in each was divided equally among its portfolio's bonds or stocks.

The First Bond Funds

In 1935, seven years before the trusts were to terminate, the Keystone organization replaced them with mutual funds having similar investment objectives, including four that (as far as can be determined) were the first bond mutual funds: B-1, invested in high- and medium-grade bonds; B-2, invested in a broad spectrum of bonds selling at a slight discount; B-3, invested in lower-priced bonds, and B-4, invested in high-yield bonds. B-4, concentrated in bonds of corporations being reorganized, seems to have been the first high-yield (or "junk") bond fund. (B-3 was merged into B-4 in 1966.)

As yields of high-grade bonds fell and remained below 3% while stock yields were relatively attractive, the new funds formed during the rest of the 1930s were essentially all balanced or equity funds. For anyone seeking to earn high current income, there was little incentive to invest in a bond fund—and, thus, little incentive for anyone to sponsor one. As things turned out, it was the beginning of a 24-year period, ending in 1958, in which high-grade bond yields would lag behind high-grade stock yields (as Table 1.2 shows) for a variety of reasons.

For both investors and the financial community, an issue even more important than either bond or stock yields (beyond, of course, the nation's economic recovery and the distant sounds of war drums in Europe and Asia) had become paramount: the basic honesty of the fund business.

After passing the Securities Act of 1933 "To provide full and fair disclosure of the character of securities sold . . . and to prevent frauds in the sale thereof," and the Securities Exchange Act of 1934 "to provide for the regulation of securities exchanges and of over-the-counter markets . . . (and) to prevent inequitable and unfair practices on such exchanges and markets," Congress in 1935 turned its attention to funds.

Concerned about dishonest practices in the investment trust/company segment of the financial services industry, it directed the SEC, which had been established in the 1934 act, to study investment trusts and investment companies and to recommend reforms.

Eventually, the SEC study's recommendations were embodied in a bill, and hearings were held that brought out not only the self-enriching practices of some unscrupulous fund promoters but also the public disagreements within the industry as to what to do about them. Following the hearings, Congress encouraged representatives of the investment company industry and the SEC to reconcile their differences. The result: substitute legislation introduced in both houses in June 1940. Called the Investment Company Act of 1940, it was passed and signed by President Franklin D. Roosevelt within two months.

In providing for the registration and comprehensive regulation of open-end investment companies, or mutual funds, the act gave investors justifiable confidence that they would be protected against fraud—but not against market fluctuations. It required funds to disclose essential information in prospectuses and periodic reports, giving shareholders what they needed to know about fund policies, management, and so on—if only they would take the time to read.

Through the 1940s, 1950s, and 1960s—through World War II and the Korean War, booms and recessions—stock funds dominated the industry. Years of economic expansion, albeit interrupted occasionally, strengthened corporate earnings as well as personal income, providing a powerful stimulus to the stock market. The Dow Jones Industrial Average, which ended 1940 at 131.13 and 1949 at 200.13, soared to 679.36 by the end of 1959 and ended 1969, with the economy at a cyclical peak, at 800.36 after coming close to 1000 on several occasions during the latter half of the decade.

Except for the war and early postwar years, most of the period from 1940 to 1965 was characterized by low interest rates, due at first to the Federal Reserve's wartime support of Treasury securities and, following the Fed-Treasury accord of 1951, to low inflation. Bond funds held little appeal.

With few exceptions, people were usually able to earn "real" interest—that is, interest above the inflation rate, which was below 2% for most of the period—by putting money into ordinary savings accounts at banks or savings institutions. A ceiling on the rate that commercial bank savings accounts could pay, set at 2.5% since 1935, was even permitted to creep up to 4% by 1964. As long as Treasury bill rates were kept artificially low, investors had little incentive to buy them, and the Fed became, by far, their largest holder.

For long-term investors, U.S. government issues also had limited attraction—whether nonmarketable savings bonds bearing a 2.9% yield or marketable securities. High-quality corporate bonds became more attractive as their yields passed those of quality stocks in 1959, but the annual volumes of new corporate issues remained low. State and local governments did issue new debt at a moderately increasing rate, but, among individual investors, these were of interest primarily to those in upper income tax brackets.

Given the environment in the corporate and U.S. Treasury securities markets, it's not surprising that bond funds—and the total bond holdings of all mutual funds combined—showed slow growth in the 25 years following passage of the 1940 act.

Nor did state and local government (or municipal) bonds offer an opportunity for faster growth because shareholders of mutual funds organized as corporations or business trusts, unlike those of funds organized as partnerships, would have had to pay federal income tax on any interest received. (During the Eisenhower administration, fund organizations asked members of Congress to pass legislation permitting the pass-through of the exemption and, as a consequence, the creation of tax-exempt municipal bond mutual funds that took the corporate or trust form. Bills were introduced but got nowhere.)

The Search for More Income

Under the circumstances, the search for high current income led mostly to the continuing growth of balanced funds and stock funds concentrating in high-yield stocks, as well as to the formation of new ones. Only a few bond funds were organized.

One mutual fund sponsor, Shareholders Management Company, took a different approach in 1963, when it changed the investment policy of the seven-year-old Kerr Income Fund to concentrate in securities convertible into common stock and changed its name to Convertible Securities Fund. It expected, thereby, to offer the prospects of both income and capital appreciation. Under the management of American Capital Asset Management since 1975, the fund is now called American Capital Harbor Fund.

Another approach taken by fund sponsors to produce income for shareholders was to invest in bonds of lower quality. According to the SEC-commissioned Wharton study of mutual fund practices during the 1952–58 period, U.S. corporate bonds accounted for 63% of the $191 million in assets of the thirteen bond and preferred stock funds in existence as of September 1958. Even more interesting was the finding that these funds had more than eight times as much invested in corporates *below* investment grade as in those that were investment grade. (State and local government bonds accounted for only 2%, and U.S. government securities, a mere 1%.)

When inflationary pressures intensified with the escalation of the Vietnam War in 1965 and the Federal Reserve pursued a more restrictive monetary policy to offset fiscal easing, interest rates began to climb significantly. Of the few announcements of new bond funds during this period, surely the most portentous was one in 1969 by Federated Investors, a Pittsburgh investment management firm. It was starting a fund whose objective would be to generate income through investment in, of all things, securities issued or guaranteed by the U.S. government!

Organized a year after Congress made the Federal National Mortgage Association (Fannie Mae) a private corporation and created the Government National Mortgage Association (Ginnie Mae) and a year before it created the Federal Home Loan Mortgage Corporation (Freddie Mac), the Fund for U.S. Government Securities thus started a major trend. It was the first of many funds that would be concentrated in federally backed pools of mortgage-backed securities, which in the 1980s were to become immensely popular among investors.

An Environment Favorable to Funds' Growth

While the 1970s were marked by extraordinary events whose impact permeated the world of finance as they dominated our lives—two oil price "shocks," searing inflation, unprecedented interest rates, the resignation of an American president—three additional developments supplied boosts to mutual funds in general and to bond funds in particular.

It was in the high interest rates resulting from the inflationary pressures that rose in the late 1960s, and became almost uncontrolled in the 1970s (as Table 1.3 indicates), that bond funds at last found an environment favorable to their growth.

Notwithstanding the axiom that high inflation makes bonds poor investments because it gnaws the purchasing power of both principal and interest payments, investors increasingly perceived bond funds as vehicles permitting them to earn high rates for a time—even if bond funds usually can't be used to "lock in" high rates. Some, no doubt, calculated that, sooner or later, inflation and interest rates would recede again, causing bond—and bond fund—prices to appreciate.

Fund promoters, ever the resourceful type, perceived what investors were perceiving and created a large number of new bond funds, starting primarily with those invested in high- and medium-quality corporate issues. Subsequently, when interest rates dropped a bit (temporarily, as it turned out), they launched funds concentrated in lower-quality, or "junk," bonds to capture their higher yields—albeit, at greater risk.

Stock prices, buffeted by the tight monetary policy used to combat inflation and by two recessions' impact on corporate profits, were extremely

Table 1.3 *Short–Term Interest Rates Versus Inflation,*
1965–1994

Year	December-to-December Changes in Consumer Price Index	Three-month Treasury Bill Yields*	Ceilings on Commercial Bank Savings Deposits**	Taxable Money Market Fund Twelve-Month Yields
1965	1.9%	4.04%	4.0%	
1966	3.5	4.98	4.0	
1967	3.0	4.41	4.0	
1968	4.7	5.48	4.0	
1969	6.2	6.87	4.0	
1970	5.6	6.58	4.5	
1971	3.3	4.44	4.5	NA
1972	3.4	4.17	4.5	NA
1973	8.7	7.26	5.0	NA
1974	12.3	8.10	5.0	NA
1975	6.9	5.94	5.0	6.36%
1976	4.9	5.11	5.0	5.29
1977	6.7	5.42	5.0	4.98
1978	9.0	7.22	5.0	7.22
1979	13.3	10.48	5.25	11.08
1980	12.5	11.96	5.25	12.78
1981	8.9	14.75	5.25	16.82
1982	3.8	11.09	5.25	12.23
1983	3.8	8.95	5.25	8.58
1984	3.9	9.92	5.5	10.04
1985	3.8	7.72	5.5	7.71
1986	1.1	6.15	***	6.26
1987	4.4	5.96		6.12
1988	4.4	6.89		7.11
1989	4.6	8.39		8.87
1990	6.1	7.75		7.82
1991	3.1	5.54		5.71
1992	2.9	3.51		3.36
1993	2.8	3.07		2.70
1994	2.7	4.37		3.75

*Annual averages
**In effect since 1933. Rates are for shortest maturities.
***Ceilings were removed April 1, 1986, pursuant to decontrol legislation enacted in 1980.
NA = Not available

Sources: U.S. Bureau of Labor Statistics, U.S. Department of the Treasury, Board of Governors of the Federal Reserve System, *IBC/Donoghue's Money Fund Directory*

volatile but went nowhere during the 1970s. The decade ended with the Dow Jones Industrial Average at 838.74—essentially where it had been at the beginning. It had managed to rise above 1000 for two periods only to fall again. Given that stocks, on the average, did not protect investors from inflation in the short run and that many investors were unwilling or unable to await better times, stock funds suffered net *redemptions* of $10.4 billion during the decade—only about half offset by capital appreciation.

Bond and income funds, on the other hand, enjoyed net *sales* of $5 billion, resulting in a 50% increase in their net assets as existing funds grew and the host of new ones were started.

In retrospect, it was modest growth for bond funds, but it was growth. It laid the foundation for future expansion, led by investment management firms such as Dreyfus, Fidelity, Franklin Resources, Massachusetts Financial Services (whose MIT had started it all 50 years earlier), T. Rowe Price, and Vanguard, and by large brokerage firms such as Merrill Lynch, which were emerging as mutual fund promoters.

Of the three major developments that stimulated the bond fund sector in the 1970s, the first was the conception of the money market mutual fund, introduced in late 1971 by the Reserve Fund. As the federal government's ceilings on the interest that savings accounts could pay were held *below* increases in the consumer price index (Table 1.3), people's savings were losing purchasing power.

Even 3-month U.S. Treasury bills ("T-bills"), whose yields were free to move to reflect conditions in the short-term, or money, market, did not keep investors whole at times. And when they did, most individuals eager to earn a real rate of interest on their savings did not have the minimum of $10,000 that it took to buy one.

The money market fund, therefore, was an investment vehicle whose time had come. Once the SEC was satisfied that the concept would work in a way that complied with the 1940 act and its regulations, the Reserve Fund's registration statement was declared effective, and its shares could be offered to the public.

The concept was a simple one: A fund would invest in high-grade debt instruments of short maturities—such as T-bills, corporations' commercial paper, and bankers' acceptances—and would be managed so that its portfolio would maintain a net asset value (NAV) per share at a constant $1.* Its principal, in other words, would be stable while its yield would fluctuate, as would its average maturity (within limits). The principal would be assured by the creditworthiness of the financial and nonfinancial corporations whose paper the fund held and by the full faith and credit of the U.S. Treasury in the case

---

*SEC regulations require, among other things, that a fund calling itself a money market fund can't invest in any security maturing in more than 397 days or have a portfolio with a dollar-weighted average maturity of more than 90 days.

of T-bills. But it would *not* be insured by the Federal Deposit Insurance Corporation (FDIC), as bank deposits are.

To attract investors, money market mutual funds offered low minimums for initial and subsequent investments, free check writing above certain amounts, and other conveniences. More important, they provided all investors—including those of modest means—access to money market interest rates that would better protect their short-term savings against inflation than savings accounts on which banks could pay only what the government permitted them to (as Table 1.3 shows). To the extent that their portfolios were invested in securities paying more—and involving more risk—than Treasury issues, their yields could exceed those of T-bills even after payment of low fund management fees.

Investors' response was enthusiastic—despite the lack of FDIC insurance. By the end of the 1970s, when inflation became much worse, money market mutual funds had become an accepted financial institution whose considerable advantages could really be appreciated. By 1980, their total assets *exceeded* those of stock and bond funds combined, a lead they enjoyed for five years.

Money market fund sponsors had to be pleased with these results; more money under their management meant more fee income for them. Moreover, they expected—correctly—that some of the new billions of dollars brought into their organizations would ultimately be moved into stock or bond funds—for whose management they charged higher fees—if and when investors were so inclined. (If and when investors redeemed stock and bond fund shares, they were expected—also correctly—to move at least some of the money into money market funds, thus maintaining the levels of assets in the companies' care.)

The next important development for mutual funds was the creation of individual retirement accounts (IRAs). Proposed by President Richard M. Nixon in a pension message to Congress one month after his re-election in 1972, they were not embodied in law until the Employee Retirement Income Security Act (ERISA) of 1974 was passed and signed by his successor, President Gerald Ford, after Nixon had resigned.

Nixon's proposal, in essence, was to encourage workers to save more toward their retirement. To induce them to supplement their expected retirement income, he proposed establishment of accounts that employees would fund with tax-deductible annual contributions. As passed, ERISA limited eligibility to those not covered by employers' pension plans, but it did enable them to "roll over" tax-free into IRAs any lump sums they received on retirement from qualified employers' plans.

Effective in 1975, IRAs were immediately a success. In the first year, according to the Internal Revenue Service (IRS), 1.2 million of 82.2 million income tax returns reported deductions for IRAs of $1.4 billion. By 1980, 2.6 million of 93.9 million returns reported deductions of $3.4 billion.

This was only the beginning. In the Economic Recovery Tax Act of 1981 (ERTA), President Reagan and Congress extended eligibility for IRAs to all workers and raised the deductible annual contribution from $1,500 to $2,000, effective 1982. In the first year of liberalization, 12 million tax returns (out of 95.3 million filed) showed contributions to IRAs of $28.3 billion. And a good chunk of the money was going into mutual funds: By the end of 1982, employees had 1.9 million IRA accounts in funds, with assets totaling $5.7 billion, according to ICI.

And even though President Reagan and Congress reversed themselves in 1986, depriving many workers covered by pension plans of the opportunity to make deductible IRA contributions, IRAs have continued to grow through annual deductible and nondeductible contributions and through rollovers of lump sums from company plans as people retired (including many who were forced to take early retirement).

By the end of 1993, mutual funds held $284 billion, or 33%, of all IRA assets in 29.3 million accounts. Over 32% of the mutual fund share was in 6.8 million bond and income fund accounts.

The third development, also emanating from Washington, was the provision in the Tax Reform Act of 1976 that at last permitted mutual funds organized as corporations or trusts to pass through to their shareholders the federal tax exemption accorded interest on municipal bonds.

Faster than you could say "tax-free income," a score or more of mutual fund groups were ready to file registration statements for their entries with the SEC. Having waited for this day since the Eisenhower administration 20 years earlier and having lobbied for this provision during this session of Congress, they were ready to do business as soon as the act became law with President Ford's signature on October 4.

Federally tax-exempt municipal bond funds promised to do for average investors what taxable stock, bond, and money market funds had done for them: provide them diversification, professional management, and convenience. They also brought within reach of many the tax-exempt interest that had been available only to those who invested in funds organized as limited partnerships or in less flexible unit investment trusts—or to those who bought individual tax-exempt securities but may not have been able to afford enough bonds to be adequately diversified.

It would be three more years before federally tax-exempt interest also would be available in municipal money market mutual funds, offering shareholders everything that taxable money market funds had, including the right to write checks on their accounts, and tax-exempt interest besides. Instead of taxable T-bills and short-term instruments of corporations, they would invest in municipal notes, tax-exempt commercial paper, or bonds that would soon mature.

As the 1980s dawned, the mutual fund industry had the organization, the variety of investment vehicles, favorable federal legislation, and the growing confidence of its shareholders in its honesty and reliability—and in its regulation by the SEC. All that the industry—and the nation—needed was a more favorable economic environment: healthy growth with stable prices instead of the third recession in a decade and even higher inflation than experienced in the 1970s.

That was soon to come—probably sooner than most people imagined amid the gloom. After the nation had gone through the agony of *another* recession in 1981–82 and the Fed at last had pushed the inflation rate down from double-digit rates to below 6%, an environment favorable to economic growth and to investment in financial assets was in place.

The Great Bull Market of the 1980s

People could invest in stocks and bonds, as well as in funds that invest in them, with the expectation of receiving a satisfactory *real* return.

The realization sank in slowly at first, but then it spread, igniting rallies in securities prices in August 1982 that spawned the great bull market of the 1980s—and the explosive growth of stock and bond funds.

To a large extent, the growth of stock and bond funds was attributable to common factors: the disposable personal income that people had available for investment as the economy grew, their increasing inclination to own interests in professionally managed portfolios instead of individual securities, the availability and growing popularity of IRAs (and other retirement plans), and the accumulation of balances in money market accounts that could easily be moved to earn higher returns.

Nor can one ignore the contagion of the bull market, becoming more infectious as prices soared, or the persuasiveness of the fund industry's marketing efforts—whether the pushing of shares by legions of salespeople representing funds with high sales loads or the advertising and promotion of no- or low-load funds.

For bond funds, the strongest appeal was, of course, the yields they could offer. Funds invested in Treasury or high-quality corporate securities, which yielded 13% to 14% or more (Table 1.4), could provide nearly as generous income after expenses while exposing investors to acceptable risk of loss. With inflation running around 4%, hard-to-believe real returns of around 10% could be achieved.

And as yields drifted lower, reflecting growing confidence that inflation had been brought under control, bond prices appreciated, enabling bond funds to chalk up impressive total returns. In 1982 alone, according to Lehman Brothers, the total returns of government bonds averaged nearly 30% and of high-quality corporates, nearly 40%.

While total returns of quality issues dropped below 10% in 1983 as bond prices slipped a bit, they returned to 15% or more in ensuing years until 1987.

Table 1.4 *Bond and Stock Yields: A Comparison, 1975–1994*

Year	U.S. Treasury Ten-Year Constant Maturities	Moody's Aaa Corporate Bonds	Moody's Baa Corporate Bonds	Standard & Poor's 500 Stock Index
1975	7.99%	8.83%	10.61%	4.31%
1976	7.61	8.43	9.75	3.77
1977	7.42	8.02	8.97	4.62
1978	8.41	8.73	9.49	5.28
1979	9.44	9.63	10.69	5.47
1980	11.46	11.94	13.67	5.26
1981	13.91	14.17	16.04	5.20
1982	13.00	13.79	16.11	5.81
1983	11.10	12.04	13.55	4.40
1984	12.44	12.71	14.19	4.64
1985	10.62	11.37	12.72	4.25
1986	7.68	9.02	10.39	3.49
1987	8.39	9.38	10.58	3.08
1988	8.85	9.71	10.83	3.64
1989	8.49	9.26	10.18	3.45
1990	8.55	9.32	10.36	3.61
1991	7.86	8.77	9.80	3.24
1992	7.01	8.14	8.98	2.99
1993	5.87	7.22	7.93	2.78
1994	7.09	7.97	8.63	2.84

Sources: U.S. Department of the Treasury, Moody's Investors Service, and Standard & Poor's Corporation

Although interest rates fluctuated—the Fed engaged in a bit of tightening in spring 1984, for example, in response to its concerns about inflationary pressures resulting from the economy's rapid growth—their trend was downward.

So was the rate of inflation. The 1.1% increase in the consumer price index in 1986 was the lowest in 20 years. It meant you could earn a real rate of 5% or so in a money market fund and 7% or more in a bond fund.

Little wonder, then, that bond funds' *sales* of shares (including exchanges within fund families) rose to $180 billion in 1986, exceeding the $135 billion of total *net assets* that the ICI had reported for the funds at the end of 1985.

There was certainly enough merchandise to go around to meet investors' demand. As Table 1.5 indicates, the federal government, state and local governments, corporations, and homeowners went on a borrowing binge, providing new securities issues for bond funds (and other investors) to snap up.

The federal government's ever-growing budget deficits generated the issues that sustained the growth of government bond funds while the torrent of government-related mortgage-backed securities satisfied the appetite of funds that were concentrated in these. And the normal demand for federally tax-exempt state and local government bonds—and municipal bond funds—was enhanced when the Tax Reform Act of 1986 eliminated a number of tax shelters, stimulating the search for alternative sources of tax-free income. (This same act deprived many workers of the opportunity to deduct annual $2,000 contributions to their IRAs from their taxable income.)

Table 1.5   U.S. Credit Market Debt Outstanding at End of Select Years, 1968–1993 (in trillions)

Type of Debt	1968	1973	1978	1983	1988	1993
U.S. government securities	$0.3	$0.4	$0.8	$1.6	$ 3.2	$ 5.2
Mortgages	0.4	0.7	1.2	1.8	3.2	4.2
Corporate bonds*	0.2	0.3	0.4	0.6	1.4	2.1
Tax-exempt obligations**	0.1	0.2	0.3	0.5	0.9	1.2
Other debt***	0.4	0.6	1.1	1.8	2.9	3.1
Total	$1.4	$2.2	$3.8	$6.4	$11.7	$15.8
Corporate equities excluding shares of mutual funds	$1.0	$0.9	$1.0	$2.0	$ 3.1	$ 6.2

*Excludes industrial revenue bonds.

**Includes industrial revenue bonds.

***Consumer credit, bank loans, open market paper, and other loans

Totals may not add due to rounding.

Note: Market values of outstanding corporate equities are shown (in italics) to permit comparison with corporate bonds.

Source: Board of Governors of the Federal Reserve System

With short-term interest rates down from their double-digit levels, investors were easily persuaded to seek higher income by switching to the new government bond funds and government-backed mortgage securities funds, which were spreading like dandelions, promoted with tempting—if misleading—phrases such as "government guarantee" and "safety."

When government bond yields fell further, the search for high income led promoters of taxable funds and their investors down the credit quality ladder—first to funds invested in corporate bonds of high and medium investment quality and then to funds concentrated in bonds of lower quality, usually called "high-yield" or "junk" bonds.

With so much attention given to maximizing yields, many investors were not made adequately aware of—or just remained oblivious to—the one risk inherent in all marketable bonds and the funds that own them: that prices fall when interest rates rise.

Since this seemed an unlikely possibility, many—especially new investors—were stunned when it happened not once but twice in 1987. They redeemed their shares, especially in government, GNMA, and municipal bond funds, whose purchases had contributed to the groups' strong growth not long before.

Actual inflation and inflation expectations gained momentum almost from the start of the year, partly because of the impact of a weakening dollar on the costs of imports, and interest rates rose to reflect the concerns of individual and institutional investors. The Fed exerted pressure on bank reserves, reinforcing the firming of rates. By April, the monthly total return of Salomon Brothers' Broad Investment Grade Bond Index, which tracks the performance of all investment-grade securities traded in the U.S. bond market, *fell* 2.45%—its worst showing since May 1984.*

After pressures in credit markets eased and the dollar firmed at mid-year, the dollar weakened again when disappointing figures on the trade deficit were released. Interest rates turned up again in anticipation of renewed Fed tightening to retard the inflationary pressures associated with a weaker dollar. In September, the Fed took action, reducing bank reserves through open market operations and raising the discount rate (the rate at which it lends money to banks), which caused short-term yields to increase further.

Investors Turn to Foreign Markets

Given the turbulence in the U.S. bond market, it was not surprising that investors would turn to the growing number of funds that were concentrated in foreign bonds. The concept had been introduced in 1981, when Massa-

---

*For more on bond indexes, see Chapter 5.

chusetts Financial Services launched the predecessor of its MFS World Governments Fund. In 1981's environment, when investors also had been discouraged by rising U.S. interest rates and falling bond prices, many were convinced they should cut losses by selling long bonds and replacing them with shorter maturities.

MFS hit on the international bond fund idea as an alternative for their consideration. As Richard B. Bailey, then MFS president, put it at the time: ". . . economies can and do move in different directions, which means national interest rates can and do move in different directions at any given time. If a fixed-income investor is free to look anywhere in the world for a favorable fixed-income environment, he can shift his money from that country in which bond prices are heading downward, and move it to that country in which bond prices are trending upward, thereby immediately becoming an offensive rather than a defensive investor. He is no longer forced to pursue a strategy which is aimed only at lessening portfolio losses, but now can actively pursue a policy of increasing values."

Investors had barely digested the impact of higher interest rates—and lower bond prices—resulting from market forces and Fed policy when stock prices, which had peaked in August, collapsed in October.

Interest rates reversed course, as many investors rushed from stocks into the expected safety of Treasury bonds, driving their prices up and their yields down, and as the Fed sought to ensure the liquidity of the financial system by easing banks' reserve positions.

Bonds recovered sufficiently in the fourth quarter to save the bond market from having a down year but not by much; the Salomon Brothers index's total return for all of 1987 was a mere 2.6%, its worst showing of the decade. (Stocks, despite the 20.5% plunge of October 19, had a better year; the Standard & Poor's 500 had a total return of 5.1%.)

Markets snapped back in 1988 despite the continuation of an inflation rate of over 4% and the Fed's efforts to bring it under control. Yields of 30-year Treasuries rose only slightly, creeping up from 8.95% at the end of 1987 to 9.00% at the end of 1988, while those of 3-month Treasury bills soared 251 basis points (1 basis point = 0.01%) from 5.86% to 8.37%, thus sharply reducing the spread between the two.

This trend continued into 1989 as the Fed pressed on, increasing short-term rates again in February—its last move to tighten, as things turned out, until February 1994. Short-term rates peaked in March 1989 above 9%, the highest levels since 1984 and even slightly higher than long-term rates. By the end of May, 30-year bonds' yields had dropped to 8.60% while yields of 3-month Treasury bills had only slipped to 8.92%, producing the flat "yield curve" in Figure 1.1.

It was an environment in which many found money market funds more attractive than bond funds. To no one's surprise, money market funds' 1989

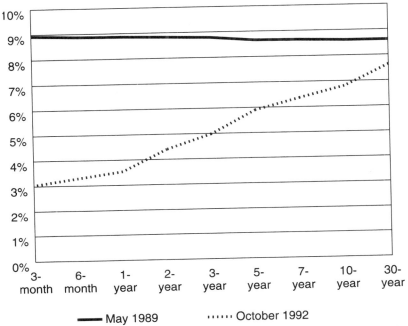

FIGURE 1.1 How Treasury Securities' Yield Curve Looks When It's Flat (May 1989) or Steep (October 1992).
End of month Treasury market bid yields at constant maturities for bills, notes, and bonds
Source: U.S. Department of the Treasury

share sales soared to the highest levels since 1981—five times as great as those of bond funds—because people realized that they could earn about as much from money market funds as from bond funds while assuming essentially no risk of losing principal.

That risk became quite real for investors in high-yield bond funds as actual and expected defaults—partly attributable to the impact of slower economic growth on companies' ability to service their debts—threw the prices of junk bonds for large losses (and lifted yields above 15%). Many investors redeemed their shares and moved the money into money market funds.

Many other investors, who assumed that money market yields would drop because they presumably could not long remain much above the 4.5% inflation rate, bought shares of short-term bond funds. They hoped to enjoy slight appreciation whenever rates would fall again.

This is just what happened as the economy's growth rate slowed and the Fed eased even though inflation didn't let up. By the end of 1989, the yields of bills and 30-year bonds had dropped to 7.80% and 7.98%, respectively, as the yield curve remained flat.

Spreads between the two expanded very slightly in the first half of 1990 as the weak economy—still growing but at a declining rate—held bills' yields stable while long bonds' yields moved up (and prices drifted down) in anticipation of accelerated inflation. Stocks continued their climb from the lows of October 1987, with the Dow Jones Industrial Average hitting an all-time closing high of 2999.75 in July.

Then everything changed. Iraq invaded Kuwait on August 2, causing oil prices to spike upward and consequently boosting the inflation rate above 6%. The economy, which had expanded for 92 months—a peacetime record—was thrown into recession despite the Fed's efforts to prevent it.

While stocks tumbled toward their October lows—the Dow dropped 21% to a closing low of 2365.10 in just three months—bond prices gradually moved up. By the end of 1990, following a December rate cut by the Fed, Treasury bill yields had fallen to 6.63% though 30-year Treasury bond yields, being stickier, had dropped only to 8.26%.

With the wider spreads, the yield curve took on a more "normal" shape.

Although the Business Cycle Dating Committee of the National Bureau of Economic Research, which defines the peaks and troughs of economic cycles, ruled in December 1992 that the recession had ended in March 1991, the recovery remained feeble for the rest of 1991. (The committee didn't rule until April 1991 that a recession had begun in July 1990.)

The Fed Eases—Again

The Fed cut rates as many as five times in 1991 to stimulate the economy—especially job growth—but with limited benefits. It did so again in July 1992 after the inflation-adjusted gross domestic product had at last returned to an annual rate of 3% or more. While in line with the economy's long-run growth rate, it was low for a period of recovery.

In pumping reserves into the banking system to promote growth—always a sensitive strategy but especially so during a presidential election year in which job creation became a major issue—the Fed seemed not to be greatly concerned about inflation, which remained around 3%.

Investors appeared to be more concerned, bidding up long-term bond prices only slightly. From the end of 1990 until the end of October 1992—days before Bill Clinton beat the incumbent George Bush—30-year bond yields had fallen only from 8.26% to 7.63%, while the Fed's easing had resulted in 3-month Treasury bill yields' plunging from 6.63% to 3.03%. That meant bill rates had been pushed down to about zero when adjusted for inflation, while the real rates on long bonds remained over 4% in reflection of inflation concerns.

The yield spread between 3-month and 30-year securities was thus widened to an unusual 460 basis points, giving the steep yield curve of Figure 1.1 its shape.

A steep yield curve, rooted in a 3% money market rate, was bound to have a predictable effect on investors: It would encourage them to go up the curve in search of the higher yields available for issues of longer maturities. People moved from money market funds into short-, intermediate-, and long-term bond funds in hopes of earning more income, not always realizing that such funds would expose them to greater risks than money market funds. (Chapter 3 will discuss these in more detail.)

Low money market rates also shooed many out of their bank savings accounts and maturing CDs into bond (or equity) mutual funds. This gave rise to concerns among the regulators of the SEC and other federal agencies about whether all who made such switches realized that the FDIC didn't insure mutual fund shares—even if they were bought from banks, which had become major factors in the fund industry.

Money market rates continued sliding in the first months of the Clinton administration until bill rates bottomed at 2.79% in April 1993. They remained around 3% for the rest of the year and into 1994, continuing to draw money out of CDs and other short-term instruments.

Before long, investors were gaining confidence that the low inflation rate might endure and that the federal government finally would succeed in reducing its budget deficit. (At 1993's end, it had done just that, thanks to receipts rising faster than outlays.) Bond yields continued to fall, with those of 30-year Treasury bonds hitting 5.78% by October 15, 1993, providing handsome returns for those who had invested in them and other long-term securities, including bond funds.

The appeal of bond funds had not merely continued in 1993. Sales of bond fund shares (including exchanges into the funds from siblings), net of redemptions, set a new record of $140 billion, well ahead of the previous record of $119 billion set in 1986, when yields were higher but inflation was lower.

Since the start of the bull market in bonds in 1982, long bonds' yields had fallen over 750 basis points. Clearly, they could no longer fall so steeply. Some began to suspect that the risk of yields rising was greater than the likelihood of their continued diving and moved at least some money from long- into intermediate- and short- term funds. Others, feeling that yields were more likely to fall abroad than in the United States, switched some money into international bond funds.

But many, seeing current inflation even sliding below 3% and perceiving economic growth to remain below-average for a recovery, found the case for moving out of long-term bonds and bond funds not compelling enough.

1994's Sea Change in the Bond Market

They were shocked, therefore, when on February 4, 1994, the Federal Reserve's Federal Open Market Committee (FOMC) decided, as its announcement said, "to increase slightly the degree of pressure on reserve positions." Intended to increase short-term money market interest rates by 25 basis points, the action was the first by the FOMC to tighten reserves since early 1989.

Members of the FOMC had acted not because the current inflation rate had accelerated—it had not—but because they saw the potential for future acceleration as operations in some sectors of the slowly growing economy seemed likely to bump against capacity limits.

While the Fed action to nip the potential for greater inflation in the bud should have reassured investors in long bonds and resulted in little, if any, increase in their yields, it had the opposite effect. They unloaded bonds, causing their prices to fall and their yields to rise. Additional rounds of Fed tightening in subsequent months had similar effects.

In only the first ten months following the sea change in the bond market, an increase of around 250 basis points, or 2.5%, in short-term money market interest rates had been accompanied by an increase of about 150 basis points in 30-year Treasury bond yields. The yield curve had become flatter.

The impact on long-term yields of the Fed's raising of short-term rates may have been a surprise for many, but the impact of higher yields on bond funds followed the usual script. Prices of long-term bonds fell more than those of short-term bonds and, therefore, the NAVs of long-term bond funds fell more than those of short-term bond funds. Share sales slumped, and redemptions increased.

Whether the trend would continue or be reversed in the event of a slowdown in the economy—and how many investors might regret redeeming or not redeeming—only time would tell.

Whatever the case, in 1994 the bond market provided another reminder, as if one was necessary, that interest rates often defy forecasters.

It also served as a reminder that bond fund investing involves risks as well as rewards and that you need to ensure that the investment objectives and risk levels of the funds in which you invest are compatible with your own.

The rest of this book will help you to make appropriate choices and reduce the likelihood of unhappy surprises.

CHAPTER 2

How Debt Securities Differ

Before you begin to consider the types of bond funds that may be appropriate for someone in your circumstances, it would be very helpful for you to understand the various types of debt securities in which bond funds invest.

By becoming familiar with the major characteristics of these securities, you will be better able to understand why bond funds perform as well—or as poorly—as they do and, therefore, to select funds that should be right for you.

There are many types of debt securities that individual investors, such as you, or institutional investors, such as mutual funds, can buy. Most of them are traded in the over-the-counter market.

Among their major differences are: the levels of income that they pay per dollar invested, the taxability of their income, their maturities, their potential for loss or gain when interest rates rise or fall, and the likelihood that their issuers could fail to pay interest or repay principal when they are supposed to.

While there are several ways to classify U.S. debt securities, the most easily understood is probably by broad categories of issuers: the U.S. government, federal agencies that guarantee or issue mortgage-backed securities (MBS), corporations, and state and local governments. (See Tables 2.1 and 2.2.) Income from the latter obligations is commonly—but not always—federally tax-exempt.

Foreign debt securities may be divided along similar lines but differ in two major respects: principal and income are subject to the risk that they will fall in U.S. dollar terms when the dollar rises in relation to the foreign currencies in which they are denominated, and income from the foreign equivalents of state and local government issues is not exempt from U.S. income tax.

Table 2.1   The Rewards of Investing in Debt Securities Maturing in One Year or More by Categories

	U.S. Government	Mortgage-Backed	Tax-Exempt	Corporate
Current income	Lowest taxable income for comparable maturities	Higher than U.S. Treasuries of comparable maturities	Lowest income for comparable maturities	Higher taxable income for comparable maturities
Exemption from U.S. income tax	No	No	Yes	No
Exemption from state and local income tax	Usually	No	Varies	No
Safety of principal	Yes	Yes	Usually	Usually
Choice of maturities	Yes	Yes	Yes	Yes
Opportunities for capital gains	Sometimes	Sometimes	Sometimes	Sometimes
Call protection	Yes	Low	Low	Low
Liquidity	Highest	Usually	Varies	Varies

U.S. Government

U.S. government securities fall into two broad categories: those issued by the U.S. Treasury or other units of the government and backed by the full faith and credit of the Treasury, and those issued by other federal units that don't enjoy that degree of backing but may have some sort of government support (such as the ability to borrow from the Treasury).

Full Faith and Credit: Treasury

The first category of debt securities is the safest because the "full faith and credit" support of the Treasury means that the federal government stands ready to levy taxes or to borrow from its citizens or foreigners to make good on its word to pay interest and repay principal on time.

The government has honored its commitment since the early days of the Republic, thanks in large part to our first secretary of the treasury, Alexander

Table 2.2 *The Risks of Investing in Debt Securities Maturing in One Year or More by Categories*

	U.S. Government	Mortgage-Backed	Tax-Exempt	Corporate
Loss of principal due to default	None	Very low	Small; it depends on issuer	Small; it depends on issuer
Failure to receive interest	None	Very low	Low	Low
Price can fall before maturity	Yes—when interest rates rise	Yes—when interest rates rise	Yes—when interest rates rise	Yes—when interest rates rise
Call/prepayment prior to maturity	Rare	High when rates fall	High when rates fall	High when rates fall
Lost purchasing power on principal and interest due to inflation	Almost certain; varies with maturity	Almost certain; varies with maturity	Almost certain; varies with maturity	Almost certain; varies with maturity

Hamilton, who laid the foundation for its creditworthiness with the Report on Public Credit, which he submitted to Congress in 1790.

He was appalled by, among other things, the fact that the bonds issued under the Continental Congress were selling at deep discounts. To promote the development of the new nation's economy and to conduct its operations, the government would have to be able to borrow money at home and abroad. That, in turn, required that its credit had to be good.

Hamilton, therefore, pushed for assuming the Continental Congress's debts at face value—over the opposition of other Founding Fathers who didn't want to give speculators windfall profits—and persuaded Congress to impose duties on imports and excise taxes to enable the government to service its debt and to pay its operating expenses. (It wasn't until 1913 that the Sixteenth Amendment to the Constitution permanently empowered Congress to tax individual and business income.)

Thus, free from credit risk, those who invest in "full faith and credit" government securities have been exposed to only one major risk: interest rate risk—the risk that an increase in interest rates will cause the securities' prices to fall prior to maturity, when they can be cashed at 100 cents on the dollar.

Don't let that "only" fool you. Interest rate risk is a serious risk. It is one that not all investors understand and that is not always clarified by all associated with the sales of mutual funds that own such paper and are promoted in literature that makes liberal use of pictures of the flag and the Capitol. Their implied majesty can't protect you from a bear market in bonds.

Of the nation's total public and private credit market debt of nearly $16 trillion (Table 1.5), U.S. government debt accounts for over $5 trillion. And of all these securities, by far the largest volume—well over $3 trillion—were issued by the Treasury itself. These securities were sold to make up yearly budget deficits resulting from the excess of outlays over receipts, and to pay off maturing securities.

Even if Congress and President Bill Clinton have at last been able to slow down the growth of the public debt in the mid-1990s by trimming deficits, you need not worry about an imminent shortage of Treasury securities. It's unlikely that any secretary of the treasury soon will be able to say, as did President Andrew Jackson's secretary, Levi Woodbury, after redeeming all outstanding interest-bearing bonds: "An unprecedented spectacle . . . A government . . . virtually without any debt."

While the maturities of Treasury securities traded in the bond market range from a few days to 30 years, the Treasury issues them in only eight distinct maturities. Other maturities, most recently 4- and 7-year, have been discontinued. The eight, their minimum denominations, and the frequencies of their auctions are:

Treasury bills (13 to 52 weeks)
  13- and 26-week bills ($10,000 minimum), auctioned weekly
  52-week bills ($10,000 minimum), every four weeks.
Treasury notes (2 to 10 years)
  2-year notes ($5,000 minimum), once a month
  3-year notes ($5,000 minimum), once a quarter (February, May, August, and November)
  5-year notes ($1,000 minimum), once a month
  10-year notes ($1,000 minimum), once a quarter (February, May, August, and November)
Treasury bonds (over 10 years)
  30-year bonds ($1,000 minimum), twice a year (February and August)

Because of the safety of principal inherent in Treasury securities, their yields are lower than those of other debt securities of comparable maturities—except for state and local government issues whose yields reflect the exemption of their income from federal tax.

But Treasury securities have other qualities.

They are the most liquid securities, meaning that individual investors or mutual fund portfolio managers can easily sell them when they want to—or have to—at low transaction costs.

Virtually all of them are noncallable, meaning that the Treasury can't call a bond with a high coupon when interest rates are relatively low to reduce its interest costs by replacing it with a bond bearing a lower coupon. When you buy a Treasury security, you lock in the rate—whether high or low.

The certainty about the period that any Treasury issue is outstanding makes it easy for a portfolio manager to calculate its duration (a measure of a bond's sensitivity to interest rate risk—see page 47) and to adjust the average duration of his or her portfolio to defend against rising rates or take advantage of falling rates.

Like other investors, fund portfolio managers have a large range of maturities from which they can select in the open market: Around 200 issues of Treasury notes and bonds, plus bills, are outstanding at any time. Of course, they also may buy new issues from the Treasury at one of its periodic auctions, paying the same prices as all other purchasers. When buying outstanding Treasury securities from dealers, they have to negotiate prices, which also include dealers' markup.

Some Treasury notes and bonds can be split into their component parts of principal and unmatured interest coupons to create zero-coupon securities. Those that are traded under the Treasury's program, introduced in 1986 and called STRIPS (for Separate Trading of Registered Interest and Principal of Securities), are also direct obligations of the government and have the same credit quality as other Treasury issues.

They are traded at discount prices that reflect prevailing interest rates, pay no interest, and are redeemable when they mature at face value. (Thus, they are similar to Treasury bills and U.S. savings bonds.) The appreciation between the discount prices and face values is, in effect, the interest on these securities and is treated accordingly as interest income by the Internal Revenue Service. A certain amount is calculated as imputed income each year and subject to income tax, unless held in a tax-deferred account.

STRIPS (and other zeros) are more volatile than coupon-bearing bonds and notes. They are used by individuals or institutions that don't need current income but want to be certain of the principal amount they will ultimately get and of the yield they will earn in the years between the time of purchase and maturity. These investors cannot be certain of their total return when buying coupon-bearing securities and reinvesting the interest payments because they cannot know at what rates the interest payments will be reinvested over time. Zeros are also popular with investors who want to speculate on interest rates and can afford to assume the high risk that inheres in them.

Full Faith and Credit: Other

Obligations issued or guaranteed by agencies or other instrumentalities of the government and also backed by the full faith and credit of the Treasury include those of the Export-Import Bank, Farmers Home Administration, Federal Housing Administration, General Services Administration, Government National Mortgage Association (GNMA, or Ginnie Mae—see the following section), the Maritime Administration, and Small Business Administration. The maturities of such obligations usually range from 3 months to 30 years.

Issues of the Treasury and GNMA alone account for over one-half of the taxable investment-grade bond market, as reflected by the Lehman Brothers Aggregate Index (Figure 2.1).

Other Government Securities

Other agencies and instrumentalities, which may be owned by public stockholders, issue debt obligations that, though perhaps perceived as being endowed with the government's support, are primarily supported only by their own credit. They may have the ability to borrow from the Treasury, however. These include the securities of the Federal Home Loan Mortgage Corporation (FHLMC, or Freddie Mac—see the following section) and Federal National Mortgage Association (FNMA, or Fannie Mae—see the following section) as well as those of the Banks for Cooperatives, Federal Farm Credit Banks, Federal Home Loan Banks, Postal Service, Student Loan Marketing Association, and Tennesee Valley Authority.

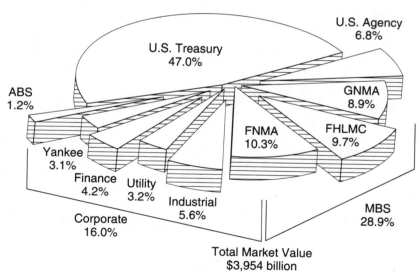

FIGURE 2.1 Distribution of the Lehman Brothers Aggregate Index, December 31, 1994
Source: Lehman Brothers Aggregate Index

However the programs of these agencies may vary, their securities have had in common the fact that they were issued under congressional authorization to raise capital needed for certain federal activities beyond that provided by appropriations or the Treasury's borrowings.

Government-Related Mortgage-Backed Securities

Because they constitute a significant share of bond fund assets and because they differ from conventional Treasury and other federal agencies' debt issues, mortgage-backed securities that are issued or guaranteed by the FHLMC, FNMA, and GNMA warrant a separate description.

There are essentially two types of such securities: (1) those issued by private lending institutions but insured by government-owned GNMA and backed by the full faith and credit of the Treasury and (2) those issued by FHLMC and FNMA, stockholder-owned corporations that were chartered by the government (5 of whose 18 directors are appointed by the president).

Since the Depression, the government has guaranteed or insured payment of interest and repayment of principal on housing mortgage loans via the Farmers Home Administration, the Federal Housing Administration (FHA), and the Veterans Administration (VA), predecessor of the Department of Veterans Affairs.

It has further helped people buy or build homes by making cash available to lending institutions so that they, in turn, could make more loans: advances by the Federal Home Loan Bank System (FHLBS) to member savings institutions and purchases by FNMA of FHA- and VA-backed mortgages from banks and other lending institutions. The FHLBS and FNMA raised the capital for these programs by selling their own debt securities to individual and institutional investors.

But, whenever the money supply became tight and interest rates rose over the years, the housing industry and home buyers had trouble getting mortgage loans to build or buy. Even when banks and other institutions had money to lend, many builders and buyers couldn't afford to borrow it.

When this happened again in the mid-1960s, President Lyndon B. Johnson and Congress took the first of several federal initiatives to channel more money into housing, thereby adding not only to credit market debt but also to the range of financial assets that you could invest in.

In 1966, they authorized FNMA to package its holdings of FHA and VA mortgage loans, bought from banks and thrift institutions, in pools and to sell "pass-through" certificates of participation in the pools to investors. ("Pass-through" meant that borrowers' monthly interest and principal payments, as well as unscheduled prepayments, would be passed through to certificate holders.)

In 1968, FNMA, which had been a government entity since 1938, was split into two organizations to expand the federal role in financing housing.

One, retaining FNMA's name, was converted into a stockholder-owned corporation that primarily would acquire pools of conventional mortgages (those not guaranteed by the government) and would have the right to borrow up to a specified limit from the Treasury.

The other, GNMA, was established as a government corporation (within the Department of Housing and Urban Development). It was authorized not only to buy FHA and VA mortgages from their originating institutions but also to stamp the government's guarantee on the institutions' certificates, embodying interest in pools of such mortgages, so they could more easily be sold to the public.

By making it attractive for all types of investors to acquire interests in FHA and VA mortgages, GNMA could improve their liquidity in the secondary market.

The investment vehicle that was developed under GNMA's auspices, and that evolved into a magnet for mutual fund sponsors and investors alike, works like this: A private, FHA-approved lender—say, a commercial bank—makes a number of mortgage loans that are insured by the FHA or guaranteed by the VA. Instead of holding these loan documents as assets in its vault for 25 or 30 years, the bank bunches $1 million worth of them, with common interest rates and maturities, in a "pool" and submits the pool to GNMA for its approval.

After receiving GNMA's—that is, the government's—additional guarantee of the timely payment of interest and repayment of principal, the bank creates $25,000 GNMA certificates, or "Ginnie Maes," representing ownership in the pool's mortgages. It sells the certificates to securities dealers and, with the proceeds, can make new mortgage loans, starting the cycle all over again.

Bond funds, which would buy them from the dealers, could provide access to these federally guaranteed securities to individuals who found their credit quality and monthly payments appealing but could not buy $25,000 Ginnie Maes on their own (or who would not be able to reinvest monthly checks in similar instruments, if they didn't need the money).

With passage of the Emergency Home Finance Act of 1970, Congress strengthened the secondary market for conventional mortgages by creating another federal agency, FHLMC, to acquire pools of these mortgages and issue securities backed by them.

Until the Financial Institutions Reform, Recovery, and Enforcement Act of 1989 (FIRREA) was approved to deal with the massive failures of savings associations, FHLMC was run by the Federal Home Loan Bank Board and owned by the 12 regional Federal Home Loan Banks (which provide a credit reserve for the thrift industry). Since then, it also has been converted into a stockholder-owned corporation and kept its federal ties.

While both FNMA and FHMLC stand behind the mortgage-backed securities they issue and both are regarded as instrumentalities of the federal government, their guarantees do not have the weight that GNMAs carry. Nevertheless, investors in Fannie Maes, Freddie Macs, and Ginnie Maes should be able to count on getting paid on time even if borrowers do not make their payments when scheduled.

While there are some largely technical differences in the securities' features that portfolio managers take into account when investing, what matters more to you are the features they have in common.

In theory, investors in mortgage-backed securities should be able to expect a monthly "pass-through" of principal and interest payments on a pool of 30-year mortgages from the issuer or its agent for 30 years.

In practice, however, mortgages are liquidated earlier. People prepay them as they move or refinance when interest rates fall, or lenders foreclose when borrowers fail to pay. Experience has shown the average life of a 30-year pool to be really no more than 12 years. (The expected life of a 15-year security is about 8 years.)

To compensate investors for the "risk" of getting money back before they want it—known as prepayment risk—the yields on mortgage-backed securities tend to run 0.5% to 1% or so higher than those for Treasury issues of comparable maturity.

To appreciate prepayment risk, consider this: When you buy a Treasury bond maturing in 12 years, you know how much interest you will get every 6 months, for how long you will get it, and how much principal you will be repaid at maturity. If you reinvest your semiannual interest because you don't need the money, you can't know what your total return will be for the 12 years, however, because you can't predict the rates of interest at which you will be reinvesting.

But when you buy a mortgage-backed security, your potential total return is even less predictable. Since you get both interest and principal payments every month and presumably would want at least to reinvest the principal, you would be plowing back a lot more money—at unpredictable rates of interest—over the security's life.

And when interest rates fall and homeowners refinance their mortgages to take advantage of lower rates, as they have done periodically in waves, prepayments are accelerated. Your income goes down as you have to reinvest money from prepayments at the lower rates then prevailing. You can't lock in higher yields, as you could with Treasuries. And instead of enjoying the appreciation that Treasuries would provide, your security's price underperforms.

Prepayment risk is greatest for the Fannie Maes, Freddie Macs, and Ginnie Maes with the highest coupon rates, which are likely to sell at premiums. Investors who bought them at prices above par (face value) can suffer losses of as much as the premiums because prepayment is guaranteed at par.

And what happens when interest rates rise? No matter how "safe" Ginnie Maes, Fannie Maes, or Freddie Macs may be, their prices fall just as the prices of other fixed-income securities do. Moreover, if you had bought securities representing interests in low-coupon pools to reduce your exposure to pre-payment risk, you would expose yourself to greater loss of principal. That's because the duration (loosely, expected life) of a low-coupon pool is longer than that of a high-coupon pool, making it more sensitive to changes in interest rates.

Corporations

Compared with governments, corporations were late in becoming major issuers of bonds. It was essential for businesses first to raise equity capital through the sale of common stocks and to establish reputations for being good credit risks.

Following in the wake of canal, turnpike, toll bridge, and water companies, railroads became a major demander of capital. By the 1850s they dominated the corporate securities market as they had to raise money for laying rail across the developing country. (When some early railroads, whose promises to pay their debts were of doubtful value, couldn't sell bonds, they had people selling stocks door-to-door.)

Then came the large steel, oil, and other industrial corporations, as well as emerging utilities: electric light and power, telephone and telegraph. All had enormous appetites for capital to build facilities and buy equipment.

By 1900, a total of $6 billion of corporate bonds were outstanding. Of these, $5 billion were accounted for by the railroads alone. If these sound like small sums, you have to remember that the total public debt at the time was only a bit above $3 billion. (Only about one-third of that was the debt of the federal government!)

The growing mix of incorporated businesses offering securities, the increasing variety in the types of these securities, and the range of companies' creditworthiness afforded investors a choice of corporate offerings that they had not previously known.

The greater selection, of course, was a mixed blessing. It confronted investors with factors that they—and their brokers—didn't have to think about when buying easily understood Treasury securities. (The choices turned out to be a preview of what you face now when considering mutual funds, whose managers have a much greater variety of issues and issuers to invest in. But I'm getting ahead of myself.)

Of all the considerations, the most important was—and remains—safety of principal. Some corporate bonds were secured by railroad cars, factories, and other assets while others (known as debentures) were not. In either case, assuming that investors would be reluctant to take possession of cabooses or blast furnaces for nonpayment of debt, they had to rely on the earning power of the companies that issued the bonds.

To help investors with the challenge of identifying the better credit risks, men such as John Moody (a statistician), Henry Varnum Poor (editor of *Railroad Journal*), and his son, Henry William, began to collect financial and operating data about companies and to publish the data regularly. Having planted the seeds for today's Moody's Investors Service and Standard & Poor's Corporation (S&P), they followed with manuals, of which the first had been Henry V. Poor's *Manual of the Railroads of the United States*, published in 1868.

In 1909, Moody went a step further by introducing a system for rating securities according to their investment qualities—a system that would eventually be recognized by the federal government and is still widely used today for issues of state and local governments as well as for those of corporations. It is heavily relied on by individual and institutional investors, including the portfolio managers of bond funds in which you may wish to invest, and it serves as a discipline for many corporate and governmental issuers of debt securities. Moody first applied the system to railroads, then to utilities and industrial companies. A predecessor of S&P launched a similar concept in 1923.

The systems, which provide for nine (Moody's) or ten (S&P's) categories, give their top ratings (Aaa, in Moody's case; AAA, in S&P's) to the most creditworthy corporations. If not quite equal to the Treasury, no one need have any doubt about their ability to service their debts. As of November 1, 1994, the bonds of only eight industrial corporations and six utilities met the grade in Moody's view. The bottom ratings go to the most speculative.

Since, as an investor, you should expect to be compensated according to the degree of risk that you accept, you'll understand that, all other things being equal, the securities accorded the highest ratings will offer the lowest yields. At the same time, you would expect to be offered the highest yields when investing in issues with the lowest ratings—and to keep your fingers crossed that you'll be paid when scheduled.

From "triple-A" through the next three grades—Aa/AA, A/A, and Baa/ BBB—bonds are regarded as being investment grade. That is to say, they are deemed to be suitable investments for conservative investors, including bond funds that can only buy investment-grade bonds. As of September 30, 1994, about 80% of outstanding corporate bonds rated by Moody's made the grade and, of these, the largest share—about 18%—were bonds of manufacturing companies, according to Salomon Brothers. Manufacturing long ago displaced

HOW CORPORATE BONDS ARE RATED

INVESTMENT GRADE
High Grade

Aaa. Bonds with this rating are judged to be the best quality. They carry the smallest degree of investment risk and are generally referred to as "gilt edged." Interest payments are protected by a large or exceptionally stable margin and principal is secure.

Aa. These are high quality by all standards. They are rated lower than the best bonds because margins of protection may not be as large or fluctuation of protective elements may be of greater amplitude.

Medium Grade

A. These bonds possess many favorable investment attributes. Factors giving security to principal and interest are considered adequate, but elements may be present that suggest a susceptibility to impairment some time in the future.

Baa. They are neither highly protected nor poorly secured. Interest payments and principal security appear adequate for the present but certain protective elements may be lacking or may be characteristically unreliable over any great length of time.

SPECULATIVE

Ba. Their future cannot be considered as well-assured. Often the protection of interest and principal payments may be very moderate and thereby not well safeguarded during both good and bad times over the future.

B. These bonds generally lack characteristics of the desirable investment. Assurance of interest and principal payments over any long period of time may be small.

Caa. Such issues are of poor standing. They may be in default or elements of danger may be present with respect to principal or interest.

Ca. These obligations are speculative in a high degree. Such issues are often in default or have other marked shortcomings.

C. This is the lowest-rated class of bonds. Issues so rated can be regarded as having extremely poor prospects of ever attaining any real investment standing.

Source: Excerpted from *Moody's Bond Record,* Moody's Investors Service

railroads as No. 1. Electric utilities were No. 2 with about 12%. (Railroads account for only 1%, just ahead of publishing.)

The remaining ratings are given to bonds that are regarded as being speculative—or junk bonds—and, therefore, inappropriate for investors who cannot or should not buy them. They range from securities whose issuers could have trouble meeting debt service during recessions—if not in good times—to issues actually in default.

While bonds of less than investment grade should be avoided by those who can't afford the risks, other investors, able and willing to study them, may spot some that are suitable for their portfolios.

Moody's and S&P assign a rating to an issue when it comes to market and then monitor the company's finances as long as the issue is outstanding. They may upgrade it when an issuer's situation improves, resulting in a higher market price (and lower yield for the issue), or downgrade it when a situation deteriorates, resulting in a lower price (and higher yield). If the downgrading knocks an issue below Baa/BBB, it is knocked out of consideration for bond funds and other investors who are limited to buying investment-grade securities.

While some corporate bonds, like some Treasury bonds, have maturities of 30 years, they have longer maturities, on the average, than Treasury securities. According to Salomon Brothers, the average maturity of all investment-grade corporates was close to 12 years in December 1994 versus about 8 years for all Treasuries with a maturity of at least 1 year. (The Treasury, in fact, began in 1993 to shorten the average maturity of its outstanding debt by restructuring its mix.)

Unlike nearly all Treasuries, however, corporate bonds may involve call risk, which is similar to the prepayment risk of mortgage-backed securities. Corporate bonds often may have provisions that they can be called at stipulated prices—usually at a premium above face value—after a period of years. Companies insert this provision in anticipation of their having spare cash to reduce debt or wishing to take advantage of lower interest rates to reduce borrowing costs.

Thus, in weighing a particular issue, it's important for investors to think not merely in terms of its maturity but also of its effective maturity, which reflects the earliest call date, when principal would be repaid and have to be reinvested. The more imminent retirement of a callable bond makes its price less sensitive to interest rate changes than a long-term bond that cannot be called (but whose income stream will be more durable).

State and Local Governments

While the constitutions or statutes of all states but Vermont require that state governments balance their operating budgets annually or biennially, they permit the states to fund construction and other capital outlays by borrowing—that is, by selling general obligation (GO) bonds that are backed by their tax bases.

Similar budget requirements and debt limits apply to offspring of the states that have the authority to levy taxes: counties, municipalities, townships, school districts, and nearly one-half of special districts.

Both state and local governments usually must ask voters to approve proposed GO bond issues, an opportunity not afforded voters by the federal government when the Treasury has to borrow (for operating expenses as well as capital outlays). Most of the time, voters approve the issues.

All told, of the 85,005 state and local government entities counted by the Bureau of the Census in its latest (1992) census of governments, over three out of four have the power to tax and to pledge future tax collections in support of bonds they may issue.

Of special districts—entities that build, own, and operate utilities, turnpikes, ports, airports, sewage treatment plants, transportation systems, and other public purpose facilities—roughly 17,000 have no power to tax. They derive their revenues from user fees and other sources, and must finance their general and capital expenditures out of these receipts, plus whatever they are permitted—and agree—to borrow.

When they undertake capital projects, they, too, sell long-term bonds. But, since their securities can't be backed by expected tax collections, the issuers pledge the revenues from their operations, giving rise to the name "revenue bonds"—a class involving greater risk for investors than full faith and credit bonds and, therefore, likely to pay higher interest.

Revenue bonds, which also are sold by state and other units of local government, account for about two-thirds of the $100- to $200-billion in new state and local government debt that has been issued annually in recent years; GOs account for about one-third. Until 1992, according to Securities Data Company, most of the proceeds were used to fund projects and programs; in 1992 and 1993, most of the money was used to refund outstanding issues bearing higher coupons.

Because income from state and local GO and revenue bonds is exempt from federal income tax—making them one of a shrinking number of sources of federally tax-free income—they have a strong appeal to many taxpayers. It's an appeal that was enhanced in 1993, when President Clinton and Congress raised tax rates for people with higher income.

Some revenue bonds, classified as "private activity bonds" by the Tax Reform Act of 1986, may subject some taxpayers to the "alternative minimum tax" (AMT) even though income from the bonds may be exempt from federal income tax. That's because the interest, which may exceed that of non-AMT bonds of comparable maturities and quality, is considered a tax preference item for purposes of calculating taxpayers' AMT.

As the term suggests, so-called AMT bonds differ from public purpose revenue bonds in that the private activities for which they are sold—such as housing, industrial and commercial facilities, hospitals, and stadiums—may be those of for-profit organizations. In fact, the bonds may be the obligations of corporations instead of the governmental units in whose names they are issued. Because the IRS, in the eyes of some government officials, defines "private" activities very broadly, it may apply the term to projects that other, presumably fair-minded people would characterize as public.

States have sold bonds since the early days of the nation—for development of canals, railroads, roads, and other improvements—but local governments long ago passed them in the rate at which they issue new securities each year.

Unlike the federal government, which has maintained its reputation for prompt payment of debts, state and local governments have periodically defaulted on their bonds or have come close to doing so.

Such events were numerous during the Depression, but they have also occurred occasionally in recent years, making it important to be mindful of credit quality when considering state and local government securities. You need only to think of Orange County, California, which filed for bankruptcy in 1994 because of losses in an investment fund, to appreciate the desirability of letting the professionals who manage bond funds—and who are backed by thorough credit research departments—pick and watch tax-exempt securities for you.

Municipal bonds—whether GO or revenue—are rated by the rating agencies in a manner similar to their ratings of corporates (page 37). Unfortunately, as Orange County illustrated, they may not always downgrade securities in a timely manner.

Governmental units that have the best prospects for meeting their debt service obligations aren't the only ones whose issues are top-rated, however.

A large number of governments seek to enhance the marketability of their bonds by buying insurance policies that assure investors of their timely debt service. If the municipal bond insurance companies' financial conditions justify it, they would be rated triple-A, too.

CHAPTER 3

The Different Types of Bond Funds

If there seem to be many types of bond funds—perhaps more than you had imagined—you're right. How many depends on how they are classified according to their investment objectives and policies.

The SEC, which regulates mutual funds under the Investment Company Act of 1940, is less concerned with the number of bond fund classifications than with the congruity of every fund's name, investment objectives, policies, and practices.

It wants to be certain that a fund's name, which often indicates a fund's type, does not mislead you into buying one that's not what you think it is.

To help you to decide whether to invest in a fund, the 1940 act and SEC regulations require every fund to disclose certain pertinent information. This information then enables others to classify the fund.

Among other things, the SEC requires every fund to:

- State its investment objectives and policies succinctly and prominently in its prospectus. For bond funds, the most common objective is, of course, income. Some fund managements may (also) specify that they aim at high current income, growth of income, tax-exempt income, capital preservation, some capital appreciation, and so on.
- Describe in the prospectus the types of securities in which it principally invests, as well as any special investment practices or techniques that it employs.
- Describe in the prospectus the principal risk factors associated with investment in the fund.

■ State semiannually in its reports to shareholders what percent of its net assets is invested in each of the different types of government and corporate debt securities, divided into those with maturities of 12 months or less (the sort that money market funds are concentrated in) and those with longer maturities.

■ State in each report the dollar-weighted average maturity (in years, to one decimal place) of the fund's portfolio securities.

Based on the fund information, the Investment Company Institute, the industry's principal trade association, has divided the universe of bond and income funds into 11 categories since 1986. They include three—income-mixed, balanced, and flexible portfolio—whose funds invest in stocks as well as bonds to earn income.

Lipper Analytical Services, a New York firm that has calculated and disseminated fund performance data since 1960, classifies bond and income funds according to investment objectives into about 25 groups (excluding single-state municipal bond funds sold in about 40 states, income, balanced, and flexible portfolio funds).

Lipper's classification system is accepted widely in the fund industry. When they report to shareholders, fund managements commonly compare the performance of their funds with Lipper data on the performance of their funds' groups. They also use the published data, as well proprietary data calculated for them by Lipper, when reporting on their stewardship to fund boards and when calculating year-end bonuses for funds' portfolio managers.

Morningstar, a Chicago fund data firm formed in 1984, which computes funds' returns and rates them for risk-adjusted performance, classifies bond and income funds into 11 categories (also excluding single-state, income, balanced, and asset allocation funds). Other data services and periodicals follow still different practices.

Because the greater differentiation among Lipper's categories could be more helpful to you in choosing the bond fund(s) that may enable you to achieve your investment objectives—while exposing you to no more than an acceptable level of risk—I use them in this book.

Table 3.1 shows you how more than 1,800 national bond funds have been distributed among the Lipper categories and how the number of funds in each category has grown in the decade from 1984 to 1994.

How do you take advantage of the classification system to find the one or more bond funds that you want or to reassure yourself that the fund(s) you own is (are) right for you?

First, by going beyond your desire to earn—and keep—the maximum amount of income and thinking of your investment goals and risk tolerance in terms of three important criteria: taxability of income, acceptability of credit risk, and acceptability of interest rate risk.

Table 3.1 *Bond Fund Categories: How They've Multiplied and Grown*

Classification	Number of Funds in Operation For		
	1 Year	5 Years	10 Years
Taxable			
Short U.S. Treasury	15	4	0
Short U.S. Government	108	33	5
Short Investment Grade	112	30	7
Intermediate U.S. Treasury	10	4	1
Intermediate U.S. Government	77	22	5
Intermediate Investment Grade	123	32	11
General U.S. Treasury	14	8	0
General U.S. Government	145	77	18
Adjustable Rate Mortgage	77	5	0
GNMA	47	32	12
U.S. Mortgage	55	20	10
A-Rated Corporate	89	47	24
BBB-Rated Corporate	69	28	14
General Bond	43	16	8
High Current Yield	93	60	32
Convertible Securities	24	20	3
Flexible Income	20	13	5
Target Maturity	11	7	0
Short World Multi-Market	37	4	0
Short World Single-Market	3	3	0
General World Income	106	26	2
Income	21	15	6
Balanced	153	57	25
Subtotal	1,452	563	188
Tax-Exempt: National			
Short Municipal	37	14	9
Intermediate Municipal	82	29	9
General Municipal	184	88	51
Insured Municipal	41	22	5
High Yield Municipal	36	22	6
Subtotal	380	175	80

Table 3.1 Continued

Classification	Number of Funds in Operation For		
	1 Year	5 Years	10 Years
Tax-Exempt: Single-State			
Alabama	6	1	0
Arizona	24	6	1
California	128	54	17
Colorado	14	6	0
Connecticut	14	5	0
Florida	67	4	0
Georgia	17	5	1
Hawaii	5	3	0
Kansas	5	0	0
Kentucky	7	3	1
Louisiana	10	5	0
Maryland	22	7	1
Massachusetts	42	18	4
Michigan	35	10	2
Minnesota	28	15	3
Missouri	11	5	0
New Jersey	32	8	0
New York	94	44	15
North Carolina	23	4	1
Ohio	37	14	2
Oregon	11	5	1
Pennsylvania	57	15	1
South Carolina	9	2	1
Tennessee	11	2	0
Texas	19	3	0
Virginia	23	5	1
Washington	7	0	0
Other states*	103	13	2
Subtotal	861	262	54
Total	2,693	1,000	322

*Includes the following 16 states: Arkansas, Idaho, Indiana, Iowa, Maine, Mississippi, Montana, Nebraska, New Hampshire, New Mexico, North Dakota, Rhode Island, Utah, Vermont, West Virginia, and Wisconsin plus Puerto Rico.
Note: Multiple classes of shares are included for some funds in some categories.
Source: LIPPER—Fixed Income Fund Performance Analysis, December 31, 1994, Lipper Analytical Services

Once you've decided how you want—and can afford—to be invested in the context of these criteria, you'll be in position to focus on fund categories and the funds that are assigned to them.

Taxability of Income

Current income—the most common principal objective for buying bond fund shares—is either subject to, or exempt from, federal income tax.

Income is usually federally tax-exempt when it's distributed in dividends by bond funds that receive interest from investing in tax-exempt, or municipal, securities.

All other distributions of investment income, whether you take them in cash or reinvest them in additional shares, are federally taxable—unless, of course, tax is deferred because you hold the shares in individual retirement accounts (IRAs), 401(k), or other retirement plans. When you take your money out, sooner or later, your patient Uncle Sam will expect his cut.

Income from federally tax-exempt funds may be taxable by state and/or local governments that impose income taxes. Patterns vary, but state authorities typically exempt income from state and local government obligations issued within the states where taxpayers live—if it exceeds a specified minimum percentage of a fund's dividend payments. But they tax income from securities issued in other states.

This has stimulated the boom in single-state municipal bond funds promising double—or even triple—tax-free income.

Whatever the situation in respect to income dividends, you are not exempt from federal, state, or local income tax when a tax-exempt fund distributes net short- and long-term capital gains that were realized from its sales of securities. They *are* taxable, as many shareholders were surprised to discover in recent years.

The reverse of funds that are federally tax-exempt but taxable at the state level occurs in some funds that own U.S. Treasury and certain other U.S. government securities. They are structured so that their income distributions are beyond the grasp of state and local governments, even if taxable at the federal level.

Thus, if you are investing only in a tax-deferred account, you will want to consider only taxable funds.

If, however, you are investing outside such tax-sheltered arrangements, you will want to calculate whether you would be better off in a taxable or taxexempt fund, not merely assume which it would be. (For pointers on how to figure this out, please see page 180.)

Credit Quality

As we saw in Chapter 2, debt securities in which bond funds invest range in credit risk from those backed by the full faith and credit of the U.S. government to high-quality corporate, municipal, and foreign government bonds, to issues with low prospects for timely interest payment or principal repayment.

No matter whether the range of current interest rates is high or low—whether, say, from 10 to 15% or from 5 to 10%—securities of the highest quality always pay the lowest interest. Those with the lowest quality pay the highest—when they pay.

If a fund is primarily or partially invested in securities low on the credit rating scale, it has to make this clear. A fund's name may not indicate its level of risk—a fund invested in junk bonds is more likely to be called a "high-yield" or "high-income" fund than a "junk bond" or "low-quality bond" fund—but the SEC requires its prospectus to spell out credit risk up front.

Naturally, if a fund is only invested in U.S. government or investment-grade corporate securities, it will be glad to say so. In fact, its name probably will reflect its policy; the phrases "U.S. Government" and "Investment Grade" appear often.

Few things have caused the SEC greater concern in this regard in recent years than implications that the full faith and credit of the U.S. government stands behind a fund's shares or surveys that indicate that many investors believe—wrongly—that the Federal Deposit Insurance Corporation insures mutual fund shares bought at a bank.

The government assures you only of timely interest payment and principal repayment for the Treasury and certain other government securities that a fund holds in its portfolio—not of the price of the fund's shares.

To help you to understand the levels of credit risk inherent in funds' holdings of corporate and tax-exempt securities, their prospectuses and reports describe their credit quality policies and portfolio securities in terms of Moody's and Standard & Poor's bond ratings (page 37).

If, for example, a fund states its policy is to hold only triple-A and double-A securities, you don't have to wonder about the degree of credit risk to which the fund's portfolio would expose you.

If, on the other hand, it aims at higher income by investing in other than investment-grade bonds—that is, bonds receiving a Ba or lower from Moody's (or BB or lower from S&P)—just stating the ratings isn't enough. The fund has to disclose clearly the risks involved in more speculative investments. (Some fund complexes have developed their own rating systems to supplement the commercial ones. T. Rowe Price describes the composition of its bond portfolios according to its quality ratings system in reports to its shareholders.)

Should you only feel comfortable being in a fund that is limited to investing in U.S. Treasury securities, your choice of a fund group is fairly obvious. Should you want to earn the higher income associated with speculative-grade bonds, your choice of a fund group is also obvious—as is the need to check your ability to accept the credit risk that's involved.

If you're in between—willing and able to assume a limited degree of credit risk and not determined to earn maximum income—you have more fund categories to choose from, as you'll soon see.

Average Maturities

Taxable or tax-exempt, the debt securities held by the bond funds that you would consider may have maturities of from one to thirty (or even more) years, depending on their investment objectives. Interest rate risk—the risk that a bond's price will fall when interest rates rise—increases with maturity or duration. So do the potential rewards when rates fall. (To understand the concept of duration, see the box.)

Although definitions may differ, short-term bond funds are often understood to have policies requiring them to invest in portfolios of securities whose dollar-weighted average maturities range from one to five years; intermediate-term funds, five to ten years, and long-term funds, over ten years. (The SEC staff suggests three years as the divide between short- and intermediate-term funds.)

Some funds state in their prospectuses that they have no explicit policies regarding maturities. This gives their portfolio managers a lot of flexibility, but makes it more difficult for you to figure out whether they'd be appropriate for you, inasmuch as you really may not know what you're buying.

All other things being equal, prices of securities having long maturities or durations fall more when interest rates rise than prices of short maturities or durations. This means that the prices, or net asset values (NAVs), of long-term bond funds that own them will fall more, too.

No long bonds—including those of the Treasury—are immune. The government's "full faith and credit" assures you of timely debt service; it doesn't insulate you from a falling bond market.

When you consider the interest rate risk associated with long-term bonds it's important, of course, to bear the potential advantages in mind, too.

When interest rates decline, as they had for most of the last decade until late 1993, those who invest in long-term bond funds enjoy greater appreciation of their funds' NAVs than do those invested in short-term funds.

Moreover, as we have also seen, the dollars and cents that long-term funds pay in income dividends tend to hold up better than the distribution rates of short-term funds when interest rates decline. For people who rely on

DURATION—A KEY TO BOND FUND RISK AND POTENTIAL RETURN

You are presumably familiar by now with the importance of the dollar-weighted average maturity of a bond fund portfolio in judging the fund's riskiness and potential return: Funds whose bonds have long average maturities tend to fall more when interest rates rise and to appreciate more when interest rates fall.

But portfolio managers and other professional bond investors use another yardstick that is even more indicative of a bond's—or bond fund's—sensitivity to changes in interest rates: duration.

It represents a more sophisticated concept than maturity, but its essence is not difficult to grasp.

Weighted average maturity is pretty simple to understand.

If you have a $100,000 portfolio divided equally among bond issues maturing in 10 years and 20 years, the weighted average maturity is 15 years. If the portfolio consists of $25,000 in 20-year maturities and $75,000 in 10-year maturities, the weighted average is 12.5 years, 2.5 years shorter because of the greater weight of the 10-year maturities.

I said nothing about the interest rates of the bonds' coupons.

But a coupon has an important effect on a bond's sensitivity to a change in interest rates. It's not the same for low-coupon and high-coupon issues of identical maturities because a high-coupon bond provides you a greater portion of your total expected cash flow—interest and principal—in earlier years.

Duration, which measures the expected life of the cash flows that you receive from a bond, is based on the present value of each of its interest and principal payments. For a 10-year bond, for example, it would be 20 semiannual interest payments and one principal payment. For a fund's portfolio, the duration would be the weighted average of the durations of all the bonds it owns.

In other words, duration measures how many years it will take you to get your money back from interest and principal when you invest in a bond. Except for zero-coupon bonds, whose durations and maturities are identical because zeros don't pay current interest, durations are always shorter than maturities. And they are likely to be shorter for callable bonds than for noncallable bonds.

It's easy to see why durations for high-coupon bonds are shorter than those for low-coupon bonds of identical maturities. If, say, you invest $1,000 in a 10-year bond that has a 10% coupon, you should get your money back sooner than if you invested $1,000 in a 10-year bond that has an 8% coupon because you'll be getting $100 cash each year instead of $80.

DURATION—
Continued

When interest rates are declining, the price of the longer-duration bond should appreciate more than the shorter-duration bond. When rates are rising, it should decline more.

Duration can be used to approximate the extent of the rise or fall. If a fund has a duration of six years, a 1% rise or fall in interest rates would result in a 6% fall or rise in its price. A 2% change would result in about a 12% rise or fall. (Actually, as the change in interest rates get larger, the changes in price are not quite symmetrical. The increases in price tend to be greater than the decreases for a rate change of the same percentage.)

Table 3.2 gives you an indication of the differences in durations of the major segments of the U.S. investment-grade bond market. It shows, for example, how much longer the durations of long-term corporates and Treasuries are than that of the market as a whole. It also illustrates how expected prepayments shorten the duration of 30-year Ginnie Maes. (Call provisions affect corporates in the same way.)

Table 3.2   *Maturity and Duration in the Investment–Grade Bond Market*

Investment-Grade Bond Market Sector	Yield to Maturity	Average Coupon	Average Maturity (Years)	Modified Duration (Years)
Treasury	7.81%	7.21%	7.99%	4.60%
10+ year Treasury	8.07	8.81	23.03	9.82
Government sponsored*	8.16	6.67	12.36	5.78
Corporate	8.72	7.85	11.85	5.88
10+ year high grade corporate**	8.77	7.84	24.11	9.45
Mortgage-backed securities	8.65	7.52	8.27***	4.98
30-year GNMA	8.73	8.07	10.15***	5.67
Salomon Brothers BIG Index	8.24	7.39	9.03	5.00

BIG = Broad investment grade
*Primarily government agency
** Salomon Brothers High-Grade (Aaa/AAA and Aa/AA) Index
***Weighted-average life.
Data as of January 1, 1995
Source: Salomon Brothers

DURATION—
Continued

When portfolio managers want to adjust their portfolios to defend against higher rates—or to benefit from falling rates—they buy and sell bonds to adjust the durations of their portfolios, addressing both maturities and coupons. (Bonds that sell at face value, or par, are likely to have coupons bearing current interest rates. Issues with higher coupons sell at premiums; lower-coupon issues, at discounts.)

Of course, a portfolio's duration can change even when a manager does nothing to cause it. If interest rates rise and bonds that were trading at par fall to a discount, the duration of a portfolio of noncallable securities is shortened. If they fall and bond prices rise to a premium, it is lengthened, making the portfolio more risky.

The effects on securities subject to call or prepayment (as is the case with Ginnie Maes) are just the opposite. When interest rates fall, the prices of these securities will also rise. But, because the chances of calls or prepayments are increased, their expected lives—or durations—are shortened.

When this book went to press, the SEC did not yet require funds to report on their durations, but it was considering proposals to require disclosure of such risk measures.

Meantime, pending such requirements, some fund companies cite them voluntarily in reports to shareholders. Those that don't should be able to provide you durations on the telephone. You can assume that most portfolio managers have them calculated regularly to help them do their jobs.

Don't rely too much on whatever figure you see or are told, however. It will be the fund's duration as of a particular day and may have changed, or be about to change, because of what the manager and/or the bond market may have done or be doing.

Ian A. MacKinnon, head of Vanguard's fixed income group, adds another word of caution: "Duration tells you what will happen to prices when interest rates change. It doesn't tell you when or how they're going to change."

bond funds for income, this is an important factor to weigh when considering what to invest in.

Investors insist on higher interest for longer maturities, as the Treasury yield curve in Figure 3.1 illustrates, because their money is subject to all sorts of unpredictable risks—especially inflation—for longer periods. Because adverse

Based on closing bid quotations (in percentages)

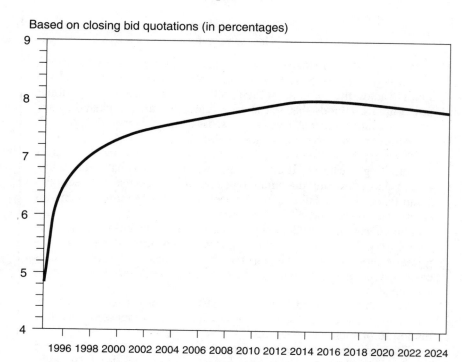

Years

FIGURE 3.1   Yields of Treasury Securities, September 30, 1994
Note: The curve is based only on the most actively traded issues. Market yields
on coupon issues due in less than three months are excluded.
Source: Treasury Bulletin, U.S. Department of the Treasury, December 1994

conditions are less likely to develop in short periods, short-term bonds—and
the funds that own these—normally pay lower interest.

Conditions are not always normal, however. There are times when long
and short rates are very close. There are other times—usually when the Federal
Reserve tries to cool down an overheated economy by slowing down growth
of the money supply—when short maturities may even have higher yields.

Unlike an individual bond, whose date of maturity you can choose when
you buy it—fairly certain that you will get your principal back then (unless the
issuer defaults, of course)—bond funds never mature. The exceptions are a
few target funds (page 64).

Thus, a fund that's managed to maintain a weighted-average maturity
of ten years will still have the same average maturity ten years from now,
unless its policy is changed. That means its risk/reward balance will remain
that of a ten-year fund for the period. On the other hand, when you buy a

ten-year bond, its risk/reward balance will change as it approaches maturity. In the last year, it should behave like a money market instrument.

To recap, maturities are important to you. In selecting bond funds according to their maturities, you influence both the interest rate risk to which they could expose you and the potential rewards—the level and durability of income—that they hold out for you.

Description of Fund Categories

Mindful of the three major criteria that you need to apply in screening fund classes and individual funds, you now are able to see which Lipper bond fund categories are most likely to have the funds that you believe would be most appropriate for you.

You'll find brief descriptions of each category, beginning with paraphrased Lipper definitions, on the following pages.

Absent an ideal way to organize the material, I have clustered the groups according to maturities or other common elements that seem to make the most sense (and have included the balanced and income fund categories, which, while not bond funds, you may wish to consider, too.)

Taxable Bond Funds

SHORT-TERM FUNDS

Short U.S. Treasury Funds: Funds that invest at least 65% of their assets in U.S. Treasury bills, notes, and bonds with dollar-weighted average maturities of five years or less.

Short U.S. Government Funds: Funds that invest at least 65% of their assets in securities issued or guaranteed by the U.S. government, its agencies, or instrumentalities with dollar-weighted average maturities of five years or less.

Short Investment Grade Bond Funds: Funds that invest at least 65% of their assets in investment-grade debt issues with dollar-weighted average maturities of five years or less.

The funds assigned to these groups by Lipper have one thing in common: their relatively short maturities, which make them least vulnerable to interest rate risk and, therefore, generally suitable for investors with relatively low risk tolerance.

Of course, when interest rates fall, the dividends they pay also tend to fall more sharply than those paid by riskier long-term funds as their maturing securities are replaced sooner by lower-yielding ones. This reduces the income of risk-averse investors who look to them for monthly checks.

Some managers may try to enhance returns by engaging in transactions that involve derivatives. They may succeed for a time, but unpredictable market developments can cause such strategies to backfire, turning funds that you might regard as low-risk investments into money losers.

Dollar-weighted average maturities vary within the groups. Some funds average close to one year, others are closer to five, and a number are smack in the middle.

Funds in each group tend to have yields and total returns higher than those of money market funds but lower than those of funds with longer maturities.

Given their relatively low interest rate risk, many investors use them as "parking lots" for money in place of money market funds when yields are generally low, even if they are not managed to maintain stable NAVs. They reckon that the higher income would more than offset a possible drop in NAV.

The major differences among the three groups lie in the credit quality of their investments.

Being primarily invested in U.S. Treasury issues, the U.S. Treasury funds have the highest quality portfolios and, all other things being equal, also provide relatively lower returns. Some may supplement their Treasury issues with those of government agencies that have the full faith and credit of the Treasury behind them.

The U.S. government funds typically blend their Treasuries with securities of other government entities, some—but not all—of which are backed by the full faith and credit of the Treasury.

Bear this in mind when a prospectus says that a fund "invests principally in securities issued or guaranteed as to principal and interest by the U.S. government, its agencies, and instrumentalities." Lest a hasty reading lead you to think otherwise, remember that this includes agencies such as Fannie Mae and Freddie Mac, which are owned by shareholders and whose securities are not guaranteed by the Treasury itself.

Although investment-grade funds may be 65% to 80% or more invested in corporates, many are widely diversified, also including government and mortgage-backed securities as well perhaps as securities backed by assets ranging from credit card receivables to airplane leases.

Some also invest in foreign securities—denominated in U.S. dollars or in foreign currencies, thereby incurring currency risk—and even in common stocks.

Funds differ in the percentages they allocate to the four investment grades: Aaa/AAA, Aa/AA, A/A, and Baa/BBB. Some concentrate on higher credit quality: Scudder Short Term Bond Fund, for example, limits its 65% core to the top two grades, while Vanguard Short-Term Corporate Portfolio must have 70% of its assets in the top three grades. Others may invest in all four investment grades in whatever proportions the portfolio managers wish.

Moreover, just because funds in the group invest primarily in investment-grade bonds doesn't mean that's all they invest in. Some, such as Dreyfus Short-Term Income Fund and Fidelity Advisor Short Fixed-Income Fund, may invest up to 35% in junk bonds. If they do have that flexibility, of course, they have to tell you so in the prospectus.

INTERMEDIATE–TERM FUNDS

Intermediate U.S. Treasury Funds: Funds that invest at least 65% of their assets in U.S. Treasury bills, notes, and bonds with dollar-weighted average maturities of five to ten years.

Intermediate U.S. Government Funds: Funds that invest at least 65% of their assets in securities issued or guaranteed by the U.S. government, its agencies, or instrumentalities with dollar-weighted average maturities of five to ten years.

Intermediate Investment Grade Bond Funds: Funds that invest at least 65% of their assets in investment-grade debt issues with dollar-weighted average maturities of five to ten years.

Most of the time, when the yield curve has a "normal" slope—that is, when bonds of long maturities yield more than bonds of short maturities—intermediate-term bond funds tend to provide higher returns than short-term funds. They also tend to fall farther when interest rates rise.

As in the case of short-term funds, Intermediate-Term Treasury and U.S. Government Funds invest only in Treasuries or in mixes of issues that include those of other government agencies, which may or may not be backed by the government. They also may include zero-coupon Treasury issues, which pay no current interest and whose prices can fluctuate widely.

Investment-grade funds have blends of governments, mortgage-backed securities, and corporates, unless they are invested in corporates alone. And, as in the case of short-term funds, they differ in how they allocate their assets among the four investment grades. American Funds' Intermediate Bond Fund of America, for example, may only buy corporates if they are rated Aaa/AAA or Aa/AA, while Warburg Pincus Fixed Income Fund may invest up to 35% in junk bonds.

Their weighted average maturities commonly range from three or five to ten years, although some try to stay in a narrower range. John Hancock Limited Term Government Fund is one that expects to maintain an average maturity of five to seven years. As you would expect by now, those closer to ten are likely to earn more—and be more risky—than those closer to three or five.

When the spreads between Treasury and corporate yields are relatively wide and managers feel comfortable assuming the credit risk of investment-grade corporate bonds, they may "overweight" funds in corporates by having above-average allocations to such issues.

On the other hand, when yield spreads are relatively narrow and managers are reluctant to invest in corporates for only slightly greater income, funds may tend to "underweight" corporates.

Another factor in the mix is call or prepayment risk. When interest rates are declining, and managers are concerned about the likelihood that corporate bonds may be called and/or that mortgage-backed securities may be prepaid, funds may try to maximize noncallable corporates and reduce exposure to the mortgage sector.

While the phrase "intermediate-term maturity" has an agreeable middle-of-the-road ring to it, it also happens to characterize most of the $4 trillion taxable U.S. investment-grade bond market.

As calculated by Salomon Brothers, whose Broad Investment-Grade Bond Index measures its performance, the market as a whole has an average maturity of around nine years. That's slightly higher than the 8-year average of all U.S. Treasury issues, which make up close to 50% of the total. Mortgage-backed securities, which make up 30%, have an average close to that of Treasuries. Corporates, which constitute slightly less than 20%, tend to be long-term, however; their average is around twelve years.

LONG-TERM AND UNSPECIFIED-TERM FUNDS

General U.S. Treasury Funds: Invest at least 65% of assets in U.S. Treasury bills, notes, and bonds.

General U.S. Government Funds: Invest 65% of their assets in U.S. Treasury and agency issues.

These groups of funds, like short- and intermediate-term U.S. Treasury and U.S. government funds, are concentrated in the safest securities—those backed by the full faith and credit of the U.S. Treasury—or those backed by agencies or instrumentalities of the government, some of which, you remember, are shareholder-owned. But, as cannot be repeated too often, the shares of the funds themselves are *not* backed by the government or insured.

Their prospectuses have to spell out the types of securities that they may own. Those invested in Treasury notes and bonds and in issues of agencies and instrumentalities that are backed by the full faith and credit of the United States usually will say so very prominently in their literature. Prospectuses of those invested in government securities that don't have such support—some of whose issuers may have the ability to borrow from the Treasury—have to make their relationship to the Treasury clear.

The common investment objective of U.S. Treasury and U.S. Government Securities Funds is "a high level of current income." Those only invested in Treasuries are likely to pay a bit less than those that own a variety of government issues. In either case, most distribute dividends monthly; others, quarterly.

In general, these funds really should expose investors to only two major risks: market risk arising from changes in interest rates, which usually reflect changes in actual or anticipated inflation rates, and prepayment risk resulting from their ownership of Ginnie Maes and other mortgage-backed securities.

If a fund also makes liberal use of a variety of derivative securities in the hope of enhancing returns, it also can run the risk of mismanaging these sometimes complex instruments and losing money.

The degree of interest rate risk—and, therefore, of course, the potential for reward—depends on the weighted average maturity or, to be more precise, the expected life of a fund's portfolio, which is reflected in the measure known as duration.

Prospectuses of the small number of General U.S. Treasury Funds tend to report the expected ranges of their weighted average maturities, and they are long: Benham Long-Term Treasury and Agency Fund, 20 to 30 years; Dreyfus 100% U.S. Treasury Long Term Fund, over 10 years; T. Rowe Price U.S. Treasury Long-Term Fund, 15 to 20 years, and Vanguard Long-Term U.S. Treasury Portfolio, 15 to 30 years.

Prospectuses of General U.S. Government Funds tend to be more ambiguous—possibly because of their holdings of mortgage-backed securities whose maturities are hard to specify because they change with interest rates. Among the few that state expected maturities, they range from 4 to 8 years for Lord Abbett U.S. Government Fund to 20 to 30 years for Overland Express U.S. Government Income Fund.

In many cases, in fact, fund statements of investment policy state that funds have no maturity restrictions, implying that portfolio managers are free to change maturities as they see fit.

Absent a statement as to the range of maturities that shareholders may expect, a shareholder report, disclosing how a fund is actually invested, may offer the only clues.

To the extent that a fund is invested in noncallable U.S. Treasury securities, it is fairly easy to come up with a hunch as to its average maturity. In such a case, it's important to remember that the manager can easily adjust this if he or she regards it desirable to cope with—or take advantage of—expected changes in interest rates.

But to the extent that a U.S. government fund is invested in mortgage-backed securities, its average maturity becomes a softer figure because of the difficulties in forecasting the possible acceleration of prepayments, which shorten the expected lives of such investments when interest rates slide.

Perhaps surprisingly, some funds in the group involve credit and currency risks because their policies permit their being invested up to 35% in securities other than U.S. government issues. Some, such as Delaware U.S. Government Fund, Prudential U.S. Government Fund, and Putnam Federal Income Trust, may hold small (even 20%) positions in corporate securities. Others, such as

Fidelity's Spartan Long-Term Government Bond Fund, may hold foreign obligations.

In implementing their investment policies, managers of a number of government bond funds may engage in strategies using derivatives such as call and put options and futures contracts to reduce the volatility of share prices, hedge against changes in interest rates, or enhance their return.

In so doing, they expose shareholders to risks that their strategies will not succeed, resulting in underperformance or even losses that to some—perhaps many—would seem incompatible with the perceived safety of government bond funds.

By selling call options against the government bonds in their portfolios, for example, managers hope to earn premium income to supplement the interest income received on the bonds—and thus to pay out more in distributions than government bond funds that invest only in government bonds.

Until the early 1990s, funds that aggressively pursued such strategies—offered by major firms such as Colonial, Dean Witter, Kemper, Massachusetts Financial Services (MFS), and Putnam—would have terms such as "government plus" or "enhanced income" in their names to indicate to investors that they were more than "plain vanilla" government bond funds.

A promotional leaflet for a Kemper fund illustrates the typical sales pitch: "It's hard to beat a portfolio of U.S. Government securities for credit safety. And when it is paired with the income-enhancing potential of futures and options, you've got a great combination."

So does one from MFS: "Higher yield through options—In addition to high current income, the Fund's goal is to provide an 'extra' level of income by writing covered-call and secured-put options against its holdings—income not available to the average investor."

As the fine print in their literature warns prospective buyers—"The use of options and futures to achieve higher returns and portfolio stability involves possible risks," MFS said—things don't always work out as planned, however.

By selling calls against bonds, "government plus" funds would risk missing out on increases in the bonds' prices when interest rates fell, as they had to do during the strong bond market of 1989–93. They had to give up securities as buyers of the calls exercised their options (unless the funds incurred the cost of buying offsetting calls), while shareholders of other bond funds were enjoying appreciation of their funds' portfolios. But when interest rates rose, the "government plus" funds' NAVs would drop, just as those of "plain vanilla" bond funds did.

Since there was no "plus" in sacrificing appreciation opportunities or losing money in closing options transactions, and since funds' names must be consistent with their policies and practices, the investment objectives of several funds were revised. These terms were deleted from their names, lest they mislead investors. (Prudential didn't drop "government plus" until mid-1994, becoming the last to do so.)

Nor were names the only problem for government funds managed to fatten monthly distributions from derivatives. In adopting new rules and amending old ones to standardize the computation of mutual fund performance data, the SEC in 1988 stipulated that a bond fund's "yield" could only include investment income from interest (and dividends, if any)—not premium income from options.

Since premium income is not considered investment income under generally accepted accounting principles and has to be treated as short-term capital gains, "government plus" funds could not advertise yields that reflected it. (Nor could a fund be called a "government high yield" fund if the "high" was attributable to more than interest from government bonds—that is, to premium income.)

The commission did permit funds to quote a "distribution rate" that included premium income in their prospectuses and sales literature—provided it's explained and accompanied by uniformly calculated yield and total return data. It prohibited the use of such rates in advertisements, however, because ads would be unlikely to contain adequate explanations.

Managements of some funds emphasizing the stability of their monthly distributions responded to falling interest rates, when income dividends had to be reduced, by including in their payments small sums that were nontaxable returns of shareholders' paid-in capital.

The practice raised at least two questions: whether shareholders understood that the funds had such policies and whether they made sense from the shareholders' point of view.

The law is clear on disclosure: Under the 1940 act, funds have to disclose the sources from which distributions are paid—whether from interest or dividend income, capital gains, or capital.

Does return of capital to keep distributions stable make sense for shareholders? Usually, not. Shareholders who invest in a fund presumably want that money working for them—not to get the money back after paying a fund to manage it for them and, as is more than likely with a government securities fund, after paying a broker a front-end load of as much as 5% to take the investment.

The fact that the return of capital is not taxed as income—since *it isn't income*—shouldn't make any difference.

A-Rated Corporate Bond Funds: Invest at least 65% of assets in corporate debt issues rated A or better or in government issues.

BBB-Rated Corporate Bond Funds: Invest at least 65% of assets in corporate and government debt issues rated in the top four grades.

General Bond Funds: Invest primarily in corporate and government debt issues, but do not have quality or maturity restrictions.

A-rated corporate bond funds are concentrated in high-grade corporate bonds and government securities to provide shareholders "high" current income consistent with "prudent investment risk" or "preservation of capital," as their prospectuses say. They invest primarily in corporate bonds that at the time of purchase carried the three highest credit ratings: Aaa/AAA, Aa/AA, or A/A.

Since the high-quality bonds owned by these funds tend to provide lower yields than speculative issues of comparable maturities, their portfolio managers face a challenge: How *can* they produce high income?

Usually, they accomplish this by formulating quality mixes that include some lower-grade securities and/or by owning longer maturities. (Of course, their investment advisers could help by holding down annual expenses.)

They may strive for higher-yielding blends of their core holdings of 65% to 90% high-quality bonds by investing proportionately more in A-rated corporate bonds than in Aaa/AAA-rated corporates or in government securities and/or by investing more in government-related, mortgage-backed securities, which yield more than Treasury issues of comparable maturities.

They may invest their remaining assets in bonds rated Baa/BBB, the lowest of the investment grades. Pioneer Bond Fund, for example, can invest up to 15% of its assets in such securities; Scudder Income Fund, up to 25%, and Vanguard Long-Term Corporate Portfolio, up to 30%.

Or they may buy bonds below investment grade (that is, Ba/BB or lower), including convertible securities. American Funds' Bond Fund of America can invest up to 34% in junk; John Hancock Sovereign Bond Fund, up to 25%; Dodge & Cox Income Fund, up to 20%, and Dreyfus A Bonds Plus and IAI Bond Fund, up to 5%.

Putnam Income Fund, which has no minimum requirement for investment-grade bonds and can invest in junk, is managed so that its average credit quality doesn't fall below A. (An informal policy guideline limits junk to 20% of assets.) It is permitted to boost income by buying higher-yielding bonds that sell at premium prices, despite the risk of capital losses when such bonds are called. The fund also may buy dividend-paying common stocks when they are more attractive; no one can predict when that might be.

As bond market conditions change, portfolio managers sometimes adjust their quality mixes. When, for example, there is little difference in yields among the top grades and they don't have to give up much income, some prefer to be cautious and have higher percentages of higher-grade issues. When spreads widen, they may lean more to Baa/BBBs—or, if permitted, Ba/BBs—in the expectation that the higher income will offset the slightly higher credit risk.

Another, concurrent strategy can involve maturities.

A fund's investment policy may require it, under "normal" circumstances, to be invested so that its portfolio can be expected to have a weighted average maturity of X to Y years and that, when deemed appropriate, it will be invested in long maturities to obtain their higher yields. The weighted average maturity of Vanguard Long-Term Corporate Portfolio, for example, can be expected to be 15 to 25 years; that of T. Rowe Price New Income Fund, 4 to 9 years.

More likely, prospectuses of funds in the A-rated group will be more ambiguous. Some, such as those of Bond Fund of America and Scudder Income Fund, say that their managers are not limited to specific maturities but are expected to invest in intermediate- and long-term bonds—a wide range. Others won't even say that much.

Whatever the case, fund managers may adjust maturities (or durations) as market conditions change by replacing bond holdings with, and/or putting fresh cash to work in, longer or shorter maturities to achieve their targets.

As the prospectus of the D.L. Babson Bond Trust, which offers two portfolios—L (7 to 15 years) and S (2 to 5 years)—states:

> Future interest rates cannot be accurately and consistently forecast. Nevertheless, when management believes that interest rates are likely to rise in the future, it will tend to shorten portfolio maturities so that it may reinvest maturing holdings as soon as possible and thereby obtain higher yields. When management believes that interest rates are likely to fall in the future, it will seek to preserve and extend the Trust's yields by lengthening the maturities of the portfolio holdings.

Funds in the BBB group have investment objectives and policies that are similar to those of A-rated Corporate Bond Funds but drop one level below A to include (more) Baa/BBB-rated corporate issues and, thus, should produce higher yields.

They incur a shade more credit risk than inheres in A-rated funds but, judging by statements about expected maturities, seem to involve a similar degree of interest rate risk.

To maximize income, some fund managers have large shares of their portfolios in Baa/BBB issues when these offer yields sufficiently higher than high-grade bonds to make them attractive. When their assessment of market conditions indicates it would be desirable—that is, when they feel shareholders won't be compensated sufficiently for accepting the risk inherent in corporate bonds—they may load up on government securities.

In addition to corporate bonds of the top four grades, governments, and money market instruments, funds in this group also are likely to invest in lower-rated bonds or other speculative securities, including convertibles, common and preferred stocks, foreign securities, options, and futures. Fidelity Investment Grade Bond Fund and Federated's Fortress Bond Fund, for example, may invest up to 35% in junk; Colonial Income Fund and Legg Mason Investment Grade Income Portfolio, up to 25%, and MFS Bond Fund, up to 20%.

As far as prospectus comments on expected maturities go, the Columbia Fixed Income Securities Fund statement is about as specific as they get: "Generally, the securities purchased will be of an intermediate maturity (less than 10 years) when interest rates are expected to rise and of a relatively long maturity (over 10 years) when interest rates are expected to decline."

Calvert Income Fund offers less guidance with the statement that its expected maturity will range between 5 and 20 years—a huge range—while Fidelity's Spartan Investment Grade Bond Fund's policy is to invest in securities having longer terms to maturity than its sibling, Spartan Short-Term Income Fund, whose weighted average maturity "is normally limited" to 3 years. Others simply say that they invest in a variety of maturities—period.

General Bond Funds, having no particular credit quality or maturity restrictions, tend to invest in both government and corporate bonds, including both investment grade and junk, as well as convertible and foreign securities.

A few of the funds assigned to this category by Lipper aim at maximizing returns while holding down volatility by investing in three broad bond market sectors that aren't expected to rise or fall in tandem: U.S. government, U.S. corporate junk, and foreign securities. (They could, of course.)

Colonial, Fidelity, John Hancock, Keystone, Massachusetts Financial, Oppenheimer, and Paine Webber use the word "strategic" in their funds' names to indicate that they adhere to this so-called three-sector strategy.

The word "strategic" doesn't have a unique definition in fund usage, however. Nor are "strategic income" funds the only ones that are concentrated in those sectors.

Putnam, which originated the concept with a closed-end fund in 1987, called its 3-sector mutual fund Putnam Diversified Income Trust, and Kemper followed this example, retaining "diversified" in the name of the fund whose investment policy was changed to this strategy in 1994. Smith Barney Shearson, perhaps showing ambivalence or foresight, covered all the bases by naming its fund Diversified Strategic Income Fund.

Other funds with "strategic" or "diversified" in their names may have similar objectives of diversification among bond market sectors to be less volatile than the individual sectors, but have different investment policies. Funds such as Dean Witter Diversified Income and Dreyfus Strategic Income may invest in three different sectors or in more sectors.

Clearly, it's important to look beyond the labels.

The General Bond Funds group also includes a few other funds with interesting investment policies.

A notable example: Fidelity's Spartan Bond Strategist, which is designed to maximize after-tax total return for high-tax bracket investors by investing in both taxable and tax-exempt securities. At least 50% of the fund's assets have to be invested in municipals so that income dividends can qualify for federal tax exemption. How much of the rest is in taxable government, corporate, or foreign bonds will depend on which sector is judged to be more attractive on an after-tax basis.

MORTGAGE FUNDS

Adjustable Rate Mortgage (ARM) Funds: Invest at least 65% of assets in ARM securities or other securities collateralized by, or representing, an interest in mortgages.

GNMA Funds: Invest at least 65% of their assets in mortgage-backed securities guaranteed by the Government National Mortgage Association.

U.S. Mortgage Funds: Invest a minimum of 65% of their assets in mortgages/securities issued or guaranteed by the U.S. government and certain federal agencies.

Funds in these groups are primarily invested in (1) securities issued by lending institutions, backed by FHA-insured and VA-guaranteed mortgages, and guaranteed by GNMA and (2) securities issued by FHLMC and FNMA, backed by conventional mortgages, and guaranteed by those stockholder-owned federal agencies. As we saw in Chapter 2, the former are backed by the full faith and credit of the U.S. Treasury; the latter are not.

Ginnie Maes, Fannie Maes, and Freddie Macs, whether representing interests in government-backed or conventional mortgages, usually have maturities of 15 and 30 years. Because of both normal prepayment rates and accelerated prepayments during periods of declining interest rates when homeowners refinance mortgages, the expected lives of the pools of mortgage-backed securities (MBS) are much less. For 30-year securities, they're usually estimated to be 12 years.

Yields of MBS typically run around 1 percent higher than those of Treasury issues of comparable maturities because of the risk of unscheduled prepayments, which funds are forced to reinvest in lower-yield MBS, reducing the income they can distribute as well as the potential for appreciation of securities in their portfolios.

MBS backed by pools of adjustable rate mortgages (ARM), introduced by GNMA in 1983, have the characteristics of short-term securities since their interest rates are reset—within specified ranges—at various intervals up to annually.

The frequencies are important in determining whether an ARM will have more stable income or more stable principal. When rates are reset often, an ARM's principal is more likely to remain stable while its interest rate fluctuates more. When they are reset infrequently, the rates remain stable but principal fluctuates more. Similarly, when market rates rise above or fall below an ARM's permitted range, its principal will fluctuate more as well.

Rates are reset based on indexes of short-term Treasury securities' market prices or calculated measures. The most commonly used Treasury securities index is the 1-year constant maturity Treasury (CMT) index, which closely reflects changes in rates. The most commonly used calculated measure is the cost of funds index (COFI) computed by the Federal Home Loan Bank of San Francisco, which operates with a lag.

ARM funds were introduced with the launchings of Federated Variable Rate Mortgage Securities Trust and Franklin Adjustable U.S. Government Securities Fund in October 1987. After the Federated fund was merged into Federated Income Trust in 1989, the Franklin fund was alone until 1990, when the Overland Express Variable Rate Government Fund was started by Wells Fargo Bank, with Stephens Inc. as administrator and distributor.

The field became more crowded in 1991. As falling interest rates stimulated demand for ARMs among home buyers and stimulated demand among investors for instruments yielding more than money market rates, other funds came along—including the first two no-load ARM funds from Benham and T. Rowe Price and load funds from firms such as Dean Witter, Federated, Keystone, Merrill Lynch, and Putnam. Before long, there were enough to warrant Lipper's creating a category for them, and by mid-1994 there were as many as 70.

The funds' goal is a simple one: to provide more yield than money market funds while holding the volatility of principal below that of bond funds with longer maturities.

Most funds in the group are primarily invested in ARMs guaranteed by GNMA or issued by FHLMC and FNMA. A number also may be invested in government-related collateralized mortgage obligations (CMOs).

Others try to enhance income by also buying nongovernment MBS and asset-backed securities with variable rates and fixed-rate government securities.

Policies also differ with respect to derivatives—in the types they use, the purposes for which they use them, and the extent to which they use them.

GNMA funds, which are primarily invested in fixed-rate Ginnie Maes, have been popular with investors for years. Their total net assets of over $45 billion exceeded those of any other taxable bond fund group in late 1994 and were second among all bond fund groups only to general municipal bond funds' assets of over $65 billion.

In fact, the group includes several of the largest mutual funds: Franklin U.S. Government Securities Series, with net assets of around $11.7 billion; Vanguard GNMA, $6 billion; AARP GNMA & U.S. Treasury Fund, $5.6 billion, and Kemper U.S. Government Securities Fund, $5.1 billion. (Another giant, the $9.4 billion Dean Witter U.S. Government Securities Trust, is classified as a General U.S. Government Fund but tends to be nearly half invested in Ginnie Maes.)

Inasmuch as all GNMA funds are concentrated in Ginnie Maes and have essentially the same investment objective—current income consistent with safety of principal and liquidity—can there be more than name difference among them? You bet.

For one thing, they vary in the minimum percentages of assets they must invest in Ginnie Maes. They range from 65% to 80%. The rest may be in other kinds of mortgage-backed or government-related securities, including U.S. Treasuries, Fannie Maes, and Freddie Macs. The AARP fund, for example, tries to be 20% in short-term (one year or less) Treasury securities to help mitigate volatility; informal policy guidelines permit this to go as high as 50%.

When they expect lower interest rates, some managers may replace some of their Ginnie Maes with Treasuries to benefit from their greater potential for appreciation.

Beyond deciding how much to invest in Ginnie Maes, which Ginnie Mae pools to invest in, and where to invest the rest of their funds' assets, managers have the challenging job of figuring out how to allocate their Ginnie Mae holdings by coupon rates.

Maximizing income would call for buying Ginnie Maes with the highest coupons. When interest rates are rising, this strategy also would run less risk of decline in principal. But when rates are falling, it would run the greatest risk of accelerated prepayments, resulting in reduced income. To the extent that GNMA certificates may have been bought at a premium, prepayments could result in realization of capital losses.

By emphasizing Ginnie Maes bearing whatever current coupon rate prevails in the market—or lower rates—managers may protect themselves more against prepayment risk if interest rates fall, but they also tend to inhibit yield and return and to run the risk of losing principal if rates should rise.

Some fund managers spend a great deal of time analyzing the characteristics of Ginnie Mae pools to determine which are most likely to incur prepayment risk because of regional or other factors. They also try to judge which pools of high-coupon Ginnie Maes are less likely to run this risk because the owners of the underlying mortgages have passed up earlier opportunities to refinance their mortgages at lower rates and, therefore, may be expected to do so again.

U.S. Mortgage Funds are similar to Ginnie Mae funds. They also seek to provide shareholders high levels of current income by investing in MBS, but they are able to choose among the three major categories: Freddie Macs and Fannie Maes as well as Ginnie Maes.

The three have in common not only their government links but also the provisions for passing through to funds (and other owners) the monthly payments of interest and principal made by mortgagors. This key feature distinguishes them from conventional debt securities on which issuers pay interest regularly but don't repay principal until they do so in one lump sum at maturity.

Not committed to invest only in securities backed by the government's full faith and credit, the group's funds have investment policies that are more narrowly focused than those of U.S. Government Securities Funds—given their MBS concentration—yet not as narrowly defined as those of pure Ginnie Mae funds.

Inherent in all three securities is the risk that mortgagors will pay off their mortgages before they mature. Whatever the reason for unscheduled prepayments—refinancing to take advantage of lower interest rates, sales, fore-closures—they deprive investors of income they had expected until maturity and necessitate reinvestment at lower yields.

Based on their assessment of the securities and of market conditions, funds' portfolios contain different mixes of Ginnie Maes, Freddie Macs, and Fannie Maes. They usually tend to have significant holdings of Ginnie Maes; some funds have devoted 50% or more of their assets to them. Others, however, have larger stakes in Freddie Macs or Fannie Maes.

Funds also differ in what they do with the money not invested in these three. Some may have 25% or more invested in U.S. Treasury securities as a cushion against falling interest rates; others also may own other government and government-related securities. Still others, giving greater weight to in-come—but not necessarily indifferent to credit risk—also invest in private mort-gage-backed securities, which may be supported by insurance or guarantees, or other high-quality corporate debt.

Like U.S. government and ARM funds, fixed-rate mortgage funds also may engage in a variety of derivative strategies to try to enhance returns or reduce volatility in their share prices.

HIGH INTEREST RATE RISK BOND FUNDS

Target Maturity Funds: Invest principally in zero-coupon U.S. Treasury se-curities.

With few exceptions, bond mutual funds do not mature on specific dates, as individual bonds do. The funds in this group constitute essentially all of the exceptions.

The group consists primarily of the funds in the Benham Target Ma-turities Trust, first offered in 1985, which mature in 1995 and every fifth year thereafter until 2020. (By the time you read this, Benham may have filed a registration statement for one to mature in 2025.)

These funds, like Scudder Zero Coupon 2000 Fund, the only survivor of a once larger Scudder target maturity group, are primarily invested in Treasury zero-coupon obligations—known as STRIPS—that mature in the target year or within a few months of its beginning or end.

As noted in Chapter 2, STRIPS (and similar securities) can be highly volatile. Because they pay no interest on a current basis, their prices fluctuate more between issue and maturity than coupon-bearing bonds, thereby exposing investors to a high degree of interest rate risk. The longer the maturities, the greater the possible fall in price. To the extent that the U.S. Treasury stands behind them, they involve no credit risk, of course.

While some investors use STRIPS or target maturity funds to speculate on interest rates—their prices rise more than other bonds when interest rates fall—a less risky strategy is to hold them to maturity, when the redemption proceeds may be needed for a particular purpose, such as tuition. (Unless

STRIPS are bought in a tax-deferred account, income taxes are payable on interest income credited—but not received—as the price of each security increases from its discounted level to its face value.)

Sponsors cannot guarantee that the funds' shares will be worth some predictable amount at maturity, but they do manage each portfolio in a way that aims to achieve a projected rate of return, called an "anticipated growth rate," and an ultimate value by the time a fund is liquidated at the end of the target year.

Unlike individual bonds, zeros don't involve reinvestment risk—that is, the risk of reinvesting semiannual interest payments at lower rates, which can happen over a long period—since interest is not paid semiannually. The Benham and Scudder funds are managed to minimize this risk for shareholders who reinvest distributions.

HIGH CREDIT RISK BOND FUNDS

High Current Yield Funds: These funds aim at earning relatively high current yields from fixed income securities. They tend to invest in lower-grade bonds but have no quality restrictions. Nor do they have maturity restrictions.

Often called junk bond funds, the funds in this group seek high income by investing in speculative—that is, relatively high-risk—corporate securities that offer high yields. Some also have capital appreciation as a secondary objective. Despite the term "junk," such funds may be suitable for a portion of your portfolio if you consider yourself able and willing to accept the credit risk they involve.

The principal securities they own are corporate bonds that are rated Ba/BB or lower—that is, below the four investment grades of Aaa/AAA, Aa/AA, A, and Baa/BBB—because the credit rating agencies have doubts as to the issuers' abilities to pay interest and repay principal when scheduled. Some issues may even be in default.

To compensate investors for taking the risks, the securities have to offer yields that are higher than those offered by higher-rated corporates or government securities. In 1983, when 10-year Treasury issues were yielding about 11%, high-yield bonds, on the average, yielded about 14%. By 1993, when 10-year Treasuries yielded close to 6%, high-yield bonds were yielding over 9%, lower in absolute terms but still higher on a relative basis. In between, the spreads between the two were as wide as 10% during the 1990–91 recession, when high-yield bonds averaged nearly 18% versus around 8% for 10-year Treasuries.

Because of the importance of their debt service being timely, the prices of high-yield bonds are very sensitive to the profitability of the issuing corporations—at times, especially for lower-quality junk, more so than to the trend of interest rates. Changes in expectations of prompt interest payments and principal repayments—whether due to profit slippage, excessive debt, or other factors—can cause junk bonds to dive.

Bonds assigned lower ratings, which include some of the best-known corporate names in the nation, fall essentially into two categories:

1. New bond issues, whether sold by emerging companies that need debt capital before attaining the financial strength entitling them to a higher rating or by established firms that want to use the cash for expansion or acquisitions.

2. Existing issues whose ratings are lowered from investment grade when their issuers have, or are expected to have, financial problems that have resulted—or could result—in default. Their prices fall until their yields become comparable to those of other bonds of similar maturities and perceived credit quality.

An ample supply of corporate junk bonds is usually outstanding. At the end of September 1994, bonds rated Ba or lower by Moody's totaled some $235 billion—about 20% of all U.S. corporate long-term debt rated by the firm.

The premise on which high current yield bond funds operate, as the prospectus for Kemper High Yield Fund says, is "that over the long term a broadly diversified portfolio of high yield fixed income securities should, even taking into account possible losses, provide a higher net return than that achievable on a portfolio of higher rated securities."

In other words, given that yields of high-yield bonds tend to run at least 3% higher than those of U.S. Treasury securities of comparable maturity, a well-diversified portfolio should generate enough income to absorb a small number of defaults and still come out ahead. The margin of 3% or more is not constant or guaranteed, however.

"The market values of such securities tend to reflect individual corporate developments to a greater extent than do those of higher rated securities, which react primarily to fluctuations in the general level of interest rates," Kemper's prospectus points out.

"Such lower-rated securities also tend to be more sensitive to economic conditions than are higher-rated securities. Adverse publicity and investor perceptions regarding lower-rated bonds, whether or not based on fundamental analysis, may depress the prices for such securities."

While the possibilities for greater income and greater gain exist among high-yield securities, investment in them clearly necessitates addressing the risks of loss of income, and even principal, which are inherent in them. They are the risks that lead the rating services to give them a low rating in the first place.

Because the means of coping with these risks—credit analysis of issuing companies, adequate diversification among many issues, economic analysis—are beyond the capabilities of an average individual investor, investing in high-yield bonds via mutual funds makes a lot more sense—if you can afford to invest in them at all.

Credit analysis isn't just looking up a rating in Moody's. It involves analyzing a company so that you can judge whether Moody's rating, on which the bond's price is partially based, may be inappropriate or on the verge of being raised or lowered. (Analysis can lead a fund manager to buy bonds of a company in default if he or she expects the company to overcome its problems and eventually pay its bondholders.)

Given that some bonds will inevitably go into default, it is critical that an investor have a sufficiently diversified portfolio to absorb the loss of income from them, and even their principal, without materially hurting the portfolio's performance. Some funds have as many as 200 issues.

Because the yields that attract purchasers of high-yield bonds are dependent on their issuers' ability to pay interest at the rates to which their coupons commit them, and because that, in turn, is commonly dependent on business conditions, it is important to be alert to the likelihood of an economic downturn. That could significantly reduce the issuers' profits or even cause them to suffer losses and result in sharp drops of their bonds' prices.

Differences among high-yield funds arise not only from the differences in their analysis of pertinent information but also from the policies on which they base their investment decisions and the skills with which they choose companies.

A key difference is in their quality mixes. Some include lower-tier investment-grade bonds by putting a quality cap of Baa/BBB on their core bond holdings. Others limit their core holdings to issues rated below investment grade. Some won't buy issues rated below B; others will.

Policies regarding the normal investment of the 20% to 35% of assets beyond their core positions also vary—that is, whether to include high-grade bonds, zero-coupon obligations, common stocks, and foreign securities.

During changes in interest rate levels or spreads, funds may make adjustments in their portfolios. When interest rates are high, some managers may take advantage of the opportunity to buy more government securities and lock in the high yields with the assurance that the bonds won't be called, as corporates often are, when interest rates fall. Quite a few also opt for quality by including more governments at a time when interest rates generally are lower but the spread between Treasuries and lower-rated bonds is narrow.

When managers sense a recession may be near, some become defensive, switching out of the issues of corporations in cyclical industries and into bonds of more "recession-proof" industries.

FUNDS LINKED, IN VARYING DEGREES, TO THE STOCK MARKET

Flexible Income Funds: Funds that emphasize the generation of income by investing at least 85% in debt issues, preferred stock, and convertible securities. Common stocks cannot consistently exceed 15%.

Income Funds: Funds that normally seek a high level of current income through investing in income-producing stocks, bonds, and money market instruments.

Balanced Funds: Funds whose primary objective is to conserve principal by maintaining at all times balanced portfolios of both stocks and bonds. Typically, their stock/bond ratios range around 60%/40%.

Convertible Securities Funds: Funds that invest primarily in bonds and/or preferred stocks that are convertible into common stocks.

However the funds in these groups may differ, all have in common objectives of both producing income and providing at least some growth through a linkage to the stock market, yet doing so in a way that results in less volatility than is characteristic of all-stock funds.

Flexible Income Funds—not to be confused with Lipper's Flexible Portfolio (or asset allocation) category—invest in whatever types of securities will provide income without exceeding the expected levels of risk that their managements deem appropriate. Given their relatively low holdings of common stocks, appreciation is likely to be limited.

The group's fund managers have the flexibility to make portfolio switches, when deemed advantageous, between fixed-income securities and equities; among short, intermediate, and long maturities; among high-, medium-, and lower-grade bonds; between corporates and governments; and between U.S. and foreign issues.

Inasmuch as high-quality bonds have long provided higher yields, on the average, than high-quality common stocks, it's not surprising that bonds tend to account for 75% to 85% of flexible income fund portfolios. Among funds in the group that own any common stocks, the shares tend to be 10% to 15%.

While a fund such as USAA Income may be 80% invested in U.S. government securities, large shares of the bonds held by the group's other funds are not highly rated at all, however. Nicholas Income Fund and Northeast Investors Trust, for example, may be 80% or more invested in bonds that are rated below investment grade or not rated. Janus Flexible Income Fund's assets may be more evenly divided between investment grade and junk bonds.

The Northeast fund doesn't only take the risk of investing heavily in speculative bonds. It borrows money on a short-term basis—equivalent to as much as 25% of its assets—to buy more bonds than shareholder's cash enables it to do. This, of course, can only be profitable as long as the return on its investments exceeds the interest cost of the borrowings.

Lipper classifies Income Funds as funds that can assume a bit more stock market risk but otherwise may invest in similar categories of securities—possibly in different proportions.

The group's largest, Vanguard/Wellesley Income Fund, is expected to be 60% in bonds with the remainder in dividend-paying common stocks. The bonds are primarily of investment grade; the stocks, blue chip. Franklin Income Fund may be similarly split between bonds and stocks, but a substantial share of its bond holdings are junk.

Fidelity Asset Manager: Income, a sibling of Fidelity Asset Manager, a huge asset allocation fund, follows a still different, more conservative approach. Its "neutral" mix calls for 20% stocks, 30% bonds, and 50% domestic and foreign short-term instruments with maturities of three years or less. The manager has the flexibility, as market conditions indicate, to vary the stock portion between 0 and 30%; bonds, between 20% and 40%; and short-term securities between 30% and 80%.

Whether defined by Lipper or by the SEC, which requires any fund calling itself "balanced" to have at least 25% of its assets in "fixed income senior securities" (that is, bonds and preferred stocks), balanced funds commonly seek growth and income (as well as growth of income) and capital preservation.

Although the SEC frowns on any fund management suggesting that its fund may be considered a complete investment program—and insists that fund literature warn that none should be so considered—a well-managed balanced fund comes close to being that: the only type of mutual fund to own if you only want, or can afford, one.

American Funds' American Balanced Fund may come close to saying that in its prospectus: "The fund approaches the management of its investments as if they constituted the complete investment program of the prudent investor."

So does Dodge & Cox Balanced Fund: "In shares of the Fund, investors acquire the kind of balanced portfolio ordinarily limited to large investment accounts. Many individuals, trustees, retirement plans and institutions have found that such a portfolio and the investment policies and continuous investment supervision provided by the Fund make it suitable for their entire long-term investment program."

Whether "balanced" is in their names or not, the funds that Lipper assigns to this group differ in what they emphasize in their investment objectives as well as in how they intend to achieve them.

To achieve their objectives, all invest in diversified portfolios of common and preferred stocks, bonds, and money market instruments. A large number state in their prospectuses that their policies don't call for the allocation of specific percentages to each asset type.

Several specify a minimum of 25% of assets in bonds or bonds plus preferred stocks—presumably to satisfy the SEC requirement—unless the need to take defensive positions leads them to invest more heavily in money market securities.

Others express targets in terms of equities, stating they will allocate no more than 60% to 75% to common stocks.

Vanguard STAR Fund, which invests in other Vanguard bond, equity, and money market funds, says it has a policy of investing 60% to 70% in the group's equity funds and 30% to 40% in its fixed income funds.

While several balanced funds speak of being flexible to change asset allocations as market conditions warrant, STAR's management has maintained fixed targets, since its inception in 1985, of 62.5% in equity funds, 25% in bond funds, and 12.5% in the money market fund.

"This policy," the prospectus says, "reflects the Board of Trustees' belief that holding relatively steady proportions of stocks, bonds and money market instruments is more likely to provide favorable long-term investment returns, with moderate risk, than frequently rebalancing STAR's investment holdings based on short-term events."

Convertible Securities Funds invest in bonds and/or preferred stocks that may be converted into specific numbers of shares of the common stocks of the companies that issued them, at specific prices, within specific periods. In a corporation's capital structure, convertibles are junior to nonconvertible bonds but senior to common stocks. Until their conversion, holders of convertible bonds or preferreds receive regular interest or dividends, respectively.

Their market values may be based on interest rates or on the market values of the common stock into which they could be converted. Like the prices of nonconvertible fixed-income securities, the prices of convertibles tend to rise when interest rates fall and to fall when interest rates rise.

When the prices of the underlying shares rise, the prices of convertibles rise and may exceed the market values that their interest or dividends would indicate. When prices of the stocks fall, the prices of the convertibles fall, too, but eventually their yields provide support.

While their interest and dividend payments make convertible securities suitable investments for those who want stable current income, their issuers offer lower interest or dividend yields than they would for nonconvertible bonds or preferreds of similar quality. That's because of the opportunities for capital appreciation arising from the conversion possibility. Yet, because of their fixed-income characteristics, the yields tends to be higher than those of the dividends paid on the stocks into which they may be converted.

Convertible securities funds state that their investment objectives are capital appreciation as well as current income, or simply total return. While a large number say they aim to have at least 65% of their assets in convertible securities, a few have higher or lower minimums. Vanguard Convertible Securities Fund, for example, says it normally will be at least 80% invested in convertibles. On the other hand, American Capital Harbor Fund, the oldest, has a fundamental policy of investing "over 50%" of its assets excluding cash, cash equivalents, and government securities in them.

To attain their objectives, the funds employ essentially two kinds of strategies: choosing the convertible securities for their portfolios' core holdings and deciding how to invest the remaining assets. The selection of convertibles typically involves consideration of how much of the portfolio should consist of high-grade issues versus those with lower credit ratings and, therefore, higher yields. Another consideration is how much to invest in securities of small- or medium-size companies in the expectation that the long-term appreciation of their stocks will be greater.

The portions of portfolios invested in nonconvertible assets are used to enhance income, prospects for appreciation, or both. They may include lower-grade debt issues, common and preferred stocks, options, futures, foreign securities, and money market instruments.

American Capital Harbor appears to be the most enthusiastic for common stocks, having a fundamental policy that permits it to devote as much as 45% of total assets to them.

Despite their potential appeal to investors who want linkage to the long-term performance of the stock market but who want to hold down their commitment to equity funds, convertible securities funds have not been hot sellers because, marketers explain, they have had trouble explaining the concept behind these funds.

In fact, in recent years, the managements of AIM's and Federated's convertible securities funds, which had performed well but remained small, converted them into AIM Balanced and Liberty Equity Income funds, respectively. Dreyfus Convertible Securities Fund, which had done poorly but was large, was merged into Dreyfus Growth and Income Fund, thereby burying its poor record.

WORLD INCOME FUNDS

General World Income Funds: Invest primarily in non-U.S. dollar (as well as U.S. dollar) debt instruments with unspecified maturities or duration.

Short World Multi-Market Income Funds: Invest in non-U.S. dollar (as well as U.S. dollar) debt instruments, keeping a dollar-weighted average maturity of less than five years.

Started in 1981, when MFS offered the predecessor of today's MFS World Governments Fund to provide investors an alternative to then plummeting U.S. bonds, the group has grown in number and size as other fund families perceived potential investor demand for foreign bonds and as investors responded.

The basic premise underlying the general funds is that at any given time some bond markets somewhere in the world are likely to be more attractive than ours—whether because of higher inflation- adjusted, or real, interest rates (in U.S. dollar terms) or the prospects for a secular decline in rates.

The U.S. government bond market, which accounts for less than 40% of Salomon Brothers' World Government Bond Index, has not been the number one performer among major markets since 1984. In fact, as Table 3.3 shows, our market's performance has only been close to the top twice since then and was the worst performer in 1987.

Attractive as investing in other bond markets may seem, it hasn't been easy. Not only have managers had to bear in mind the interest rate and credit risks associated with investing in U.S. bonds; they've also had to contend with occasional turbulence in world currency markets that could undermine their strategies. (To say nothing of risks of expropriation of corporate property or renunciation of debts!)

What bittersweet achievement it can be for a portfolio manager to get certain key things right—a country's interest rate outlook, the upgrading of major corporate issues—only to have hostilities erupt somewhere, causing people to flee to the dollar and strengthening it against other major currencies.

Unlike most U.S. bond funds, which have current income as their principal—if not only—objective, general world income funds are also able to hold

Table 3.3 *How Our Government Bond Market Compared with Other Major Markets, 1984–1994 (total returns in U.S. dollars)*

Year	Best Return		Worst Return		U.S. Market
1984	U.S.	14.3%	Switzerland	(14.6%)	14.3%
1985	France	50.5	Australia	(12.1)	20.9
1986	Japan	40.1	U.K.	14.8	15.7
1987	U.K.	46.6	U.S.	1.9	1.9
1988	Australia	28.8	Switzerland	(12.7)	7.1
1989	Canada	16.2	Japan	(14.3)	14.4
1990	U.K.	30.9	Canada	7.7	8.6
1991	Australia	23.5	Switzerland	0.7	15.3
1992	Japan	10.8	Italy	(13.9)	7.2
1993	Japan	27.6	Sweden	2.9	10.7
1994	Belgium	12.2	Canada	(9.9)	(3.4)

Source: Salomon Brothers

out the potential of capital appreciation because of the gains they expect from changes in currency exchange rates, interest rates, or—ideally—both.

To achieve their objectives, most of the funds state they will normally be 65% to 80% invested in U.S. and foreign government and corporate bonds. They differ in how much of their assets to devote to U.S. securities and how to split their holdings between governments (including supranational entities such as the World Bank) and corporates.

Policies also differ with respect to credit quality—that is, whether and how much to allocate to bonds below investment grade—corporate or governmental. Emerging countries' debt securities, which involve higher risks and higher yields, are increasingly appearing in portfolios, and a few new funds are concentrated in them.

While most of the group appear to have intermediate maturities, a few have long weighted averages.

To obtain adequate diversification, virtually all funds say they must be invested in at least three currencies, including multinational currency units such as European Currency Units (ECUs). In actuality, most have invested in quite a few more.

To cope with the risks that foreign currencies could decline against the U.S. dollar, reducing the dollar value of their funds' holdings (and, therefore, their funds' NAVs), managers often use derivative instruments—put and call options, futures contracts, and forward currency contracts—for hedging purposes.

For example, when a manager expects to engage in a currency exchange transaction in connection with the purchase or sale of a security, he or she may enter into a forward contract to secure the exchange rate at which the purchase or sale will be made. A manager also may buy or sell foreign currency futures contracts, options on them, or options on foreign currencies to hedge against the risk of fluctuations in the market value of some—if not all—of a fund's foreign bonds that could result from changes in foreign exchange rates.

While some may contend that, in the long run, the ups and downs of the dollar cancel each other out, making hedging unnecessary, the benefits of hedges can be significant if they work out as intended. They, however, do involve costs that shave a fund's return—a good reason not to try to protect against all potential changes in exchange rates. But, of course, they also can fail to work out. A manager may have made a wrong guess on what the dollar would do against one or more currencies. In such a case, the fund's return could be impacted more substantially.

To provide the potential rewards of foreign bond markets but with less interest rate risk, several companies, led by Alliance Capital Management in May 1989, have begun to offer what Lipper calls Short World Multi-Market Income Funds. They would hold down interest rate risk by investing in short-term securities.

The prospectus for Alliance Short-Term Multi-Market Trust said it would invest in high-quality debt securities with remaining maturities of not more than three years. It added that the fund "is designed for the investor who seeks a higher yield than a money market fund or certificate of deposit and less fluctuation in net asset value than a longer-term bond fund." (A comparison with other types of short-term bond funds might have been more relevant.)

A strategy known as cross-hedging was to protect its return from higher-yielding foreign securities against currency risk. In a promotional leaflet for its multi-market fund group, Alliance explained how this was supposed to work:

> Cross-hedging seeks to take advantage of the differences in currencies that tend to move in a similar direction against the U.S. dollar. Today these countries primarily are members of the European Monetary System (EMS). These nations have agreed to target the exchange rates of their currencies within a specific range.
>
> For example, a portfolio manager will buy high current yielding bonds in one currency, such as the British pound, but will hedge that currency by selling forward an equivalent amount of a lower yielding currency, such as the French franc, that moves with the pound. This technique dampens volatility that may result from exchange rate movements and enables the investor to capture most of the difference in yield between the pound and the franc.
>
> Most multi-market fund managers do not cross-hedge with the thought of making money on currency fluctuation—they try to neutralize it.

Everything seemed to follow the script until the second half of 1992, when the European currency mechanism came unglued and devaluations of some currencies wrecked their tendency to move in harmony with others. While the crisis naturally led to a sharp reduction in the use of cross-hedging to reduce the volatility of short-term world income funds, the funds have survived—albeit, with diminished appeal.

Tax-Exempt Bond Funds

About 1,500 bond funds (including share classes of multi-class funds), with net assets of close to $250 billion, are eligible in the SEC's eyes to call themselves tax-exempt and to imply that their distributions are exempt from federal income taxation.

That's because their fundamental policies require them to be invested so that at least 80% of their income is federally tax-exempt or to have at least 80% of their assets in tax-exempt securities.

Also known as municipal bond funds, they are concentrated in the debt securities of states, counties, townships, school districts, special districts, and authorities created by state governments as well as municipalities.

The state and local government bond market is a large market—each year $100 billion or more of such securities are issued to raise new capital (in addition to billions sold to refund old bonds)—and tax-exempt bond funds have been the leading purchasers.

Interest payments that investors receive from issuers of municipal bonds are almost always exempt from federal income tax; when funds, in turn, distribute their investment income (after deducting expenses) to their shareholders, the exemption is passed through. From time to time, there has been some tinkering with the exemption for nonconventional municipal bonds, but the exemption has remained essentially intact.

Exemption from federal income tax isn't the only benefit of owning municipal bonds, directly or indirectly through mutual funds. If you are subject to state and local income taxes, you also are likely to be exempt from such taxes on the interest income attributable to securities issued in your state. You may be liable, however, for state and local taxes on income attributable to other states' securities. Hence, the development and expansion of single-state municipal bond funds and the promotion of double tax-exempt and even triple tax-free income.

No exemption is accorded capital gains, however—whether it is distributions of capital gains that funds have realized when selling securities or those that you realize when selling fund shares. They can be taxable at all three levels of government.

The Tax Reform Act of 1986 (TRA86) changed and complicated the municipal bond picture in several ways. For one thing, it narrowed the definition of public purpose obligations after state and local governments had issued billions of dollars' worth of bonds for projects that were more private activities (housing, pollution control, sports and convention facilities, and others) than traditional government activities. It ended the tax exemption for the interest received from certain types of private activity bonds, and it designated the interest from others as tax preference items. This exposed investors in such bonds, or in mutual funds that invested in them, to the possibility of paying the alternative minimum tax (AMT) if they had too many preference items.

TRA86 also eliminated a number of tax shelters, thereby expanding the demand for tax-exempts among those who find them a convenient, alternative way to earn nontaxable income.

This demand, already increasing as more people have their income taxed federally at 28%, was greatly strengthened, of course, when President Clinton and Congress approved higher tax rates in 1993 for those with high taxable income ($140,000, if married and filing jointly; $70,000, if married and filing separately, and $115,000, if single).

Owing to the tax-exempt feature, issuers of municipal bonds are able, under normal market conditions, to offer lower interest rates than are offered for comparable taxable bonds. How much lower is a function of supply-demand balances in the bond market. (Because of the lower yields, municipals make no sense for individuals' tax-sheltered portfolios, such as IRAs; for tax-exempt institutional investors; or for others not required to pay U.S. income tax.)

Given the commitment to earn a desired level of current income for shareholders that is consistent with the level of risk a fund may accept, a portfolio manager makes several types of choices:

- General obligation versus revenue bonds—General obligation bonds are serviced out of appropriations and backed by the credit and tax base of the issuing unit of government. Interest and principal on revenue bonds are paid from the revenues of the facilities that were built with the money received from their sale. Industrial development bonds, issued by state and local governments but guaranteed by corporations for whose projects they were sold, are a form of revenue bond.

  General obligation bonds account for around 35% of all new municipal issues, according to Securities Data Company, but typically they account for a smaller percentage of long-term bond funds. For one thing, the supply of revenue bonds is normally greater in longer maturities, while the supply of general obligation bonds is greater in intermediate maturities. Thus, managers looking for longer maturities are more likely to invest in revenue bonds, all other things being equal. Those looking for shorter maturities are more likely to find them among general obligation bonds. Moreover, general obligation bonds offer a slightly lower yield, even when maturities and other key factors are comparable, because of the perception that, with taxing authority behind them, they are a better credit risk.

- Purposes of revenue bonds—They cover a wide range: airports, turnpikes, harbor improvements, electric utilities, gas utilities, waste treatment, water works, hospitals, housing projects, single- and multifamily housing mortgages, university buildings, to name a few. Within each sector there may be further choices—nuclear versus nonnuclear electric utilities, for example. Since some sectors are regarded as better credit risks than others during any given period, fund managers buy or sell in accordance with their analyses of the risk-reward balances (or policies regarding credit risks).

- Credit quality—Both general obligation and revenue bonds are rated for credit quality by Moody's and Standard & Poor's. As with corporates, municipals rated Aaa/AAA through Baa/BBB are regarded as being of investment grade. And as with corporates, the higher-grade securities offer a lower yield; the lower grades, a higher yield. Even given the support of underlying tax bases, the general obligation bonds of some state and local governments are judged not to be as good risks as others.

Some funds have policies that permit investment only in municipals of investment grades, which tend to be more liquid.

- Maturities—Municipal bonds are frequently issued for terms as long as 30 years—as long as the longest Treasury issues—but maturities of 40 years and even more are offered from time to time.
- State versus local governments—All other things being equal, state securities may be more desirable than local obligations because the markets for state securities tend to be larger and more liquid.

In dealing with these and other variables, managers run their portfolios to achieve similar investment objectives in ways that have both similarities and differences, reflecting a variety of management policies, managerial styles, and assessments of the commonly available data before them.

While they generally are active in managing their portfolios—not just passively buying bonds and holding them—they vary in the extent to which they are active, in the emphasis they give alternative strategies—and, of course, in their effectiveness.

SHORT AND INTERMEDIATE FUNDS

Short Municipal Bond Funds: Invest in municipal debt issues with dollar-weighted average maturities of less than five years.

The funds constituting this group try to offer investors yields that normally are slightly higher than those offered by tax-exempt money market funds but that involve the risk of only slight fluctuation in prices.

To minimize market risk when short-term rates are rising or to benefit from higher short-term rates when they may have hit a cyclical peak, managers adjust their average maturities.

Some have more maneuvering room than others. Vanguard Municipal Bond Fund's Short-Term Portfolio, the oldest (started in 1977), aims at an average of between one and two years and will buy securities with an effective maturity of five years or less, for example. Its sibling, the Limited-Term Portfolio, is expected to maintain a weighted average maturity of between two and five years and will buy securities with an effective maturity of ten years or less.

Merrill Lynch Municipal Bond Fund's Limited Maturity Portfolio buys securities with a maximum maturity of four years and tries to maintain an average maturity of less than two.

Consistent with managements' aims to minimize the risks involved in investing in these funds, they generally insist on investment-grade quality. They may even limit the percent of assets that can be invested in the lowest investment grade, Baa/BBB, and most likely will limit how much can be invested in municipal junk bonds.

Intermediate Municipal Bond Funds: Invest in municipal debt securities with dollar-weighted average maturities of five to ten years.

These are funds that, under normal circumstances, provide a lower yield and more stability than long-term tax-exempt funds but a higher yield than funds invested in municipals of shorter maturities.

They target various average maturities, which they adjust with interest rates—within limits—when it seems appropriate.

Vanguard's Intermediate-Term Portfolio, by far the largest in the group, with $5 billion of the group's $16 billion in assets, is expected to maintain a dollar-weighted average maturity between seven and twelve years and can buy individual securities of any maturity.

American Funds' Limited Term Tax-Exempt Bond Fund of America, Dreyfus Intermediate Municipal Bond Fund, and Franklin Federal Intermediate-Term Tax-Free Income Fund hold their ranges to between three and ten years; Legg Mason Tax-Free Intermediate-Term Trust, between two and ten; and Merrill Lynch Municipal Income Fund, five to twelve years. Fidelity Limited Term Municipals' policy caps its weighted average maturity at twelve years but specifies no minimum.

Differences in the credit risks that funds incur appear to be slight. They generally want primary holdings to be rated at least A, but differ in whether, and how much, remaining holdings may include bonds rated Baa/BBB or lower.

LONG AND UNSPECIFIED TERM FUNDS

General Municipal Bond Funds: Invest at least 65% of their assets in municipal debt issues in the top four credit ratings.

This is by far the largest category of national (as distinct from single-state) municipal bond funds, accounting for about half of the number and net assets. Within the group, there are differences in quality requirements, policies on maturities, and other aspects of management emphasis.

Being widely diversified through investment in securities from across the country, they are less exposed to geographic risk than funds concentrated in a single state and dependent on its economy. (Consider the problems of Orange County, California, which emerged in 1994, for example.) But their income may not be exempt from state and local income tax, as single-state bond funds are, because of their limited investment in the securities of any single state.

Scudder Managed Municipal Bonds may have the highest quality standards of all, stating that, under normal market conditions, 100% of its investments in municipal securities will be rated Baa/BBB or higher and at least 75% will be rated A or higher.

Others express their quality standards in different ways: the percentages (less than 100%) that have to be Baa/BBB or higher, Aa/AA or higher, A or higher, within the Baa/BBB rating, and/or the percentages that may be less than Baa/BBB—that is, municipal junk.

Whatever the ratings, the bonds held by the funds in this group are primarily long-term bonds. Of the fund managements commenting on maturity policies in their prospectuses, the largest number tend to aim at having portfolios with weighted averages of 10 or 15 to 25 years or more. They differ in their apparent inclination to adjust average maturities up and down in response to, or anticipation of, changes in interest rates. Some tend to stay at the upper end of the range to benefit from higher yields. Others stay at the lower end of the range.

Within the context of their quality and maturity policies, managers employ several different techniques with varying degrees of aggressiveness.

Some manage their portfolios actively, seeking to take advantage of market developments, yield disparities, and variations in the creditworthiness of issuers, and thereby raising their portfolio turnover rates. Others are more inclined to just buy for high yields and hang on, looking for the highest total return.

The premise on which active management—that is, frequent buying and selling—is based is that the market is inefficient in pricing securities. Regardless of whether prices are moving up or down, yield spreads fluctuate between discount and premium bonds, between Aaa/AAA and Baa/BBB bonds, between bonds of different sectors, between bonds of high-tax states and low- or no-tax states.

Watching these changes, the more active managers try to spot undervalued securities for purchase before others do and to identify bonds in their own portfolios that have become overvalued so that they can unload them before the market marks them down.

Of course, managers sometimes make switches to enhance the quality of their portfolios. When quality spreads among investment-grade bonds become narrow enough, they replace lower- or medium-grade holdings with higher-grade securities in the conviction that they're not being sufficiently rewarded for taking higher credit risks. When spreads widen during an economic boom, they switch to lower-grade bonds in the belief that their higher yields are not in jeopardy.

Some managers replace bonds when they want to adjust the maturities of their portfolios as the prospects for interest rates change. When they expect rates to rise, they shorten maturities to reduce volatility and place themselves in position to pick up bonds offering higher yields—if their expectations turn out to be correct. On the other hand, when it looks as if interest rates are falling, they lengthen maturities to gain capital appreciation.

Active trading for any purpose, of course, can result not only in higher transaction costs for the fund but also in the realization of short- and/or long-term capital gains that are passed along in taxable distributions to shareholders, who may not always be thrilled to receive them inasmuch as they thought they were invested in tax-free funds.

Of the funds whose prospectuses mention the private activity bonds, which subject investors to the possibility of paying alternative minimum tax, a few state they want to avoid them altogether. A larger number say they will invest in them to a limited degree, such as a maximum of 20%.

Others, such as Alliance Municipal Income Fund's National Portfolio, take an opposite position. It was organized in 1986 for the purpose of investing in AMT-subject bonds, and may be 90% or more invested in them. "Only 0.2% of taxpayers are subject to the AMT," Susan Keenan, portfolio manager, explains. "For the benefit of all the others who don't pay the tax, we see this as an opportunity to offer a higher yield—some 50 to 75 basis points—without additional risk."

Insured Municipal Bond Funds: Invest at least 65% of their assets in municipal debt issues whose timely payment is insured.

These funds are primarily invested in long-term municipal bonds whose timely interest and principal payments are covered by municipal bond insurance. It is intended to protect the funds against loss in the event of a state or local government unit's default, leaving the securities in the funds' portfolios exposed essentially only to interest rate risk—not, to be sure, an insignificant one.

The funds point out in their literature, sometimes in bold print, that insurance does *not* protect investors against fluctuations in the market prices of the bonds held by the funds, the share prices of the funds themselves, or their yields. They also note, if not always prominently, that the insurance is no more reliable than the credit of the insurance companies that write the policies.

Investing by, and in, tax-free insured bond funds involves three types of insurance:

1. New issue insurance is what state and local governments (or their underwriters) obtain if the issuers qualify, if it would help them to sell new bond issues, and if it would reduce borrowing costs. If the premium would cost less than the government would save in interest owing to the higher rating (usually Aaa/AAA) resulting from the coverage, insurance would seem to be called for. If the cost would exceed the savings, it would not. Once the premium is paid, coverage remains in force as long as the bonds are outstanding (with their resale value enhanced) and the insurance companies are in business.

2. Secondary market insurance is purchased by investors—such as mutual funds—to cover eligible bonds already outstanding as long as they are outstanding.

3. Portfolio insurance is bought by funds to cover bonds in their portfolios that are not already insured by policies of the first two types for as long as the funds own the bonds.

First Investors Insured Tax Exempt Fund and Merrill Lynch Municipal Bond Fund's Insured Portfolio were the first mutual funds to concentrate in insured tax-exempts. They commenced operations in August 1977 and October 1977, respectively—six years after AMBAC Indemnity Corporation introduced new issue insurance for municipal bonds.

Because investor demand for the new type of fund took time to build, as did the insurance companies' ability and willingness to undertake this new type of business, First Investors and Merrill Lynch had the field to themselves for several years.

Others followed in the 1980s, no doubt encouraged by the thought that investors would want the protection of insurance after the Washington State Public Power Supply System defaulted on two of its bond issues in 1983.

In building their core portfolios, funds follow different patterns. Some buy insured municipals of investment grade (a few will buy only Aaa/AAAs), others buy uninsured investment-grade bonds for which they obtain insurance to raise their grade, and the rest do both. (They may round out their portfolios with uninsured, high-grade short-term securities.)

It's not enough that the bonds that funds buy have ratings that meet their standards. It's also important that no one have a doubt about the claims-paying abilities of the insurance companies providing the coverage.

Major companies besides publicly held AMBAC that write such insurance include Financial Guaranty Insurance Company, a wholly owned subsidiary of GE Capital, and Municipal Bond Investors Assurance Corporation, which has the largest share of the new issue business and is 88.8%-owned by public stockholders. (The remaining shares of MBIA are held by Aetna Casualty and Surety Company and Credit Local de France. Other financial institutions held large positions in AMBAC and MBIA until a few years ago.)

Most funds make certain the insurance companies are rated triple-A, and several say they check periodically to ensure that they remain triple-A.

Fund managers are able to raise their yields without raising their portfolios' credit risk by buying uninsured bonds that are rated Baa/BBB—and, therefore, offer higher yields than Aaa/AAAs—and having triple-A rated insurance companies cover them.

They're also able to take advantage of the fact that outstanding insured triple-A bonds are available in the market at lower prices in relation to their coupon rates than uninsured triple-As, enabling them to earn an additional 20 to 30 basis points for every dollar invested.

Why would uninsured triple-As provide a lower yield, implying lower risk, than insured triple-As?

"It's a paradox," says Ian A. MacKinnon, head of the Vanguard Fixed Income Group. "Maybe the market doesn't believe the insurance."

The cost of insurance is felt by tax-exempt funds—and, in turn, by their shareholders—in one or two ways. For bonds that are insured when funds buy them, premiums are reflected in the prices paid. For uninsured bonds, funds pay the premiums directly.

Portfolio insurance costs run from 0.2% to 0.4% of the value of the bonds insured, according to fund prospectuses. How much they can add to a fund's expenses depends not only on the premium rate but also on the portfolio's composition—that is, on how much of the portfolio consists of bonds for which the fund obtained coverage.

Insured municipal bond funds tend to invest in bonds of long maturities, as general municipal bond funds do. In 1992, T. Rowe Price, however, introduced the first fund with bonds of 5- to 10-year, or intermediate, maturities to provide investors both insurance protection and the likelihood of less volatility.

High Yield Municipal Bond Funds: Invest 50% or more of their assets in lower-rated municipal debt issues.

These are the municipal bond funds that try to provide the highest current return by investing in bonds that combine two kinds of risk: long maturities and low credit ratings.

They span a wide spectrum in terms of credit quality. At one end you have funds such as Vanguard Municipal Bond Fund High-Yield Portfolio, which must be 80% invested in investment-grade securities but can be 20% in junk, and Scudder High Yield Tax Free Fund, which must be at least 65% invested in securities rated investment grade, but can be 35% in the top two junk grades, Ba/BB and B/B.

At the other end you have funds such as Franklin High Yield Tax-Free Income Fund, which invests primarily in securities rated Ba/BB or lower but may invest substantially in Baa/BBB when enough lower-grade bonds are not available.

Most are in between, selecting both medium- and low-quality securities for their portfolios' core holdings.

The funds generally reserve the flexibility to invest in high-grade bonds when yield spreads are narrow or when medium- or lower-quality bonds are not available; they advise shareholders that current income might be reduced as a result. Most also say they may buy lower grades than the quality range from which they normally choose when it's justified.

Fund managements credit their research staffs for helping them to identify the high-yield securities to be bought—and those to be avoided—by supplementing the work of the rating agencies.

If diversification is essential to the prudent management of any tax-exempt mutual fund group, it's this one, given the credit risks inherent in low-grade bonds. They have a diverse list to choose from: hospitals, other health care, housing, public utilities, industrial development, and pollution control bonds.

IDS High Yield Tax-Exempt Fund, at $6 billion the largest in the group, has long emphasized revenue bonds of governmental units that provide essential services, such as water and sewer systems and toll roads. "Because of their revenue stream, we believe these types of bonds are subject to minimal default risk," Kurt Larson, portfolio manager, said in a report to shareholders, adding that he has avoided the general obligation bonds of large cities, which, he believes, are more risky.

SINGLE-STATE MUNICIPAL BOND FUNDS

The more than 1,000 federally tax-exempt funds in this group (including share classes for multi-class funds) have assets in the aggregate of more than $110 billion—more than any other bond fund category.

They are structured for investors who are subject to state (and perhaps local) income taxes, who may be exempt from such taxes on interest income from securities issued by their own state governments and by local governments within their states, and who want to invest only in such securities. (By investing in national municipal bond funds, they usually do not receive enough income attributable to their own states' securities to benefit from double or triple exemption.)

The first single-state municipal bond funds, DMC Tax-Free Income Trust-PA and Franklin California Tax-Free Income, were started shortly after corporate municipal bond funds were launched in late 1976. By now they exist in a large majority of the more than 30 states that impose income taxes on other states' securities but not on their own.

Most are fairly small, but quite a few exceed $1 billion in assets, led by the $13 billion Franklin California Tax Free Income Fund. Understandably, California and New York have many more funds than other states.

Single-state municipal bond funds involve greater credit risk than national funds because, by definition, they lack geographic diversification. Questions about their credit risk are commonly associated with cyclical weakness or secular decline in a state's or area's major industry, but they also can be raised by other events, such as a court ruling, the threat of a taxpayer rebellion that could jeopardize appropriations required to service general obligation bonds, or, as we saw in the case of Orange County, imprudent management of a government's investments.

In recognition of the risk, most fund managements tend to invest primarily in bonds rated Baa/BBB or higher. Some try to go no lower than A. Quite a few offer insured bond portfolios as their only, or as additional, choices in certain states.

Some fund managements seek to provide higher current income, at greater credit risk, by offering high-yield funds that may invest significantly—but not exclusively—in medium- and lower-grade bonds.

Single-state funds have tended to be primarily invested in bonds that give their portfolios weighted average maturities of 15 to 25 years, thereby involving significant interest rate risk. Increasingly, fund sponsors also have been offering single-state funds that are concentrated in intermediate-term bonds.

CHAPTER 4

How Bond Funds Have Performed Overall—and Why

Now that you have seen how the investment objectives, policies, and practices of various types of taxable and tax-exempt bond funds compare, you'll want to see how they have performed for shareholders—and why they have performed as well or as poorly as they did.

By definition, performance data tell you about the changes in the value of an investment in a fund and about its income in previous years. Past total return and yield data, however, do not foretell future performance, which may be better or worse.

Since you can't rely on any other indicator for an accurate forecast either, the record of past performance is important. It tells you how consistently a fund behaved during good *and* bad markets. The record that you study should be long enough to reflect both. That could be as long as five years; it could be longer.

Without this information, you know too little to make rational investment decisions. Even with this information, you cannot be sure, but at least you can get a reasonable idea of how similarly invested funds, pursuing similar policies involving similar types and degrees of risk, may perform under comparable conditions in the future.

What You Need to Know about Performance Measures

The single most important measure of any mutual fund's performance is its total return.

The SEC defines total return as "the average annual compounded rate of return over (a certain period of years) that would equate the initial amount invested to the ending redeemable value" according to a specific formula. This definition assumes that all dividends and distributions by the fund have been reinvested.

Expressed in simpler terms, it is the change in a fund's share price (or NAV) plus reinvested income.

Although income may be very important to you, total return is a more meaningful figure than yield, which you may want to focus on (or, perhaps more likely, which some sales person or fund marketer is trying to tempt you with).

The reason for not focusing on a fund's yield is that it can be manipulated. It doesn't take a lot of skill, for example, to buy a high-yield bond to get large interest payments every half year. But this involves the risk that the bond's price will slip, offsetting part of that high income. Since total return reflects both price change and income, it will indicate whether a manager may have taken too much risk to boost income.

It's also important to know whether or not total return data that you see or hear have been adjusted for loads. Load funds' total return data that appear in the press usually do *not* reflect their sales loads. Thus, they overstate what you actually would have earned on your investment and are not comparable with those for no-load funds.

When funds advertise their returns, however, the SEC requires them to publish annual rates of total return for 1, 5, and 10 years in a way that *does* reflect any sales charges.

Even so, you don't look at funds' total returns in isolation. You also need to compare them with returns for benchmarks that measure the performance of the securities the funds own to get a sense of whether the funds performed as well as could have been expected, by investing in the relevant bond market sectors, after taking into consideration prevailing market conditions.

Starting in mid-1993, the SEC has required mutual funds to compare their performance with appropriate benchmarks in prospectuses or annual reports. Bond fund results have increasingly been compared to the performance of bond indexes calculated by firms such as Lehman Brothers and Salomon Brothers.

Some fund companies have used the broad measures for the total U.S. taxable investment-grade bond market, Lehman's Aggregate Bond Index or Salomon's Broad Investment-Grade (BIG) Bond Index. Others have used indexes for subsets of the broad market—such as short-term corporates or long-term Treasuries—or for other sectors, such as tax-exempt and high-yield debt securities.

A fund whose total return comes within 0.5% or so—a margin for expenses—of an index for the sector in which it is invested may be regarded as doing essentially as well as the index. One that exceeds its benchmark consistently may be regarded as doing really well, presumably demonstrating the skill of its manager.

Of course, a measure of a fund's income flow is also important. For this, however, the measure to focus on is the annualized 30-day yield, which the SEC requires funds to compute on a uniform basis, not the rate at which dividends were paid in the latest 12 months.

That's because the SEC-basis yield takes into account not only the fund's net income from interest but also its yield to maturity and any sales loads.

By insisting that funds factor in the yield to maturity, the SEC makes certain that provision is made for amortizing the premiums of bond prices in a fund's portfolio. Thus, if a fund owns a bond with a high coupon and a market value higher than its face value—that is, a premium price—the yield calculation has to provide for the eventual decline in its market price to par when it matures.

Before looking at the performance data for bond funds, let's recall the investment environment in which they were managed.

The Performance of Debt Securities

As Table 4.1 and Figure 4.1 show, the years from 1984 through 1994 provided quite a roller-coaster ride for debt securities—and for those who managed and invested in them.

The period began with 13-week Treasury bills yielding an average of 9.3% in January 1984 and 30-year Treasury bonds yielding 11.8%. Other Treasury issues' yields were in between. Taxable securities of comparable maturities, but without the full faith and credit of the Treasury behind them, yielded more depending on their quality and call (or prepayment) risk.

The period ended with bills averaging 5.8% in December 1994 and the long bonds averaging 7.9%, reflecting drops of 3.5% and 3.9%, respectively, and a slightly narrower spread between the two.

While rates followed a generally downward course until late 1993, they fluctuated in the interim, with the bills' monthly average rates going as high as 10.9% in August 1984 and as low as 2.9% in October 1992. The 30-year bonds' yield ranged between 13.94% on May 30, 1984, and 5.78% on October 15, 1993.

Total returns—that is, reinvested interest plus (or minus) capital appreciation (or depreciation)—ranged from around 30% to negative 7.6% and 5.7%, respectively, for long-term (10-year or longer) Treasury and investment-grade corporate securities. In three of the years, 1987, 1990, and 1994, Treasury bills outperformed them—and even stayed ahead of increases in the consumer price index.

To see how taxable investment-grade debt securities behaved in the aggregate—including all maturities of one year or longer and also taking in

Table 4.1 *Annual Rates of Total Return of Debt Securities Compared with Cost of Living, 1984–1994*

Year	FI Funds	SB/BIG	L/T Corp.	L/T Treas.	Mortgage	T-bills	CPI
1984	10.9%	15.0%	16.9%	14.9%	15.8%	10.0%	3.9%
1985	19.8	22.3	29.2	31.5	25.7	7.8	3.8
1986	12.7	15.4	19.3	24.1	13.4	6.2	1.1
1987	1.3	2.6	0.5	(2.8)	4.1	5.9	4.4
1988	7.9	8.0	11.0	9.3	8.8	6.8	4.4
1989	9.4	14.4	15.7	19.0	15.2	8.6	4.6
1990	4.3	9.1	6.6	6.4	10.9	7.9	6.1
1991	18.1	16.0	20.7	18.5	15.7	5.8	3.1
1992	7.9	7.6	9.9	7.9	7.4	3.6	2.9
1993	9.7	9.9	14.2	17.3	7.0	3.1	2.7
1994	(3.3)	(2.9)	(5.7)	(7.6)	(1.4)	4.2	2.7

FI Funds = taxable fixed income mutual funds; SB/BIG = Salomon Brothers Broad Investment-Grade Bond Index; L/T Corp. = Corporate bonds with maturities of over 10 years; L/T Treas. = Treasury securities with maturities of over 10 years; Mortgage = Mortgage securities; T-bills = 3-month U.S. Treasury bills; CPI = Percent changes in consumer price index (December to December)

Sources: Lipper Analytical Services, Salomon Brothers, U.S. Bureau of Labor Statistics

other federal government issues and mortgage securities—look at the returns for Salomon Brothers' BIG Index.

It showed only positive total returns from 1980, the first year for which it was calculated, until 1994, and in the last decade it ranged between 22.3% in 1985 (topped previously only by 31.8% in 1982) and the negative 2.9% in 1994. In 1987, when it achieved only a 2.6% return, it was supported by mortgage securities, the same investments that in other years, such as 1993, held the BIG Index down. In 1994, no bond market sector enjoyed positive results.

Table 4.2 shows how returns on principal and interest have figured in the total return of the index and its broad components since it was introduced in 1980, indicating the conditions that funds' portfolio managers (and perhaps you as an individual investor) have been able to exploit or have had to contend with.

Note, for instance, that in 1982, when bonds had their best year of the period, investment-grade corporate securities and mortgage securities (such as

Monthly averages (in percentages)

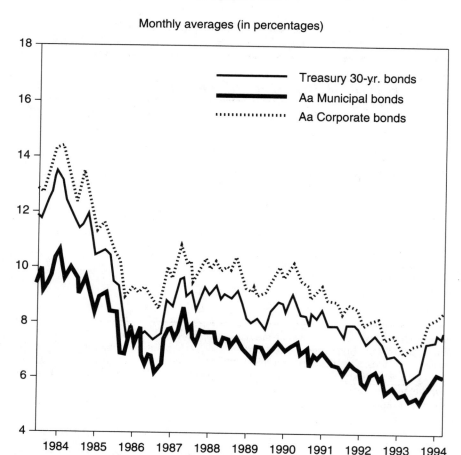

FIGURE 4.1   Average Yields of Long-Term Treasury, Corporate, and Municipal Bonds

Source: Treasury Bulletin, U.S. Department of the Treasury, December 1994

Ginnie Maes) had interest income of 16% and 17%, respectively, and the returns on their principal were even higher.

Note also that in 1987, the worst year of the period until 1994, interest was high enough to offset loss of principal and produce positive—albeit modest— total returns.

In that year, mortgage securities held the BIG Index up, thanks to a smaller principal drop and higher interest income. In contrast, a surge of mortgage prepayments caused mortgage securities to suffer a small drop in principal in 1993, while other securities enjoyed higher returns and boosted the index. As all sectors turned down in 1994, mortgages—with the smallest drop in principal and highest income—turned down the least.

Table 4.2   *Returns on Principal and Interest for Taxable Investment-Grade Securities, 1980–1994*

	Total Investment-Grade Bond Market*		
Year	Principal	Interest	Total Return
1980	(7.2)	10.1	2.8
1981	(5.7)	12.2	6.5
1982	16.6	15.2	31.8
1983	(3.2)	11.5	8.2
1984	2.3	12.7	15.0
1985	9.8	12.5	22.3
1986	5.2	10.3	15.4
1987	(6.3)	8.9	2.6
1988	(1.3)	9.3	8.0
1989	4.6	9.8	14.4
1990	(0.2)	9.3	9.1
1991	6.6	9.4	16.0
1992	(0.6)	8.1	7.6
1993	2.3	7.6	9.9
1994	(9.6)	6.8	(2.9)

	Treasury Securities		
Year	Principal	Interest	Total Return
1980	(4.7)	9.8	5.2
1981	(2.6)	12.2	9.5
1982	12.9	14.6	27.5
1983	(4.5)	11.2	6.7
1984	2.1	12.4	14.5
1985	8.8	12.2	20.9
1986	5.8	9.9	15.7
1987	(6.5)	8.5	1.9
1988	(1.9)	8.9	7.1
1989	4.9	9.5	14.4
1990	(0.3)	8.9	8.6
1991	6.4	8.9	15.3
1992	(0.4)	7.6	7.2
1993	3.6	7.0	10.7
1994	(9.7)	6.3	(3.4)

*Broad Investment-Grade Bond Index

Table 4.2 *Continued*

Government Sponsored Securities			
Year	*Principal*	*Interest*	*Total Return*
1980	(4.0)	9.6	5.6
1981	(1.2)	11.2	10.0
1982	12.6	13.5	26.1
1983	(3.0)	11.5	8.5
1984	2.0	12.4	14.4
1985	5.9	11.9	17.9
1986	4.2	10.1	14.3
1987	(5.5)	8.8	3.3
1988	(1.6)	8.9	7.4
1989	4.1	9.3	13.4
1990	0.6	9.0	9.6
1991	6.8	9.0	15.8
1992	(0.3)	7.9	7.5
1993	3.8	7.5	11.3
1994	(10.3)	6.7	(3.6)

Corporate Securities			
Year	*Principal*	*Interest*	*Total Return*
1980	(10.6)	10.3	(0.3)
1981	(9.5)	12.3	2.7
1982	21.1	16.1	37.2
1983	(2.6)	11.5	8.9
1984	3.0	13.1	16.1
1985	12.1	12.9	25.0
1986	6.4	10.6	17.0
1987	(7.1)	9.1	2.1
1988	(0.3)	9.8	9.5
1989	3.9	10.0	14.0
1990	(2.2)	9.5	7.3
1991	8.5	10.0	18.5
1992	0.3	8.6	8.9
1993	4.0	8.1	12.1
1994	(10.8)	7.2	(3.5)

Table 4.2   Continued

| Year | Mortgage Securities | | |
	Principal	Interest	Total Return
1980	(10.1)	10.6	0.5
1981	(11.6)	12.8	1.2
1982	24.2	17.1	41.4
1983	(1.3)	12.1	10.9
1984	2.5	13.3	15.8
1985	12.4	13.2	25.7
1986	2.6	10.8	13.4
1987	(5.4)	9.5	4.1
1988	(1.0)	9.8	8.8
1989	4.8	10.4	15.2
1990	1.0	9.9	10.9
1991	5.7	9.9	15.7
1992	(1.4)	8.7	7.4
1993	(1.1)	8.1	7.0
1994	(8.7)	7.3	(1.4)

Source: Salomon Brothers

Bond Funds: Similarities and Differences

The BIG Index's returns have a close correlation with those for intermediate-term securities because the investment-grade bond market as a whole has had a weighted average maturity in the intermediate range. The performance of taxable bond funds has followed a pattern close to that of the index. On the average, they, too, tend to have an intermediate weighted average maturity.

During the ten years from 1985 through 1994, as indicated in Table 4.1, bond funds, on the average, beat the index in only two years (1991 and 1992). While you can expect their average annual returns to slightly lag those of the BIG, its broad components, or other relevant indexes for at least two major, understandable reasons, larger lags may be due to inferior management and/or risky policies. They would be less defensible than these reasons:

1. Bond funds keep portions of their assets in lower-yielding Treasury bills or other cash equivalents, which are not included in bond indexes, to meet redemption requirements or to await opportunities to put just-received money to work. (T-bills are not a drag on performance, of course, when the bond market goes down, as you saw in 1994.)

2. Bond funds are encumbered by investment advisory fees and other expenses—some, as you'll soon see, a lot more than others. If a bond fund's total return is to match an appropriate index's, its portfolio has to be managed so that the expenses are offset.

Because it's important to focus on longer-run tendencies instead of on year-to-year fluctuations when considering investments in mutual funds, the performance of debt securities during 1985–94 is presented in Table 4.3 in terms of average annual returns for the entire 10-year period and for the two 5-year periods that it comprised.

It shows that taxable bond funds, on the average, had total returns of around 9% per year during the decade and that returns during the second 5-year period, when interest rates were lower, tended to be lower for funds as well as for classes of individual securities. (When you form conclusions based on data for any span of two or more years, always remember to check how much they may have been influenced by the choice of the period.)

As indicated by the data for long-term Treasuries, long-term securities outperformed intermediate- and short-term securities (as well as the BIG Index), as you would expect during periods when interest rates fell. This contrasted with the years when increases in interest rates caused bond prices to fall.

The data also show, as if you need further proof, that Treasury bills and money market funds do not constitute very rewarding long-term investments, even if they involve no principal risk and if their returns do manage to stay

Table 4.3   Total Returns for Investment Alternatives Comparison of Recent 5– and 10–Year Periods Compound Annual Rates

	1985–89	1990–94	1985–94
Money market mutual funds	7.2%	4.6%	5.9%
13-week U.S. Treasury bills	7.1	4.9	6.0
Taxable fixed income mutual funds	10.0	7.4	9.1
7–10-Year U.S. Treasury securities	13.3	7.8	10.5
10+-Year U.S. Treasury securities	15.6	8.1	11.8
Broad Investment-Grade Bond Index	12.3	7.8	10.0
Consumer Price Index	3.7	3.5	3.6

Sources: Lipper Analytical Services, Salomon Brothers, U.S. Bureau of Labor Statistics

ahead of inflation. (After income tax, they can result in real—that is, inflation-adjusted—losses if you're in a high tax bracket.)

Differences among Fund Groups

Did all categories of bond funds behave similarly over the last decade? If not, how did they differ?

You'll find a mixed pattern among taxable bond fund groups, as depicted in Table 4.4, but a generally predictable one. You may even be surprised by how well the returns that include the reinvestment of dividends held up when you consider that they reflect the 1994 bear market in bonds, the worst in years.

Bond funds involving the greatest interest rate risk—that is, funds that tend to be invested in long-term maturities—had better returns than those invested in intermediate-term bonds. Those, in turn, had better returns than funds invested in short-term bonds.

Funds involving high credit risk, the high current yield funds, provided greater rewards than those concentrated in the least risky securities: those of the U.S. government.

Funds partially invested in common stocks—such as flexible income funds—or those having some linkage to stocks—such as convertible securities funds—excelled pure bond funds on average as they reflected the booming stock market.

Of course, if you receive your dividends in cash instead of reinvesting them—or if you plan to do so—you'll be more interested in the principal-only returns.

For 1994, to be sure, they don't make pleasant reading. No group escaped the impact of the higher interest rates that resulted from the nation's economic expansion and the Federal Reserve's efforts to cool it down. Short-term funds were off, on average, 5% to 6%—except for Short World Multi-Market Income Funds, which were down over 10%. Long-term funds were off more, as you would expect. They were off over 10%, on average, too.

Average annual results for the latest five years were also affected, as 1994 replaced 1989 in that time frame. Only six categories had positive average returns for the period, but the average drops were slight. ARM Funds, which are supposedly managed for stable principal, were down an average 1.8%, more than any other category.

Over the last ten years, as many as four categories had negative average returns. Three of them—Short-Term Investment Grade, GNMA and U.S. Mortgage—were off less than 1%. Some funds in those groups were up, however. The largest average drop, 2.3%, was that of High Yield Funds. The best-performing group, Convertible Securities Funds, had an average annual

Table 4.4 Annual Rates of Return with and without Reinvested Dividends for Periods Ended in 1994

	Taxable Funds—by Fund Categories						
	Total Reinvested			12 Month Yield	Principal Only		
Fund Category	10 Years	5 Years	1 Year		10 Years	5 Years	1 Year
Short U.S. Treasury	*	6.4%	(0.2)%	5.0%	*	0.1%	(5.0)%
Short U.S. Government	7.5%	6.1	(1.7)	5.2	0.0%	(0.4)	(6.5)
Short Investment-Grade	7.6	6.4	(0.4)	5.7	(0.1)	(0.5)	(5.7)
Intermediate U.S. Treasury	8.3	7.0	(3.3)	5.8	0.9	0.1	(8.5)
Intermediate U.S. Government	8.2	6.5	(3.7)	6.0	2.0	(0.2)	(9.1)
Intermediate Investment-Grade	9.1	7.2	(3.4)	6.0	0.6	(0.1)	(8.8)
General U.S. Treasury	*	6.9	(5.8)	6.3	*	0.2	(11.3)
General U.S. Government	8.5	6.6	(4.6)	6.5	0.3	(0.8)	(10.4)
ARM	*	4.8	(2.2)	4.9	*	(1.8)	(6.7)
GNMA	8.5	6.8	(2.5)	7.0	(0.6)	(1.0)	(8.8)
U.S. Mortgage	8.5	6.5	(4.2)	7.1	(0.6)	(1.5)	(10.4)
Corporate A	9.4	7.2	(4.6)	6.5	0.4	(0.1)	(10.4)
Corporate BBB	9.6	7.9	(4.5)	6.9	0.4	(0.1)	(10.5)
General Bond	9.5	7.9	(6.0)	7.6	0.8	(0.3)	(12.5)
High Yield	9.9	10.6	(3.8)	9.9	(2.3)	(1.1)	(12.4)
Convertible	10.9	9.5	(3.8)	4.3	4.8	4.4	(7.7)
Flexible Income	10.2	7.5	(3.7)	7.1	0.0	(1.0)	(10.0)
Target Maturity	*	7.9	(8.1)	2.1	*	7.1	(9.8)
Short World Multi-Market	*	8.1	(4.3)	7.1	*	0.4	(10.4)
World Income	10.1	7.5	(6.5)	6.4	1.0	(1.1)	(11.9)
Balanced	11.7	7.9	(2.5)	3.0	NA	NA	NA
Income	10.9	8.0	(2.9)	4.5	NA	NA	NA
CPI	3.6	3.5	2.7	NA	NA	NA	NA

*Funds not in operation for the full period.
CPI = Consumer price index
NA = Not available or applicable
Sources: Lipper Analytical Services, U.S. Bureau of Labor Statistics

Table 4.5 Annual Rates of Return with and without Reinvested Dividends for Periods Ended in 1994

| | Tax-Exempt Funds—by Fund Categories | | | | | | |
| | Total Reinvested | | | 12 | Principal Only | | |
Fund Category	10 Years	5 Years	1 Year	Month Yield	10 Years	5 Years	1 Year
Short Municipal	5.8%	5.3%	(0.3)%	4.1%	0.2%	0.2%	(4.2)%
Intermediate	7.6	6.2	(3.5)	4.8	1.2	0.6	(7.9)
General Municipal	9.0	6.3	(6.5)	5.6	1.8	0.1	(11.4)
Insured Municipal	8.8	6.2	(6.5)	5.4	1.8	0.2	(11.2)
High-Yield Municipal	8.8	6.2	(5.0)	6.7	1.2	(0.7)	(10.8)

Source: Lipper Analytical Services

increase in principal of 4.8%, primarily reflecting the decade's strong stock market.

Allowing for the fact that their interest income is exempt from taxation by the federal government—and perhaps also by state and local governments—municipal bond funds (Table 4.5) gave a good account of themselves. Their returns—whether including or excluding reinvested dividends—compared well with the returns from taxable funds.

For the ten years, muni funds also ran true to form, with the longer maturity funds showing higher returns than the shorter ones. The short funds even slightly outperformed Short U.S. Treasury Funds on a principal-only basis for 1994 and the last five years.

Comparing the Funds

So much for the fund group averages. Since you can only invest in individual funds, you'll want to know which bond funds have been the leading performers in the various groups, exceeding group averages, and why. You'll see that in the next two chapters.

Whether these funds will remain leaders or be replaced by others that didn't make the lists, no one can say for certain. Even if all don't stay on top, scanning such historic data should help you to get an idea of what to look for when checking rankings in the future.

Most of the tables in the next two chapters show the average annual rates of total return for multi-year periods ended in 1994 for the top ten funds in each Lipper category, ranked according to 5-year performance. (The tables are limited to funds that are generally available to individual investors, including funds that are not available directly but that individuals can buy, as indicated, through discount brokers and/or others.) If there weren't ten, fewer funds are listed. In cases where few, if any, funds have been in operation for five years, data for shorter periods are used.

Consistent, genuinely superior long-term performance is what you want to look for when considering mutual funds in which to invest for the long term. For bond funds, such performance is best demonstrated in results for periods long enough to include rising and falling interest rates. Periods of five years often satisfy this objective.

Points to Remember

Some general comments are in order before we look at the tables.

Historic data. Obviously, performance data published in a book such as this will have been superseded by results for subsequent periods by the time you read it.

Nonetheless, I offer them so that you can compare the performance data of funds in various classifications. Even if these funds don't produce similar absolute results and retain their December 31, 1994, rankings in the years to come, they may remain leaders within their groups and their relative positions may change little.

Even if these were the most recent results, as fresh as today's newspaper, performance data would still be historic data and you could not rely on them with certainty to predict future performance.

Large differences in the performance of peer funds may not have been due only to the skills of their managers; they may also have been due to other factors, including differences in the investment policies that the managers have had to follow. In such cases, Lipper sooner or later reclassifies funds—if a more suitable class is available.

Yield. Because of the importance attached to annualized yields, calculated for the most recent 30-day period according to the SEC formula previously mentioned, I thought it would be useful to show both it and the 12-month dividend distribution rates that many still call yield.

A relatively high 30-day yield doesn't necessarily signify superior management. It could mean the absence of a sales load, low (or partially waived) expenses, and/or high risk-taking (such as a longer duration or lower average credit quality than peer funds). Conversely, a relatively low yield doesn't necessarily signify inferior management. It could mean the opposite: a high load, high expenses, and/or low risk-taking.

As in the case of total return, the absolute yields may have changed by the time you read this, and they may change again in future periods, but the rankings among peer funds may not change much.

Changes in objectives or managers. Funds may have significantly changed investment objectives or policies during the period(s) for which total return figures and yields are provided and, thus, tables may reflect results achieved when funds belonged in other categories. They also may have changed investment advisers or portfolio managers during the period(s), causing changes in performance that may not be self-evident. Footnotes indicate both types of changes when reported by funds.

Front-end sales charges. Note not only that funds impose maximum front-end loads as high as 5% or more but also that no-load funds regularly appear among leaders. If fewer no-loads make some lists, it may be because there are fewer of them in some categories—not because load funds provide superior management. Inasmuch as Lipper's (and other services') total return data are not adjusted for loads, they overstate what investors in load funds have actually earned on their money.

Deferred sales loads. A number of funds impose deferred sales loads instead of front-end loads, reducing the proceeds from sales by the stated percentages and thereby reducing capital gains or increasing capital losses. Among funds having two classes of shares, deferred sales charges are usually imposed on Class B shares.

Deferred sales charges usually are levied according to a sliding scale, falling each year the shares are held until they're eliminated after a specified number of years—often five. If a fund performs poorly during the time the load is in effect, you have to weigh the cost of redeeming shares versus the cost of holding them.

Sales loads on reinvested dividends. Some funds also charge a sales load for shares bought, year after year, through dividend reinvestment, thereby further reducing the returns of shareholders who choose to reinvest instead of taking dividends in cash.

Franklin Resources, a leading sponsor of funds that has long imposed this load, dropped it in 1994.

Operating expenses. The annual expenses of a mutual fund, which all shareholders bear, are expressed as a percent of its average net assets. Unlike one-time sales charges, which are not reflected in Lipper's total return data, annual operating expenses *are* reflected. As you glance at the tables, you can see how low or high expenses can help or hurt relative performance.

Since 1988, the SEC has required every fund to divide operating expenses into three categories—management fees, Rule 12b-1 fees, and all others—and to report them prominently in its prospectus. This makes it easy for shareholders to see why a fund's expenses are high. Rule 12b-1 fees cover distribution and other expenses incurred under a plan adopted by a fund in accordance with an SEC rule.

Class B shares or funds only imposing deferred sales loads commonly have higher annual expenses because they usually involve 12b-1 fees. The

12b-1 money is paid, year after year, to brokers and others in the distribution chain in lieu of compensation out of a front-end load. (It has nothing to do with compensating portfolio managers and, therefore, cannot be considered an incentive to their superior performance.)

Load funds aren't the only ones, by the way, that charge 12b-1 fees. Some no-load funds do, too; they must limit their fees to 0.25% of average net assets, however, to be permitted to be called no-load.

Waived and reimbursed expenses. In many cases, all or portions of a fund's scheduled expenses have been reimbursed or waived by its investment adviser. Without such reimbursements or waivers, its expense ratio would have been higher while total return and income would have been lower.

Firms frequently follow this practice to attract investors in the hope of building up assets under management on which full advisory fees would eventually be charged.

I've indicated where expenses have been held down by waivers and/or reimbursements so that you can make a more meaningful comparison of fund returns and so that you won't be led to expect a fund's temporarily inflated performance to continue indefinitely. If expenses are totally waived or reimbursed, sooner or later they'll be imposed. If they are partially waived or reimbursed, sooner or later they are likely to go up.

CHAPTER 5

How Different Types of Bond Funds Have Performed—and Why: Taxable Bond Funds

The discussion of how and why bond funds have performed as they have in recent years is organized by groupings of funds' investment objective categories, as classified by Lipper Analytical Services, primarily on the basis of maturities and credit quality. This should help you to focus easily on the ones you may want to consider.

In this chapter, you'll find the many categories of taxable bond funds that may be appropriate for any type of account you are considering (depending on your goals and risk tolerance). Tables list their top 5- or 3-year performers.

In Chapter 6, you'll find the categories of federally tax-exempt bond funds that, depending on your federal income tax bracket, may be appropriate for any type of account *other than* IRAs and other tax-deferred retirement accounts.

Short-Term Funds

Funds that are concentrated in bonds of short (1- to 5-year) maturities are mostly of recent origin, although some date back more than ten years.

As the long downward trend in interest rates was nearing a turning point, they were offered increasingly to attract investors who wanted higher yields than money market funds could provide but were concerned that funds invested in longer maturities would involve too much interest rate risk.

Vanguard, whose Short-Term Corporate Portfolio, started in 1982, had long been a leading fund in the Short-Term Investment-Grade group, introduced its Short-Term Federal Portfolio in 1987 and its Short-Term U.S. Treasury Portfolio in 1991. Both have become the largest in their respective categories, no doubt due in large part to the competitive advantage of Vanguard's low annual expenses, which are especially significant when funds are invested in lower-yielding, short-term securities.

Overseen by Robert F. Auwaerter, a vice president in Vanguard's fixed income group, the three funds have a "normal" duration (page 47) of 2.5 years—about average for the categories. This means that if interest rates rise 1%, the funds' NAVs would fall about 2.5%; if they fall 1%, the NAVs would rise about 2.5%. If Auwaerter (or another portfolio manager) expects interest rates to rise, he may make portfolio changes to reduce the duration and, thus, the extent of the drop in NAV that could occur; if he expects rates to fall, he may raise the duration slightly.

Whether invested in U.S. Treasury securities, a range of U.S. government issues, or investment-grade corporates, short-term funds have performed, on the average, about as expected: moderate income along with a bit of appreciation. As interest rates were declining, it was not surprising that their returns would decline, too, inasmuch as managers had to replace maturing securities with new issues bearing lower coupons.

Among the funds invested only in Treasury issues, whose leaders are shown in Table 5.1, differences in performance were due largely to differences in average maturities. As rates were coming down, those with maturities approaching three years topped funds that kept maturities shorter.

Of the Short-Term U.S. Government Funds—those that may invest in other government securities in addition to Treasuries—the one with the best records for the 1, 3, and 5 years ended in 1993, Piper Jaffray's Institutional Government Income Portfolio, proved the axiom about something seeming to be too good to be true.

While he and the group's other managers had a wide range of government issues in which to invest, Piper Capital Management's Worth Bruntjen tried aggressively to enhance the fund's return. He devoted "a significant portion" of the fund to mortgage-backed derivative securities such as inverse floaters and principal-only and interest-only paper.

As long as interest rates fell, the strategy worked well, as the record demonstrates. But when the Federal Reserve began to raise short-term rates in February 1994, the strategy backfired. By December 31, 1994, the fund was down over 28%—a loss that can only be regarded as stunning in a group that is presumed to offer low risk because of its association with government securities. (Its 5-year annual average return was pulled down to 3.8% from 13.8% at the end of 1993.)

The fund's performance certainly was stunning to anyone who invested in it based on the investment objective stated on the cover of its March 26, 1993, prospectus: "high level of current income consistent with preservation of capital." (It was unchanged in the prospectus as of May 23, 1994.)

Table 5.1 *Short–Term U.S. Treasury Funds*

Fund (Maximum sales load)	Total Return			12- Month Yield*	30- Day Yield**	Operating Expense Ratio***
	1990– 1994 (Annual Rate)	1992– 1994	1994			
Columbia U.S. Government Securities (NL)	6.7%	3.9%	0.0%	4.6%	6.8%	0.81%
Dreyfus 100% U.S. Treasury Short Term (NL)	6.5	4.5	(0.3)	7.9	6.9	0.11ᵃ
AIM Limited Maturity Treasury (1%)	6.0	3.6	0.9	4.3	6.7	0.47ᵇ
Group average	6.4	3.7	(0.2)	5.0	6.7	

NA = Not available; R = Deferred sales charge.
NL = A no-load fund whose shares can be bought or sold without sales charge. Some impose annual 12b-1 fees of more than 0.25% of average net assets and may not be described as true no-load funds. Most other funds impose charges at the time of purchase (including Class A shares) or at the time of redemption (including Class B shares).
*Income dividends paid during the previous 12 months, divided by the latest net asset values.
**Annualized yields calculated according to a Securities and Exchange Commission formula that reflects sales loads, amortization of discounts and premiums, and other factors.
***Annual fund operating expenses as a percent of average net assets.
ᵃExpenses are after partial waiver of fees or reimbursement of expenses by investment adviser.
ᵇIncludes Rule 12b-1 fees.
ᶜFund was not in operation for all of the period.
Note: Tables 5.1–5.22 and 6.1–6.5 exclude funds that are not generally available to individual investors or may not be listed in daily newspapers because they have less than $25 million in net assets. Group averages reflect performance data for such funds, however.
Sources: Total returns and yields, Lipper Analytical Services; sales loads and operating expense ratios, fund companies

No prose in the prospectus had given investors a clear warning of what they might expect, although in the middle of page 6 there was this inconspicuous passage: "The Fund would be adversely affected by the purchase of such (inverse or reverse floating collateralized mortgage obligations) in the event of an increase in interest rates..." And the September 30, 1993, annual report had said—after commenting on how derivatives had contributed to performance: "The fund will experience moderate price volatility...." It appeared to be intended, however, as a general statement, urging investors to regard the fund as a long-term investment—not as a forecast of 1994's plunge.

Table 5.2   *Short–Term U.S. Government Funds*

Fund (Maximum sales load)	Total Return 1990–1994 (Annual Rate)	1992–1994 (Annual Rate)	1994	12-Month Yield*	30-Day Yield**	Operating Expense Ratio***
Oppenheimer Limited-Term Govt. A (3.5%)[d]	7.6%[e]	4.2%	0.5%	7.4%	7.0%	1.02%[b]
DFA 5-Year Govt. (NL)[f,g]	7.4	4.0	(3.2)	5.1	7.5	0.31
Dreyfus Short-Intermediate Govt. (NL)	7.3	4.5	(0.8)	7.2	7.1	0.40[a]
Federated Intermediate Govt. Institutional (NL)[h]	6.8	3.9	(1.9)	5.2	7.2	0.54
New England Limited Term USG A (3%)	6.7	3.3	(2.1)	6.3	6.4	1.14[b]
Vanguard Short-Term Federal (NL)	6.7	4.0	(0.9)	5.6	7.5	0.26
Franklin Short-Intermediate USG Securities (2.25%)	6.6	3.9	(2.2)	4.9	6.7	0.73[a,b]
IDS Federal Income (5%)	6.5	3.9	(0.3)	5.7	7.2	0.76[b]
Thornburg Ltd.-Term USG A (2.5%)	6.4	3.7	(2.1)	5.9	6.3	1.01[a,b]
(Fidelity) Spartan Ltd. Maturity Govt. (NL)[f]	6.4	3.7	(1.0)	5.9	7.1	0.65
Group average	6.1	3.3	(1.7)	5.2	6.3	

[d]Current name and investment objective were adopted in May 1994.
[e]Oppenheimer Management became investment adviser in April 1990.
[f]Minimum initial investment: DFA, $100,000; Fidelity Spartan, $10,000.
[g]Shares are available to clients of qualified fee-based investment advisers who may require lower minimum initial investments.
[h]Minimum initial investment: $25,000. Lower minimums may be available through broker-dealers or banks, which may impose fees or transaction charges.
See Table 5.1 for other footnotes.

Managements of other funds in the group appeared to be less aggressive, content to invest in varying blends of Treasury notes, securities backed by fixed- and adjustable-rate mortgages, less risky collateralized mortgage obligations (CMOs), and issues of a variety of government agencies.

Short-term investment-grade funds (Table 5.3) also invest in corporate securities—sometimes including junk bonds—to earn their usually higher yields.

Table 5.3 *Short–Term Investment Grade Funds*

	Total Return					
Fund (Maximum sales load)	1990– 1994 (Annual Rate)	1992– 1994	1994	12- Month Yield*	30- Day Yield**	Operating Expense Ratio***
PIMCO Low Duration Institutional (NL)ᵈ	7.6%	5.3%	0.6%	6.3%	7.6%	0.43%
Vanguard Short-Term Corporate (NL)	7.2	4.7	(0.1)	5.7	7.7	0.26
Babson Bond Portfolio S (NL)	7.1	4.3	(2.1)	7.4	NA	0.68ᵃ
Portico Short-Term Bond (2%)	7.0	4.7	1.0	5.8	6.8	0.75ᵃ
Prudential Structured Maturity A (3.25%)	6.9	4.2	(1.2)	6.2	6.8	0.80ᵇ
Connecticut Mutual Income Account (2%)	6.8	4.7	(0.4)	7.4	7.7	0.63ᵃ
Scudder Short Term Bond (NL)	6.8	3.5	(2.9)	6.9	7.7	0.68
Strong Short-Term Bond (NL)	6.7	4.7	(1.6)	6.9	8.3	0.84ᵃ
Compass Short/ Intermediate (3.75%)	6.6	4.3	(0.5)	5.3	6.4	0.84
Bernstein Short Duration Plus (NL)ᵈ	6.5	4.1	0.6	4.8	7.3	0.66
Group average	6.4	3.8	(0.4)	5.7	6.5	

ᵈMinimum initial investment: PIMCO, $500,000; shares are also available through discount brokers who require a lower minimum but may impose a sales charge; Bernstein, $25,000. See Table 5.1 for other footnotes.

Several funds own securities of foreign corporations; some, only issues denominated in U.S. dollars to avoid currency risk.

The percentages of corporates vary. As its name implies, Vanguard's Short-Term Corporate Portfolio is around 80% invested in them. Scudder Short Term Bond Fund, on the other hand, may have only 15% corporates. Thomas M. Poor, who has managed it since 1989, when Scudder created the fund by restructuring an unsuccessful target maturity fund due to mature in 1994, is permitted to be eclectic. Among other things, he also buys asset-backed securities, collateralized by credit card receivables and home equity loans.

Intermediate–Term Funds

Owing to their longer weighted average maturities, which may range from five to ten years, and their longer durations, which may average four to six years, funds in these U.S. Treasury, U.S. government, and investment-grade categories have tended to outperform their short-term counterparts (Tables 5.4–5.6). They also have tended to be more volatile. Their mixes of bond types, however, have been quite similar, as, therefore, has been their relative credit quality.

Although you would expect U.S. Treasury funds to be concentrated in traditional Treasury notes and bonds—the investments of the highest credit

Table 5.4   Intermediate–Term U.S. Treasury Funds

Fund (Maximum sales load)	Total Return			12- Month Yield*	30- Day Yield**	Operating Expense Ratio***
	1990– 1994 (Annual Rate)	1992– 1994	1994			
Dreyfus 100% U.S. Treasury Intermediate Term (NL)	7.4%	4.6%	(4.0)%	7.5%	6.8%	0.73%[a]
T. Rowe Price U.S. Treasury Intermediate (NL)	7.0	3.9	(2.3)	6.1	7.2	0.70
Benham Treasury Note (NL)	6.9	4.0	(2.3)	5.2	7.3	0.51
Group average	7.0	4.3	(3.3)	5.8	6.5	

See Table 5.1 for footnotes.

Table 5.5 *Intermediate–Term U.S. Government Funds*

Fund (Maximum sales load)	Total Return			12- Month Yield*	30- Day Yield**	Operating Expense Ratio***
	1990– 1994 (Annual Rate)	1992– 1994	1994			
Vanguard Bond Index Fund Total Bond Market Portfolio (NL)	7.4%	4.6%	(2.7)%	6.8%	7.8%	0.18%
Winthrop Focus Fixed Income (4% R)	7.3	4.4	(3.7)	5.9	6.1	0.90[a,b]
Warburg Pincus Intermediate Maturity Govt. (NL)	7.2	4.2	(1.7)	5.9	6.9	0.60[a]
EV Traditional Government Obligations[d] (4.75%)	7.1	4.2	(1.7)	8.4	5.6	1.52[b]
Principal Preservation Govt. Portfolio (4.5%)	6.9	3.7	(5.4)	6.9	6.4	1.00[b]
Paragon Intermediate-Term Bond A (4.5%)	6.8	3.6	(4.4)	6.9	7.1	0.74
Legg Mason U.S. Govt. Intermediate (NL)	6.7	3.6	(1.9)	5.3	6.8	0.90[a,b]
Parkstone Intermediate Govt. Obligations Institutional (NL)[e]	6.5	3.4	(2.3)	5.8	6.8	1.02[a,b]
Quest for Value USG Income A (4.75%)	6.4	3.2	(3.1)	5.6	6.1	1.20[a,b]
Midwest Intermediate Term Govt. Income (2%)	6.3	3.3	(6.3)	5.8	6.9	0.99[b]
Prudential Govt. Securities Trust— Intermediate Term Series (NL)	6.3	3.6	(2.5)	6.8	6.2	0.80[b]
Group average	6.5	3.5	(3.7)	6.0	6.5	

[d]Formerly Eaton Vance Government Obligations Fund.
[e]Institutional shares are available only to customers of certain banks' trust departments. Other share classes are available to investors generally with 4% maximum sales loads or deferred sales charges.
See Table 5.1 for other footnotes.

quality—a few have taken minor positions in other securities guaranteed by the government. To enhance its total return, the Benham Treasury Note Fund invests in STRIPS (the zero-coupon obligations derived from certain Treasury notes and bonds), but limits its holdings to 35% because they pay no current interest. To raise the yield of its U.S. Treasury Intermediate Fund, T. Rowe Price invested in some Ginnie Maes, which, of course, exposed the fund modestly to prepayment risk and caused losses when securities bought at premiums were sold at par.

Performance among the funds also has differed in part because of differences in weighted average maturities. Those of the Benham and Price funds and the Dreyfus 100% U.S. Treasury Intermediate Term Fund have tended to run around three to four years—well below their expected maximums of seven (Dreyfus and Price) and ten (Benham). That of Vanguard's Intermediate-Term U.S. Treasury Portfolio has been closer to seven.

U.S. Government Funds, too, have achieved varying results—not many of them impressive—because of the wide range of their average maturities at a time when the yield curve was fairly steep and because of their different securities mixes. Few of the group's funds matched Lehman's Intermediate Government Index return of 7.3% over the last five years. Expenses also may have mattered, as Table 5.5 would indicate.

John Hancock Limited Term Government Fund, known as Hancock U.S. Government Securities Fund until July 1993, epitomized not only the range of maturities in the intermediate category—making meaningful comparisons difficult—but also the inadequately disciplined use of words in fund literature that can frustrate investors.

In reporting to its shareholders, Hancock acknowledged that the fund underperforms others in the intermediate group because its average maturity is kept shorter to keep the NAV more stable. (Its 5-year average annual return was 6%.)

The prospectus says the fund may have an average maturity of five to seven years—which would qualify as intermediate, to be sure. In her June 30, 1993, report to shareholders, however, portfolio manager Anne C. Hodsdon said "we limit our average maturity to five years or less" and said the fund actually was running around three to four years. That would make it a short-term fund, in Lipper's classification system.

Nor is that all. In the December 31, 1992, report, she asserted: "The Fund is more appropriately considered a cash alternative, and it has performed well on that basis." Like a money market fund, in other words. Shareholders might have wondered about that comment in 1994, when the fund was down—albeit, only 1.3%—while money market funds were, of course, up.

The average maturity of Prudential's Intermediate Term Series has been kept at around four years or less. That's intermediate, according to SEC guidelines; hence the name, Prudential says. Prudential hasn't helped to clarify

Table 5.6   *Intermediate-Term Investment Grade Funds*

Fund (Maximum sales load)	Total Return			12-Month Yield*	30-Day Yield**	Operating Expense Ratio***
	1990–1994 (Annual Rate)	1992–1994	1994			
PIMCO Total Return Institutional (NL)[d]	9.0%	6.0%	(3.6)%	5.9%	7.3%	0.41%
Harbor Bond (NL)	8.8	5.7	(3.8)	5.9	7.2	0.77[a]
New England Bond Income A (4.5%)	7.9	4.9	(4.2)	6.6	7.5	1.04[b]
Portico Bond IMMDEX (2%)	7.9	5.0	(3.1)	6.5	7.9	0.75[a]
Bernstein Intermediate Duration (NL)[d]	7.6	4.8	(3.2)	5.6	7.4	0.66
Merrill Lynch Corp. Bond—Intermediate Term A (1%)	7.6	4.9	(3.9)	7.2	7.8	0.58
Dreyfus/Laurel Premier Managed Income A (4.5%)	7.6	5.7	(5.2)	6.8	7.1	0.95[b]
Fidelity Intermediate Bond(NL)	7.5	5.2	(2.0)	6.5	6.8	0.79
Westcore Bonds Plus (4.5%)	7.2	4.0	(2.8)	6.3	6.7	0.79[a]
SteinRoe Intermediate Bond (NL)	7.1[e]	4.6	(2.6)	6.9	7.4	0.70
Warburg Pincus Fixed Income (NL)	7.1	5.5	(0.8)	7.1	8.4	0.75[a]
Group average	7.2	4.4	(3.4)	6.0	6.9	

[d]Minimum initial investment: PIMCO, $500,000; shares are also available through discount brokers who require a lower minimum but may impose a sales charge. Bernstein, $25,000.
[e]Current investment policy and name were adopted in April 1990.
See Table 5.1 for other footnotes.

things by declaring in its May 31, 1993, report to shareholders that the fund's duration "will likely remain in the short-term, three-year range" or by stating in its April 1, 1994, prospectus that investment in securities with maturities ranging from two to five years "is currently anticipated," although it could go out to 10 years.

The Eaton Vance and Colonial U.S. Government funds have invested primarily in government-related mortgage-backed securities to earn higher-than-Treasury yields, while the Hancock, Prudential, and Warburg Pincus funds have invested mostly in Treasury issues. Legg Mason U.S. Government Intermediate-Term Portfolio has tried to boost returns by investing up to 25% in investment-grade asset-backed and other corporate securities.

The group's leading fund, Vanguard Bond Index Fund's Total Bond Market Portfolio, is unlike the other top-performing intermediate-term U.S. Government Funds. It's managed to replicate the investment performance of the Lehman Aggregate Index (box), which, you may recall, reflects the behavior of the entire taxable U.S. investment-grade bond market.

The fund is certain never to outperform the Lehman index—but also fairly certain never to underperform it by more than its expense ratio. It is classified as an intermediate-term U.S. Government fund because the total taxable investment-grade bond market has a weighted average maturity of around 9 years and because government and government-related securities account for over 80% of its total market value.

Since its inception in 1986, the performance of the Vanguard fund (which tracked the similarly constructed Salomon Brothers BIG Index through May 1993) suffered in comparison with intermediate-term funds concentrated in Treasury and corporate issues during periods of falling interest rates. That's because mortgage-backed securities, which make up over 25% of the investment-grade market, were hurt when many holders of high-yield mortgages refinanced them during periods of falling interest rates.

The intermediate-term investment grade bond market as a whole, of course, also takes in corporate securities, which, when selected by skillful managers, can help to provide returns exceeding those of government funds.

Two of the group's leading performers are PIMCO Total Return Fund and Harbor Bond Fund, both managed by William H. Gross, a managing director of Pacific Investment Management Company. Gross says he has the same "bogey" (or target) for both: a total return of 1% above that of the Lehman Aggregate Index.

To achieve the superior average annual returns that you see for his funds in Table 5.6, Gross credits three factors: timely changes in the portfolios' maturity and duration (which may range from three to six years), timely rotation among sectors, and the inclusion of "high quality junk" bonds (up to 10% of assets). He also may invest in foreign bonds when he finds them attractive, as he did until early 1994.

Gross, who describes himself as "one-third mathematician, one-third economist, and one-third horse trader," says he makes portfolio switches to adjust durations when he believes them desirable on the basis of both his secular (or long-run) outlook for interest rates and his expectation of short-run fluctuations.

BOND INDEXES: BENCHMARKS FOR PORTFOLIO PERFORMANCE

"How's the bond market?"

You get the quick answer to that question every day when print and electronic media tell you what the yield is on 30-year U.S. Treasury bonds and whether it has gone up or down.

You know that prices of those bonds are up when the yield is down, and vice versa. But you may not read or hear about yields—or prices— of Treasury securities with shorter maturities (with the possible exception of 13-week bills) or the huge variety of other issues which may, or may not, move in tandem with the long bonds.

To know how well the bond market is doing, you need more information. You need to know how much the price of each security is up or down, and how much interest income each has earned, for a given period.

In other words, you need to know the market's total return.

Given that there are close to 5,000 issues just in the taxable investment-grade market—that is, excluding taxable junk bonds and tax-exempt securities—this is not easy to calculate. It certainly isn't as easy to calculate as the popular Dow Jones Industrial Average, which includes the stock prices of only 30 corporations.

Happily, a few firms do it. In fact, they calculate not only an index for the $4 trillion taxable investment-grade bond market, but also other indexes that measure the performance of its government, mortgage-backed, and corporate components. Given the importance of interest rate risk that varies with bond maturities, they also provide indexes for component sectors by maturities and for combined components, such as government/corporate.

These indexes provide the most meaningful benchmarks by which to judge the performance of a bond fund portfolio manager. When you know, say, the total return of an index of intermediate-term corporate bonds for one year and you make an allowance for reasonable fund expenses of up to 0.5%, you know what sort of return you should expect of an intermediate-term corporate bond fund that you may own. (Since indexes cover unmanaged batches of securities, they involve no management or other fees.)

The best known indexes are probably those of Lehman Brothers and Salomon Brothers.

BOND INDEXES—
Continued

Lehman introduced its widely-followed Government/Corporate Index in January 1973, when it included some 3,600 issues having an average yield of about 7%. (Today it includes more than 4,000.) In January 1986—after a great year for the bond market—it followed up with mortgage-backed obligations and created the Aggregate Index, which represents the aggregate of the two—that is, the total investment-grade market. Moreover, Lehman also calculated returns back to the end of 1975 to provide a 10-year historical framework. (From time to time, the firm also included additional, but small, market sectors.)

Salomon, which had introduced its High-Grade Bond Index in 1969 and its World Bond Index (WBI) in 1981, came out with its Broad Investment-Grade (BIG) Bond Index, covering essentially the same broad market as Lehman's Aggregate, in 1985. It calculated historic data back to 1980. In 1986, Salomon offered the widely-followed World Government Bond Index (WGBI). The WGBI was created to provide superior coverage of world markets. The firm intended to discontinue the WBI but has maintained it because of investor interest in a few of its sectors.

There may be slight differences between comparable Lehman and Salomon index returns from time to time because of differences in the time of day they obtain security prices, requirements for inclusion, reinvestment assumptions, and so forth. They may be of interest to professional money managers but are too complicated to describe briefly here. More important, they should not give you concern.

It matters more how close a fund's performance comes to that of a relevant benchmark index (with which the SEC requires comparison) than whether the benchmark index is calculated by Lehman or Salomon.

Actively managed funds that have been strong performers besides Gross' pair include New England Bond Income Fund and Merrill Lynch Corporate Bond Fund's Intermediate-Term Portfolio. Both have been primarily invested in corporate bonds.

For investors who want the risk/reward characteristics of an intermediate-term fund and the advantages of an index fund (such as very low expenses) but want to avoid mortgage securities, Vanguard introduced its Intermediate-Term Bond Portfolio in 1994. It's designed to track Lehman's Intermediate Government/Corporate Index (just as its siblings track Lehman's similar short- and long-term indexes). The intermediate-term fund's weighting at the end of 1994: 62% U.S. Treasury and agency securities, 38% corporates.

Long-Term and Unspecified-Term Funds

What Lipper classifies as General U.S. Treasury and General U.S. Government funds are funds that are invested in securities similar to the Short- and Intermediate-Term U.S. Treasury and General U.S. Government funds but that have (1) longer average maturities or (2) unspecified maturities.

During periods when interest rates are rising and the yield curve is steep—that is, when yields on long bonds are significantly higher than those on short bonds—the funds with longer average maturities should excel.

This would help to explain why Vanguard Long-Term U.S. Treasury Portfolio, Dreyfus 100% U.S. Treasury Long Term Fund, and Stagecoach U.S. Government Allocation Fund, whose portfolios averaged 20 years or more, would have outperformed T. Rowe Price U.S. Treasury Long-Term Fund and Flag Investors Total Return U.S. Treasury Fund Shares, with averages under 15 years (Table 5.7). Expenses also varied.

General U.S. Government Funds' performance (Table 5.8) is less predictable. The funds vary not only in maturities but also in their mixes of government and government-related securities from U.S. Treasury and agency securities (including high-risk zero-coupon Treasury obligations) to Ginnie Maes and other mortgage-backeds. Moreover, some funds permit their managers to invest some money in corporates.

This flexibility, as well as the range of skills of the managers who exercise it and the range of expenses, which commonly approach or exceed 1% annually, would explain the wide range of total returns from the best to the worst. In the five years ended December 31, 1994, for example, they ranged from Strong Government Securities and Heartland U.S. Government Securities funds' 8.6% to 3.3% annually—the latter less than the 4.6% an average taxable money market fund produced with less risk.

The group has more funds than any other Lipper category of taxable bond funds—174 (including multiple classes of shares)—of which all but a handful are load funds. Thus, it is easy to suppose that quite a few were created more to give brokers and other salespeople products that would be easy to sell because of their perceived association with the government than to give investors funds that offer relatively predictable rewards and risks, as U.S. Treasury funds do.

Dean Witter U.S. Government Securities Trust had nearly $8.2 billion in net assets at the end of December 1994, down from over $12.2 billion a year before but still the group's largest. Its performance was hardly superlative, however: a below-average annual total return of 5.7% for the last five years (due in part to the burden of expenses exceeding 1% because of 0.7% 12b-1 fees).

Strong Government Securities Fund, the top five-year performer with an average annual total return of 8.58%, invests not only in government and

Table 5.7   *General U.S. Treasury Funds*

	Total Return					
Fund *(Maximum sales load)*	*1990–* *1994* *(Annual Rate)*	*1992–* *1994*	*1994*	*12-* *Month* *Yield**	*30-* *Day* *Yield***	*Operating* *Expense* *Ratio****
Vanguard Long-Term U.S. Treasury (NL)	8.9%	7.2%	(7.0)%	7.3%	7.9%	0.26%
Dreyfus 100% U.S. Treasury Long Term (NL)	7.6	4.4	(9.2)	7.6	7.1	0.78[a]
Stagecoach USG Allocation A (4.5%)	7.5	5.1	(6.9)	6.5	6.6	0.99[a,b]
Flag Investors Total Return US Treasury A (4.5%)	7.1	4.5	(4.0)	7.0	6.3	0.77[b]
T. Rowe Price US Treasury Long- Term (NL)	6.9	4.0	(5.8)	7.2	7.4	0.80[a]
Midwest Treasury Total Return A (4%)	5.1	2.4	(7.1)	5.1	5.6	1.25[b]
Founders Govt. Securities (NL)	5.0	2.1	(7.5)	5.7	6.7	1.18[b]
Group average	6.9	4.3	(5.8)	6.3	6.8	

See Table 5.1 for footnotes.

mortgage-backed securities but also in corporates. At times, Treasuries have accounted for most of the portfolio; at other times, MBS. The corporates have ranged from zero to the 20% of assets that portfolio manager Bradley C. Tank is permitted to invest in them. Tank credits his relative performance primarily to keeping durations within an intermediate range of 4 to 6.5 years to control interest rate risk, enabling him to be somewhat defensive when rates rise but to benefit to some degree from appreciation when rates rise.

Heartland U.S. Government Securities Fund, another top five-year performer with a return of 8.55%, has been aggressively managed by William J. Nasgovitz and Patrick J. Retzer. They have successfully changed maturities, as they thought appropriate, ranging from 2.9 to 16.4 years. They also have changed securities types. Having been permitted to invest up to 35% in con-

Table 5.8 *General U.S. Government Funds*

Fund (Maximum sales load)	Total Return			12- Month Yield*	30- Day Yield**	Operating Expense Ratio***
	1990– 1994	1992– 1994	1994			
	(Annual Rate)					
Strong Govt. Securities (NL)	8.6%	6.0%	(3.4)%	6.5%	7.4%	0.83%[a]
Heartland U.S. Government Securities (NL)	8.6	5.4	(9.6)	6.7	6.9	1.06[a,b]
Fidelity Government Securities (NL)	7.9	4.8	(5.2)	6.7	7.0	0.69
Advantage Govt. Securities (4% R)	7.9	5.4	(9.8)	6.6	7.1	1.31[a,b]
Voyageur USG Securities A (4.75%)	7.9	3.8	(5.6)	7.2	6.7	0.96[b]
Overland Express USG Income A (4.5%)	7.8	3.8	(4.8)	7.2	6.4	0.53[a,b]
Financial Horizons Govt. Bond (5% R)	7.6	4.1	(3.7)	5.9	7.6	1.36[a,b]
SIT U.S. Government Securities (NL)	7.6	4.8	1.7	6.3	6.9	0.80[a]
State Street Research Govt. Income A (4.5%)	7.6	4.4	(2.9)	6.8	6.9	1.05[b]
Lord Abbett U.S. Govt. Securities (4.75%)	7.5	3.9	(4.3)	9.5	5.5	0.89[b]
Group average	6.6	3.5	(4.6)	6.5	6.5	

See Table 5.1 for footnotes.

vertible or nonconvertible corporate bonds—even including up to 25% junk, which isn't what you'd expect of a "government" fund—they have tended to be 10% to 15% in corporates but have gone up to 25%.

In running Advantage Government Securities Fund, Margaret D. Patel has achieved similar results (despite higher expenses) by sticking to government securities, switching emphasis among coupon-bearing Treasuries, STRIPS, and mortgage-backeds. Like some competitors, she was essentially only in Ginnie Maes for a while.

Fidelity Government Securities, on the other hand, cannot own any mortgage-backeds. It's limited to investments in Treasury and other government securities whose income is exempt from state and local income tax in most states. The fund's "neutral" mix is 70% agencies and 30% Treasuries, but Curt Hollingsworth, who managed the fund from 1990 until early 1995, tended to split the assets closer to fifty-fifty when agencies' yield advantage was too slim.

Corporate bond funds, classified by Lipper into two categories—those primarily invested in corporate bonds rated in the top three investment grades and those primarily invested in bonds rated in any of the four—have had similar average 10-year returns of around 10%, as you see in Tables 5.9 and 5.10.

The top performers in the A-rated group during the period of secular decline in interest rates have generally been those with the longest weighted average maturities and durations, such as Vanguard Long-Term Corporate Portfolio, Smith Barney Investment Grade Bond Fund, and Dreyfus A Bonds Plus. Their average maturities have tended to run 15 to 20 years or even longer. Alliance Corporate Bond Portfolio has led the BBB-rated group with a similar long average.

On the other hand, managers of American Funds' Bond Fund of America, Scudder Income Fund, and Merrill Lynch Corporate Bond Fund's Investment Grade Portfolio have tended to hold their weighted average maturities to around ten years or less.

Maturities weren't the only factor accounting for differences in performance. The funds also differed in the types and creditworthiness of the bonds in which they invested.

Some bought higher-yielding callable corporate bonds to boost their income payments and saw them going to premium prices as interest rates fell. But as the bonds were called by their issuers, which seized opportunities to refinance debt at lower rates, the funds had to replace them with lower-yielding securities and perhaps even to suffer capital losses.

Funds whose managers emphasized noncallable bonds may have received lower interest and paid lower dividends, but they were able to retain their bonds and to sustain their income payments better.

The Vanguard and Merrill Lynch funds tended to go more heavily (that is, over 70%) for corporates in the top three tiers. Others had significant (that is, 25% to 35%) allocations of government securities, including risky Treasury zeros. The Smith Barney fund, as well as some of those in the BBB-rated group, had 25% or more of assets in Baa/BBB bonds.

And while you might have expected funds in the BBB-rated group to have substantial percentages of junk bonds, as the Alliance bond fund has had,

Table 5.9 *Corporate Bond Funds—A–Rated*

Fund (Maximum sales load)	Total Return			12- Month Yield*	30- Day Yield**	Operating Expense Ratio***
	1985– 1994 (Annual Rate)	1990– 1994	1994			
Vanguard Long-Term Corporate (NL)[d]	10.4%	8.8%	(5.3)%	7.7%	8.3%	0.30%
Bond Fund of America (4.75%)	10.6	8.5	(5.0)	8.3	8.0	0.71[b]
Dodge & Cox Income (NL)	[c]	8.1	(2.9)	7.1	7.9	0.54
Putnam Income A (4.75%)	9.7	8.0	(3.3)	8.0	7.8	1.01[b]
Smith Barney Investment Grade B (4.5%R)	10.2	8.0	(9.4)	7.5	8.1	1.58[b]
John Hancock Sovereign Bond A (4.5%)	9.8	7.9	(2.7)	8.1	7.4	1.25[b]
Kemper Income and Capital Preservation A (4.5%)	9.7	7.9	(3.4)	7.9	7.0	0.97
Scudder Income (NL)	9.7	7.9	(4.4)	6.2	7.2	0.92
Sentinel Bond (5%)	9.4	7.8	(4.9)	6.7	6.8	0.92[b]
Dreyfus A Bonds Plus (NL)	9.8	7.8	(6.2)	7.1	7.5	0.90
Group average	9.4	7.2	(4.6)	6.5	7.0	

[d]Formerly Vanguard Investment Grade Corporate Portfolio.
See Table 5.1 for other footnotes.

junk also has constituted 20% or so of the assets of A-rated funds such as Bond Fund of America and Putnam Income Fund. Some managers have focused on Ba/BB bonds, expecting to catch issues that would be raised to investment grade as their issuers strengthened their balance sheets and improved their cash flows.

Bonds of foreign companies and governments also have been appearing in A-rated and BBB-rated bond fund portfolios as managers sought to enhance returns. Some bought only those denominated in U.S. dollars, while others

Table 5.10   *Corporate Bond Funds—BBB–Rated*

Fund (Maximum sales load)	Total Return			12- Month Yield*	30- Day Yield**	Operating Expense Ratio***
	1985– 1994 (Annual Rate)	1990– 1994	1994			
Fortress Bond (1%)[d]	c	11.3%[e]	(3.4)%	8.3%	9.1%	1.04%[a]
Alliance Corp. Bond A (4.25%)	11.0%	10.0	(12.8)	9.6	9.1	1.30[b]
MAS Fixed Income (NL)[f]	10.6	8.8	(5.5)	5.7	8.6	0.49
INVESCO Select Income (NL)	10.0	8.6	(1.2)	7.6	8.3	1.00[a,b]
Fidelity Investment Grade Bond (NL)	9.7	8.5	(5.4)	7.3	7.2	0.76
William Penn Quality Income (4.75%)	c	8.5	(4.2)	7.8	6.3	0.45[a]
Standish Fixed Income (NL)[g]	c	8.4	(4.9)	6.7	8.5	0.39
IDS Selective (5%)	10.3	8.2	(4.4)	6.8	7.2	0.72[b]
SteinRoe Income (NL)	c	8.1	(3.9)	7.7	8.3	0.82[a]
Westcore Long-Term Bond (4.5%)	c	8.1	(7.1)	6.7	6.8	0.89[a]
Group average	9.6	7.9	(4.5)	6.9	7.3	

[d]Plus a 1% deferred sales charge if shares are redeemed within 4 years.
[e]Current investment objective was adopted in June 1992.
[f]Minimum initial investment: $1,000,000. Lower minimums are available when bought through discount brokers, who may impose a transaction charge.
[g]Minimum initial investment: $100,000.
See Table 5.1 for other footnotes.

such as Fidelity Investment Grade Bond Fund also bought those denominated in foreign currencies.

The funds assigned to the General Bond Funds category are a heterogenous bunch and, thus, across-the-board comparisons of their performance (Table 5.11) aren't meaningful.

Several of them follow so-called three-sector strategies—domestic high-yield corporate, foreign, and U.S. government bonds—on the theory that these sectors' market movements are not highly correlated; one or two can be up

Table 5.11 General Bond Funds

	Total Return					
Fund (*Maximum sales load*)	1985– 1994 (*Annual Rate*)	1990– 1994	1994	12- Month Yield*	30- Day Yield**	Operating Expense Ratio***
Phoenix Multi-Sector A (4.75%)	c	10.3%	(6.9)%	8.0%	8.0%	1.09%[a,b]
FPA New Income (4.5%)	11.0%	9.9	1.5	6.8	NA	0.74
Putnam Diversified Income A (4.75%)	c	9.8	(5.6)	8.8	9.4	1.01[b]
Oppenheimer Strategic Income A (4.75%)	c	9.7	(4.5)	9.8	9.7	1.09
IDS Bond (5%)	10.7	9.1	(4.3)	8.3	8.4	0.68[b]
Dreyfus Strategic Income (3%)	c	8.1	(6.3)	7.3	7.3	0.84[a,b]
IDS Strategy Income (5% R)	9.6	7.8	(6.3)	6.9	7.7	1.60[b]
Colonial Strategic Income A (4.75%)	9.3[d]	7.7[d]	(3.7)	9.1	8.7	1.21[b]
John Hancock Strategic Income A (4.5%)	c	7.6[e]	(3.0)	9.6	8.8	1.41[b]
Managers Bond (NL)[f]	9.5	7.5	(7.3)	8.9	8.6	1.15
Group average	9.5	7.9	(6.0)	7.6	7.7	

[d]Investment policy was changed in 1987 and 1991.
[e]Current investment policy and name were adopted in August 1991.
[f]Minimum initial investment for individuals: $10,000. Shares are also available through investment advisers or broker-dealers who may impose a different minimum as well as transaction fees or other charges.
See Table 5.1 for other footnotes.

while the other two or one can be down. They are known as "strategic income" or "diversified income" funds, which may be confusing since there are also "strategic income" and "diversified income" funds that follow other strategies.

The three-sector concept is still too new to indicate whether the funds will be able to consistently live up to the expectations of sponsors such as Colonial, John Hancock, Oppenheimer, and Putnam: higher returns with less volatility than one would expect of any of the three sectors alone. "Each market has had tough years—and great ones, too," says Colonial's Carl Ericson.

Mortgage Funds

Funds that primarily invest in mortgage-backed securities (MBS) are divided in two ways. One is based on whether the mortgages that constitute their collateral have adjustable or fixed interest rates; the other, on whether and how the U.S. Treasury will stand behind them in case homeowners fail to make mortgage payments.

They have appealed to investors because the yields for their underlying MBS have tended to run 1% or so higher than U.S. Treasury securities of comparable maturities and because the timely payments of interest and principal have been backed by the Treasury, in the case of Ginnie Maes, and by stockholder-owned government agencies, in the cases of Fannie Mae and Freddie Mac. The higher yield is to compensate investors for the prepayment risk that inheres in MBS.

The most favorable environment for these securities usually prevails during periods when interest rates are relatively stable. It is then that investors realize their yield advantage. When rates rise, their principal drops just like the principal of ordinary bonds of comparable maturities. And when rates fall, as they did in 1993, waves of accelerated prepayments resulting from mortgage refinancing may cause their principal and income payments to decline, just when ordinary noncallable bonds' prices are appreciating.

(In an excellent piece on MBS investment fundamentals in the March 31, 1994, annual report for The Benham Group's MBS funds, co-managers Jeffrey Tyler and Randall Merk noted: "MBS durations shorten [when falling interest rates result in higher prepayments], while Treasuries benefit from longer durations. . . . Higher interest rates reduce prepayments, which is good, but the lower level of prepayments causes MBS durations to extend longer, which is bad when rates are rising. . . . By contrast, Treasury durations generally shorten slightly. . . .")

In the SEC registration statement for the first fund concentrated in adjustable rate mortgages (ARMs), which was declared effective on October 5, 1987, the Franklin Group gave its goals as high current income and lower volatility of principal. By the time the predecessor of today's Franklin Adjustable U.S. Government Securities Fund was ready to offer shares to the public a couple of weeks later, the intervening stock market crash had given these goals added appeal.

Others formed ARM funds with similar objectives in ensuing years — first, Overland Express Variable Rate Government Fund, managed by Wells Fargo Bank, in 1990; then several competitors in 1991, including the no-load funds of Benham and T. Rowe Price.

They were generally marketed as short-term bond funds—that is, as funds that could offer higher yields than money market funds but would be less volatile than long-term bond funds because the interest rates of the ARM securities in their portfolios would be reset yearly or even more frequently.

How much more the yield and how much less the volatility would depend on the frequency with which the ARM rates, which may be linked to 1-year Treasury bills or securities indexes, would be reset. It also would depend, as things turned out, on how extensively the funds were invested in derivative securities to enhance yield or reduce risk, exposing them to losses when unexpected developments occur in the market.

When interest rates are declining, ARM fund managers want to be primarily in ARMs with annual resets to sustain their income flows; when rates are rising, managers want to be in ARMs with more frequent resets to boost their yields.

Until 1993, ARM funds performed more or less according to the script but lagged the average short-term bond funds invested in fixed-rate government or corporate securities. In 1993, however, the flood of principal prepayments hurt. Their impact was magnified on certain derivatives held by some of the funds. Those that had paid premium prices for their securities had to absorb losses. As short-term funds enjoyed gains in principal averaging about 1%, the principal values of ARM funds fell by an average of 1%; thus, the group's average total return of 3.8% was 2% lower than the average for short-term funds.

In 1994, when interest rates rose sharply, portfolios that had been primarily invested in securities linked to less frequent reset schedules—to sustain income flows when rates were falling—were caught at a disadvantage. Funds that owned inverse floaters, a type of derivative that enhances yields when rates are stable, suffered even more. While the average fund in the group was off 2.2%, some were down 20%.

Was anything to be learned from 1994's experience?

"We underestimated the unpredictability of the Fund's behavior under unfavorable market conditions, particularly the difficulty of translating the complex nature of ARM securities into a low-risk mutual fund setting," Merk and Newlin Rankin, co-managers of the Benham ARM fund, which was off only 1.2%, acknowledged in a candid report to shareholders.

"We also underestimated the potential impact of even a small derivatives position on an ARM portfolio."

The two categories of funds concentrated in securities that are backed by fixed-rate, government-related mortgages have longer average maturities and perform more like intermediate- or long-term bond funds—with an important exception.

Although most of the mortgages that make up the collateral of Ginnie Maes or other mortgage-backed securities (MBS) may have 30-year terms, their expected lives, on the average, may fall short of 10 years. That's because of the likelihood that they'll be prepaid sooner for one reason or another: people move to other cities, buy bigger or smaller homes, and so forth.

Like managers of other bond funds, the managers of MBS funds have to be skillful—and lucky—in deciding which securities to buy and sell as well

Table 5.12 *Adjustable Rate Mortgage Funds*

Fund (Maximum sales load)	Total Return			12- Month Yield*	30- Day Yield**	Operating Expense Ratio***
	1990– 1994 (Annual Rate)	1992– 1994	1994			
Kemper Adjustable Rate USG A (3.5%)	6.1%[d]	3.5%[d]	(0.4)%	5.0%	5.1%	1.03%
Federated ARMS Inst.(NL)[f]	6.0[e]	2.8[e]	0.3	5.0	5.7	0.55[a]
Franklin Adjustable USG Securities (2.25%)	4.2	1.1	(2.0)	3.7	5.5	0.79[a,b]
Putnam Adjustable Rate USG (3.25%)	3.9[g]	1.4[g]	(0.2)	4.1	4.5	1.07[b]
Managers Short Govt. (NL)[h]	3.7	0.4	(6.1)	7.2	5.1	0.87[a]
Group average	4.8	1.7	(2.2)	4.9	5.6	

[d]Current investment policy and name were adopted in January 1992.
[e]Current investment policy and name were adopted in January and April 1992.
[f]Minimum initial investment: $25,000. Lower minimums may be available through broker-dealers or banks, which may impose fees of transaction charges.
[g]Current investment policy and name were adopted in June 1991.
[h]Minimum initial investment for individuals: $10,000. Shares are also available through investment advisers or broker-dealers who may impose a different minimum as well as transaction fees or other charges.
See Table 5.1 for other footnotes.

as when to buy and sell them. Like their peers, they know that no one can consistently predict interest rates correctly and that they will always have to cope with unexpected fluctuations in rates.

But unlike the others, they also have to deal with an even greater challenge: the uncertainty of how many people with high-interest mortgages will refinance them to save money when interest rates fall, greatly accelerating prepayments of MBS pools and hurting the performance of GNMA and U.S. Mortgage Funds.

"As difficult as it is to predict interest rates, it's impossible to predict what millions of homeowners are going to do," says Paul G. Sullivan, a retired senior vice-president of Wellington Management Company, who managed the Vanguard GNMA Portfolio from 1980 to 1994.

Looking at Table 5.13, which shows the performance of the leading GNMA funds for the five years ended in 1994, you may see that, even though the GNMA securities in which the funds invested have much in common, the funds produce different returns and yields for shareholders. They differed in 1993, when interest rates fell and the group was buffeted by rounds of refinancing, and they differed in 1994, when rates were rising.

In addition to differences in operating expenses (which can exceed 1%), the variations in performance were largely a function of differences in their investment policies and in portfolio managers' assessments of interest rate prospects.

Those who aim at high yields, often at the urging of marketers who find that higher yields make funds easier to sell, are likely to invest in high-coupon Ginnie Maes. They, however, run the risk of sharp reductions in dividends and of capital losses when many homeowners refinance mortgages during a period of falling interest rates and they have to reinvest in lower-coupon GNMA pools, as occurred in 1993. On the other hand, when rates rise, the prices of the securities in their portfolios are likely to fall less.

Those who stress total return and protection of shareholders against sharp reductions in dividends and capital losses during a refinancing stampede may lean more toward low-coupon Ginnie Maes that are less likely to be refinanced. Unless their expenses are very low, they, of course, can't offer comparable yields. And, when interest rates rise, the prices of their securities, which have longer durations, tend to fall more.

(Several also may succeed in holding down the risks of prepayments by identifying higher-coupon GNMA pools whose securities are less likely to be prepaid: those for single-family homes whose owners didn't refinance—for whatever reason—when they had previous opportunities, those made up of recent mortgages issued to homeowners who may not yet be able to pay the costs of refinancing or of old mortgages whose holders are too close to paying them off to bother, or those for multi-family housing.)

Some managers may adjust their blends of Ginnie Maes as market conditions change—sometimes primarily higher coupon, sometimes lower coupon, and sometimes closer to the market rate at which new Ginnie Maes are issued. When refinancing hit 10% GNMA pools, for example, they may have sold those securities and replaced them with 8.5% Ginnie Maes. As interest rates fell and those Ginnie Maes became vulnerable to refinancing, managers switched to new securities with 7% or 7.5% coupons.

While a number of funds are fully invested in Ginnie Maes—except for 5% to 10% in cash reserves—others are less concentrated in them. Thus, performance differences also can arise from differences in the other types of securities that may constitute 25% to 35% of their assets.

They may be Treasury issues because managers want, or have, to own securities backed by the government's full faith and credit. Being noncallable,

Table 5.13   GNMA Funds

Fund (Maximum sales load)	Total Return 1985– 1994 (Annual Rate)	1990– 1994	1994	12- Month Yield*	30- Day Yield**	Operating Expense Ratio***
Vanguard GNMA (NL)	9.5%	7.6%	(1.0)%	7.1%	7.4%	0.28%
Benham GNMA Income (NL)	c	7.5	(1.7)	6.9	7.7	0.54
Smith Barney USG Securities A (4.5%)	9.4	7.5	(1.5)	7.6	NA	0.74[b]
Smith Barney Monthly Payment Govt. Portfolio A (4.5%)	c	7.4	(1.5)	6.8	NA	0.81[b]
(Dreyfus) Premier GNMA A (4.5%)	c	7.4	(2.9)	6.4	6.2	0.78[a]
Dreyfus Investors GNMA (NL)	c	7.2[d]	(1.1)	7.6	7.6	0.00[a]
Princor Govt. Securities Income (4.75%)	c	7.1	(4.9)	6.7	6.7	0.96[b]
Franklin U.S. Government Securities (4.25%)	9.0	7.1	(2.7)	7.8	7.3	0.67[b]
Federated GNMA Institutional (NL)[e]	9.2	7.1	(2.5)	7.7	7.4	0.57
Lexington GNMA Income (NL)	8.8	7.1	(2.1)	7.2	7.7	0.98
T. Rowe Price GNMA (NL)	c	7.1	(1.6)	7.6	7.1	0.76
Group average	8.5	6.8	(2.5)	7.0	6.6	

[d]Current investment objective and name were adopted in August 1991.
[e]Minimum initial investment: $25,000. Lower minimums may be available through broker-dealers or banks, which may impose fees or transaction charges.
See Table 5.1 for other footnotes.

the Treasury securities may enhance total returns when interest rates decline, but, of course, do provide lower yields and could hurt performance when rates rise again. David H. Glen of Scudder, Stevens & Clark, who normally tries to invest 20% of the AARP GNMA and U.S. Treasury Fund in short-term Treasury securities, raised that to nearly 35% to moderate its share price fluctuation when the bond market became turbulent in 1994's first half.

GNMA fund managers also may invest in other government-related MBS, Fannie Maes and Freddie Macs, which involve prepayment risks similar to those of Ginnie Maes but different credit risks. Timely payment of interest and principal, you'll recall, is guaranteed by the Treasury only on Ginnie Maes.

Portfolio managers who really have ample leeway among the three major MBS categories—as well as other securities—are those who run the funds that Lipper classifies as U.S. Mortgage Funds (Table 5.14). Of course, their leeway also may make it more difficult for investors to know what to expect in performance and volatility than in the cases of "plain vanilla" GNMA funds.

Given the differences in the degree of their government backing and the types of mortgages that collateralize them—FHA and VA in the case of Ginnie Maes, conventional mortgages in the cases of Fannie Maes and Freddie Macs—the three types of MBS also perform a bit differently. In 1994, for example, Ginnie Maes had an average total return of minus 1.3%, according to Salomon Brothers, while Freddie Macs and Fannie Maes returned minus 1.5% and minus 1.6%, respectively.

Since these securities can't be expected to move precisely in tandem, fund managers are usually trying to spot MBS pools that may be regarded as underpriced.

Perhaps an even more important factor in the differences in performance is the latitude managers have to invest in Treasury issues. Smith Barney Managed Governments Fund, for example, moved from 60% MBS in mid-1993 to 5%—with 95% in Treasuries—when manager James E. Conroy wanted to reduce the fund's exposure to accelerated prepayments. By early 1994, believing the risk reduced, he was at 80% MBS and 20% Treasuries.

Nor can you ignore the fact that some of the funds go in for risky derivative securities, which can have adverse consequences, as is epitomized by Managers Intermediate Mortgage Fund.

For the five years ended in 1993, the fund led the category, according to Lipper, with an average annual total return of 13.0%. By the end of 1994, when it had posted a total return of minus 25.1%, it had fallen to 20th of 20 funds with a five-year average return of 3.8%.

Managed since 1986 by Worth Bruntjen of Piper Capital Management, the fund had suffered a decline in 1994's first half because of its substantial stake in derivatives—securities that earlier had helped the fund. It was a fate similar to that suffered by Piper Jaffray Institutional Government Income Portfolio, which Bruntjen also runs (page 100).

Table 5.14   *U.S. Mortgage Funds*

Fund (Maximum sales load)	Total Return 1990–1994 (Annual Rate)	1992–1994 (Annual Rate)	1994	12-Month Yield*	30-Day Yield**	Operating Expense Ratio***
Smith Barney Managed Govts. A (4.5%)	7.8%	4.3%	(1.9)%	6.4%	7.1%	1.03%[b]
Standish Securitized (NL)[d]	7.6	3.9	(2.1)	6.4	7.6	0.45
Fidelity Mortgage Securities (NL)	7.5	4.7	1.9	6.0	8.6	0.79
Alliance Mortgage Securities Income A (4.25%)	7.4	3.7	(6.1)	7.4	6.8	1.00[b]
Oppenheimer Mortgage Income A (4.75%)	6.9[e]	3.5[e]	(0.8)	8.1	7.4	1.34[b]
Federated Income Institutional (NL)[d]	6.7	3.3	(1.6)	7.3	7.6	0.57
Van Kampen Merritt USG A (4.65%)	6.7	2.9	(5.1)	8.6	NA	0.87[b]
Victory Fund for Income Portfolio (2%)[f]	6.6	2.6	(1.2)	7.5	7.4	1.12[b]
Merrill Lynch Fed. Sec. D (4%)[g]	6.6	3.1	(3.3)	6.3	7.3	0.83[b]
(Federated) Govt. Income Securities (1%)[h]	6.2	2.9	(1.9)	7.5	7.5	0.85[a]
Piper Government Income (4%)	6.2	1.4	(9.1)	8.5	7.4	1.06[a,b]
Group average	6.5	2.9	(4.2)	7.1	6.8	

[d]Minimum initial investment: Standish, $1 million. Federated institutional class, $25,000; lower minimums may be available through broker-dealers or banks, which may impose fees or transaction charges.
[e]Current investment objective and name were adopted in May 1993.
[f]Formerly Investors Preference Fund for Income.
[g]These shares were designated Class A prior to October 21, 1994.
[h]Plus a 1% deferred sales charge if shares are redeemed within 4 years of purchase.
See Table 5.1 for other footnotes.

Target Maturity Funds

These funds, the only group of mutual funds that are scheduled to mature on certain dates as bonds do, are primarily invested in zero-coupon securities—mostly U.S. Treasury issues—which are sold at deep discounts from face value, do not pay current interest, and rise to face value at maturity. The difference between purchase price and value at maturity constitutes the return.

Most of the group's funds are sponsored by the Benham Group, which introduced them in 1985, targeted to mature every fifth year beginning in 1990.

Since the initial public offering of funds, they have performed according to form. When interest rates were in a downward trend, the longest maturities provided the highest returns. As Table 5.15 indicates, they also have been the most volatile, falling the most in periods when interest rates rose, as happened in 1994.

While the funds cannot perform precisely as individual zeros because of fund expenses, shareholder purchases, and redemptions, they are managed to come as close as possible to their "anticipated growth rate."

High Credit Risk Funds

Table 5.16, which shows the total returns for the high current yield bond funds that led their category for the five years ended in 1994, illustrates how annual average total returns for long periods can create the illusion of consistent performance.

Looking at the bottom line of the table, you could be led to believe that these funds usually have average annual total returns of around 10%, since that was about the average for both 5- and 10-year periods, and that 1994 must just have been a below-average year.

Data for each of the latest five years would have shown a quite different picture: *negative* average total returns for the group of 11.1% and 3.8% for 1990 and 1994, respectively (and far worse principal-only returns of concern to those who take their dividends in cash instead of reinvesting them); positive returns of 36.4% in 1991, 17.7% in 1992, and 19.3% for 1993.

Data for individual funds would have shown similar inconsistency. Dean Witter High Yield Securities led the pack in 1991 with a total return of 67.2%, was fourth with 24.2% in 1992, and second in 1993 with 31.6%. If you had only looked at any of those figures, you could not have known that the fund had been the group's worst performer in 1989 with a *negative* 13.6% and in 1990 with a *negative* 40.1%.

As a consequence, it was 59th of 60 for the five years ended in 1993 with an average total return of 7.2%—not much above the 5.6% for the average

Table 5.15   *Target Maturity Funds*

| | Total Return | | | | | |
Fund (Maximum sales load)	1990–1994 (Annual Rate)	1992–1994	1994	12-Month Yield*	30-Day Yield**	Operating Expense Ratio***
Benham Target Maturities Portfolio 2005 (NL)	8.8%	6.7%	(8.9)%	—	7.4%	0.64%
Benham Target Maturities Portfolio 2000 (NL)	8.4	5.3	(6.9)	—	7.3	0.59
Benham Target Maturities Portfolio 2010 (NL)	8.3	7.0	(11.6)	—	7.5	0.68
Benham Target Maturities Portfolio 1995 (NL)	8.0	5.0	0.8	—	6.5	0.61
Scudder Zero Coupon 2000(NL)	7.7	4.9	(7.9)	2.8%	7.1	1.00[a]
Benham Target Maturities Portfolio 2015 (NL)	7.4	6.5	(14.1)	—	7.5	0.68
Benham Target Maturities Portfolio 2020 (NL)	6.3	6.6	(17.7)	—	7.5	0.70[a]
Group average	7.9	5.7	(8.1)	2.1	7.1	

Note: No 12-month yields (i.e., dividend distribution rates) are given for Benham funds because they declare reverse share splits to offset payment of each annual dividend.
See Table 5.1 for other footnotes.

money market fund. And that, of course, doesn't reflect the net return to investors: it doesn't take into account the fund's maximum sales charge of 5.5% or the income taxes that shareholders would have paid on dividend distributions (unless invested in IRAs).

Following 1994, when it had a total return of minus 7.2%—placing it 79th among 93 funds—its 5-year average *rose* to 8.7%. The down year deleted from the time frame (1989) had been worse than the newly-added year.

What the figures for the good years indicate is that funds invested in speculative securities—commonly known as junk bonds—can reward shareholders for assuming the risks that inhere in them. The figures for the bad

Table 5.16 *High Current Yield Funds*

Fund (Maximum sales load)	Total Return 1985–1994 (Annual Rate)	1990–1994	1994	12-Month Yield*	30-Day Yield**	Operating Expense Ratio***
Fidelity Advisor High Yield A (4.75%)	c	16.1%	(1.5)%	7.6%	8.3%	1.11%[b]
Fidelity Capital & Income (NL)[d]	12.0%[e]	13.7[e]	(4.6)	9.3	8.7	0.97
Liberty High Income Bond A (4.5%)	11.5	13.6	(1.7)	10.0	10.5	1.20[a]
Oppenheimer Champion High Yield A (4.75%)	c	13.4	(0.1)	8.6	8.1	1.24[b]
Advantage High Yield Bond (4% R)	c	13.1	(2.2)	10.0	10.0	1.40[a,b]
Merrill Lynch Corporate Bond— High Income Portfolio A (4%)	12.0	12.9	(2.7)	10.9	11.4	0.55
MainStay High Yield Corporate Bond (5% R)	c	12.9	1.5	9.0	9.3	1.61[b]
Putnam High Yield Advantage A (4.75%)	c	12.8	(5.2)	11.3	9.7	1.14[b]
Kemper Diversified Income (4.5%)	9.7	12.7	(3.8)	9.4	8.2	1.04
PaineWebber High Income A (4%)	10.2	12.5	(11.7)	12.3	12.9	0.93[b]
Group average	9.9	10.6	(3.8)	9.9	10.1	

[d] A 1.5% fee is imposed for redemption of shares held less than 365 days.
[e] Current investment objective and name were adopted in December 1990.
See Table 5.1 for other footnotes.

years, on the other hand, indicate that the risks of downside volatility can be great and should be assumed only by those able and willing to do so.

Those who invest in order to receive the funds' high dividends must be prepared for the inevitable periods of decline in principal, which provide those who reinvest dividends the opportunity to pick up shares at lower prices.

To understand the performance of high-yield funds, you have to recall a few basics. These funds invest primarily in bonds that are judged by Moody's and Standard & Poor's to be below investment grade, which means that there is doubt—from a little to a lot—about their issuers' abilities to pay interest until maturity and to repay principal on time at maturity.

In Moody's terms, for example, they may be rated in the lower five ratings—from Ba ("judged to have speculative elements") through C ("extremely poor prospects of ever attaining any real investment standing")—instead of the top four: Aaa through Baa.

What kinds of companies would have bonds rated so low? As summed up in the July 1, 1994, prospectus for T. Rowe Price High Yield Fund, they typically fall into four categories: "small companies that lack the history or capital strength to merit 'investment-grade' status, former blue-chip companies that have been downgraded due to financial difficulties, companies electing to borrow heavily to finance (or avoid) a takeover or buyout, and highly indebted ('leveraged') companies seeking to refinance their debt at lower rates." Many have familiar names; you probably use some of their products or services.

If there's a chance that issuers of bonds given low ratings may default on their obligations, why invest in them at all?

Because they have to offer higher yields than higher-quality securities to compensate investors for the risk that they may not actually get a dime of interest or have their principal repaid.

Given that the risk of default is greatest when the economy goes into a recession, the premium that junk bonds offer over 10-year Treasuries—a common benchmark—is greater then than when the economy is strong, profits are rising, and some junk bonds actually are upgraded to investment grade.

It should be no surprise, therefore, that the greatest spread—8.5% to 9.0%—occurred during a recession in January 1991, when 10-year Treasuries yielded about 8.0% while high-yield bonds yielded an average of 17.0% to 18.0%, depending on which index you used. Nor should it be a surprise that the spread had narrowed to 3% by 1994.

As the economy recovered from the 1990–91 recession and bond yields fell, bond prices rose, resulting in generous total returns for high-yield bonds—well above their double-digit yields. Prices of a number of bonds also increased because they were upgraded as companies' profits and creditworthiness improved. In many cases, companies strengthened balance sheets by issuing additional common stocks to replace debt and/or refinanced old high-cost debt with new debt issues at the prevailing lower interest rates.

Although it was a euphoric time for junk bond managers and their shareholders, it was not a perfect time. As yields fell, the high dividends had to come down, too. Moreover, when companies took advantage of call options to pay off high-coupon securities and replace them with bonds bearing lower coupons, bond fund managers were forced to reinvest the proceeds in lower-yielding bonds.

When the economic recovery had gained momentum at the start of 1994, high-yield bonds and the funds that own them experienced the impact of increases in interest rates to which they, too, are not immune—even if credit quality considerations often are the principal determinant of their prices.

As interest rates on Treasury securities rose, yields on junk bonds rose, too, bringing their prices down and causing junk bonds to report negative total returns for a brief period.

Ironically, the highest-quality junk—bonds rated Ba/BB—fell more, on the average, than low-tier junk, according to Salomon Brothers. In fact, the lowest tier bonds showed positive average returns (provided, of course, that issuers could maintain debt service).

While ironic, it all makes sense when you consider how the bonds differ in duration, the measure of sensitivity to changes in interest rates. Given comparable maturities, higher-quality junk bonds with lower yields have longer durations than lower-quality junk bonds with higher yields. Thus, the higher-quality bonds would be expected to fall more when interest rates rise.

This would explain, for example, why the Vanguard High Yield Corporate Portfolio would do relatively worse when the economy is strong and credit quality is less of a concern—and relatively better when the economy is in recession and defaults pick up. Earl E. McEvoy, a senior vice president of Wellington Management Company and the fund's portfolio manager since 1984, has had to operate within tight quality constraints: 80% of assets rated B or better, no bonds rated less than Caa/CCC. He also could, and did, buy some investment-grade corporates or Treasuries. The result: a portfolio with a weighted average quality of Ba/BB, one level below investment grade.

On the other hand, Vincent T. Lathbury III, who has managed the Merrill Lynch Corporate Bond Fund's High Income Portfolio since 1982 with a bit more flexibility, has had smaller shares of his fund's assets in investment-grade securities and Ba/BB bonds. The result: an average B quality and superior long-term performance. "B has been our bread and butter," he says.

For a contrast with these two, consider Fidelity Capital & Income Fund. Since changing its name, investment objective, and investment policy in December 1990, this fund (formerly Fidelity High Income Fund) has aggressively pursued both income and growth (instead of primarily high current income). Manager David Breazzano deliberately seeks companies in distress that could be turned around for a portion of his portfolio. (When acquiring large positions, he may participate in their restructuring.) Such companies, the cover page of the June 25, 1993, prospectus pointed out, "present higher risks of untimely interest and principal payments, default, and price volatility than higher-rated securities, and may present problems of liquidity and valuation."

In deciding what to buy or sell, junk bond fund managers don't concern themselves only with meeting their credit quality criteria, whether through reliance on rating services or through their own companies' credit analysis, to identify issues that may be due for upgrading or downgrading. They also may make portfolio switches to change average maturities to adjust fund durations or rebalance their weightings among industrial sectors, adding bonds of companies in cyclical industries during recoveries and of companies less sensitive to the business cycle when business conditions are softening.

They also may invest portions of assets in bonds that pay no current interest (because they're zero-coupon obligations or "pay-in-kind"—PIK— bonds), foreign securities, and/or even common stocks.

Those whose yields have tended to be above average probably have been aiming at high current income for their shareholders and emphasized high-coupon bonds. Those whose yields have tended to be lower may have been aiming more at high total return, including some capital appreciation.

Stock Market–Linked Funds

Funds that are linked, in varying degrees, to the stock market have given a good account of themselves in recent years. That's hardly surprising inasmuch as stocks have been in an uptrend in an average of seven out of eight months since August 1982.

Based on their asset mixes, there are essentially two types of such funds: those invested in different proportions of bonds and common stocks, and those invested in bonds and preferred stocks that are convertible into common stocks.

Lipper classifies the first bunch into three categories: (1) flexible income funds, which seek to produce income by investing at least 85% in debt issues, preferred stocks, and convertible securities, and which cannot invest more than 15% in common stocks; (2) income funds, which seek income by investing in bonds, stocks, and money market instruments without limits on any asset class; and (3) balanced funds, which also emphasize capital preservation and whose assets may be similarly distributed among classes. (Balanced funds typically have 60%/40% stock/bond ratios. The SEC specifies that they must have at least 25% of assets in fixed income securities.)

Within each group, there are wide differences in investment objectives and policies.

Among flexible income funds (Table 5.17), USAA Income Fund has done well over the years by being about 65% in mortgage-backed securities, 15% in investment-grade corporate or government bonds, and the balance in high-yield common stocks. It, of course, has been susceptible to MBS pre-payments when mortgage refinancing accelerated, as in 1993.

Northeast Investors Trust and Nicholas Income Fund have invested primarily in high-yield bonds in the last decade or so. Until 1992, the Northeast fund had no more than 1% of assets in common stocks; then it began to add to its positions, building them to about 20% by early 1994. When expected returns from bonds have been high enough, Chairman Ernest E. Monrad has used the fund's ability to borrow money for investment from banks, thereby

Table 5.17 *Flexible Income Funds*

	Total Return					
Fund (Maximum sales load)	1990–1994 (Annual Rate)	1992–1994	1994	12-Month Yield*	30-Day Yield**	Operating Expense Ratio***
Northeast Investors Trust (NL)	11.1%	14.1%	2.2%	10.3%	9.0%	0.70%[d]
Nicholas Income Fund (NL)	8.7	7.6	(0.2)	9.4	NA	0.59
Janus Flexible Income (NL)	8.6	7.9	(2.9)	8.2	8.8	0.93[a]
Smith Barney Diversified Strategic Income B (4.5% R)	8.2	4.9	(3.5)	8.3	NA	1.57[b]
Vanguard Preferred Stock (NL)	7.7	4.1	(8.0)	8.0	8.3	0.51
USAA Income Fund (NL)	7.7	4.1	(5.2)	7.7	7.7	0.41
MFS Strategic Income A (4.75%)[e]	7.1[f]	3.9	(5.9)	6.0	7.0	1.83[a,b]
Comstock Partners Strategy O (4.5% X)	6.0[g]	4.7	(3.5)	6.5	NA	1.07
Maxus Income (NL)	5.9	3.9	(4.4)	7.5	NA	1.90[b]
Group average	7.5	5.6	(3.7)	7.1	7.2	

X Closed to new investors.
[d]Excludes 0.36% interest expense.
[e]Current investment policy and name were adopted in 1994.
[f]A closed-end fund until August 1991.
[g]A closed-end fund until May 1991.
See Table 5.1 for other footnotes.

supplementing shareholders' capital and enhancing returns. As of September 30, 1994, short-term borrowings were equal to 9.3% of net assets. Average interest: 4.58%. Albert O. Nicholas' less aggressive fund usually has invested about 75% to 85% in nonconvertible junk bonds—of intermediate maturity to mitigate interest rate risk—10% to 15% in cash equivalents, and the rest in convertibles and a few stocks.

A still different strategy has been followed by Ronald V. Speaker in managing Janus Flexible Income Fund, which he has kept more than 80% invested in bonds—about one-half junk bonds and most of the balance in investment-grade corporates.

Leading performers in the Income Funds group (Table 5.18) also have been invested in a variety of ways. The $5.7 billion Vanguard/Wellesley Income Fund, the largest, is usually about 60% to 65% invested in long-term investment-grade bonds and 35% to 40% in dividend-paying blue-chip stocks whose average yield greatly exceeds that of the stocks making up the S&P 500 Index. For most of the years since its inception in 1970, the fund has followed this strategy; for all but four of the years—1994 being the most recent—the fund has had positive returns.

Others have looked more to junk bonds for income. The $4.8 billion Franklin Income Fund, which is even 22 years older than Wellesley, owes its record to being 55% to 60% invested in bonds—about one-half in junk and the rest in government and foreign securities—and a comparable 35% to 40% in common stocks.

Berwyn Income Fund had been about half in investment-grade bonds and the other half in junk, preferred and common stocks, and cash until May 1993, when shareholders authorized a change in investment policy eliminating the 50% minimum for investment-grade bonds and the 50% limit on junk. A 25% "cap" on dividend-paying common stocks was retained.

Taking a different approach, Seligman Income Fund has devoted a large and growing share of assets to convertible securities, exceeding 40% by the end of 1993. Nonconvertible bonds make up another 35% to 40% of assets; their mix has been changing in recent years with government securities being added as utilities were cut back.

Required to be at least 25% invested in bonds, but often 40% or more invested in them, balanced funds are likely to lag the S&P 500 Index in years that stocks perform a lot better than bonds. But they may perform as well as the index while involving less volatility in periods when bond and stock returns are not far apart. This is probably what you'd expect, since capital preservation is usually—but not always—one of their main investment objectives.

Individual funds' returns (Table 5.19) have varied all over the lot, depending on their bond/stock ratios and on the bonds and stocks that their managers selected. Bonds range from intermediate to very long and from U.S. Treasury issues to high-yield corporates, or junk. Some funds also have foreign

Table 5.18 *Income Funds*

Fund (Maximum sales load)	Total Return			12-Month Yield*	Operating Expense Ratio***
	1985–1994 (Annual Rate)	1990–1994	1994		
Berwyn Income (NL)	c	11.6%	(1.1)%	6.8%	0.93%
Franklin Income (4.25%)	11.8%	11.1	(6.4)	8.5	0.69[b]
Seligman Income A (4.75%)	10.9	9.0	(5.4)	5.8	1.03[b]
Prairie Managed Assets Income (4.5%)[d]	c	8.7	(2.0)	5.9	1.00[a]
Vanguard/Wellesley Income (NL)	11.8	8.5	(4.4)	6.4	0.33
Putnam Managed Income A (5.75%)	c	8.3	(1.2)	6.1	1.03[b]
Advantage Income (4% R)	c	7.3	(5.3)	4.8	1.77[a,b]
Pioneer Income (4.5%)	10.1[e]	6.9[e]	(4.3)	7.4	1.06[b]
Value Line Income (NL)	10.4	6.7	(4.4)	3.4	0.88
Keystone Custodian Fund, Series K-1 (4% R)	10.4	5.8	(4.7)	4.0	1.71[b]
Group average	10.9	8.0	(2.9)	4.5	

[d]Formerly First Prairie Diversified Asset Fund.
[e]Formerly Mutual of Omaha Income Fund. Pioneering Management became investment adviser in December 1993.
See Table 5.1 for other footnotes.

bonds. Equities range from large to small companies, from long-established to young and growing, and include both growth and value stocks.

"Our equity position in the fund will range from a low of around 50% of the portfolio to a maximum of 75%," chairman James W. Ratzlaff and president Robert G. O'Donnell of American Funds' American Balanced Fund wrote in their 1993 report to shareholders.

"When common stocks appear attractively valued relative to alternative investments, the fund will move toward the 75% range. In similar fashion,

Table 5.19   *Balanced Funds*

Fund (Maximum sales load)	Total Return 1985–1994 (Annual Rate)	1990–1994	1994	12-Month Yield*	Operating Expense Ratio***
CGM Mutual (NL)	14.8%	10.7%	(9.7)%	4.2%	0.93%
AIM Balanced A (4.75%)	8.8[d]	10.5[d]	(5.4)	2.6 .	1.67[a,b]
Fidelity Advisor Income & Growth (4.75%)	[c]	10.1	(5.1)	2.3	1.51[a,b]
Eclipse Balanced (NL)	[c]	10.0	(0.1)	3.1	0.69[a]
MainStay Total Return B (5%R)	[c]	9.9	(2.4)	2.5	1.79[b]
Conn. Mutual Total Return Account (5%)	[c]	9.8	(2.1)	4.0	1.02
Dodge & Cox Balanced (NL)	14.0	9.8	2.0	3.9	0.58
T. Rowe Price Balanced (NL)	12.5[e]	9.4[e]	(2.1)	3.8	1.00[a]
Fidelity Balanced (NL)	[c]	9.0	(5.3)	3.3	1.01[a]
Kemper Total Return A (5.75%)	11.3	8.7	(9.2)	2.6	1.06
Group average	11.7	7.9	(2.5)	3.0	

[d]Current name and investment policy were adopted in October 1993.
[e]The fund, which commenced operations March 27, 1991, acquired all of the assets of Axe-Houghton Fund B on August 31, 1992. As a result of the transaction, all performance data for prior periods reflect the performance of Fund B.
See Table 5.1 for other footnotes.

when stocks appear to be at the upper end of their historic valuation level, the fund's equity position will typically move down toward 50%.

"While this approach often causes the fund to lag in very strong up markets, it also aids the fund in conserving your capital in the inevitable difficult periods that occur."

Some managers structure their portfolios in a way that will raise income—by investing in long-term bonds, for example—while others manage more for growth, believing that shareholders can redeem shares to get the cash they need if income dividends are too low.

CGM Mutual, formed as an equity fund one week after the 1929 stock market crash and a few months after Vanguard/Wellington Fund, the oldest balanced fund, has been a top performer for years under the direction of G. Kenneth Heebner. (CGM Mutual, known originally as Shaw-Loomis-Sayles Mutual Fund, is the first existing fund to have used the word "mutual" in its name. It began to buy bonds in the early 1930s.)

Heebner's performance in the last decade, in which he beat the S&P 500, is attributable to at least three major elements: (1) concentration of the equity portion into around 20 stocks that often turned out to be real winners; (2) timely shifts to a higher percentage of bonds (government and/or corporate) when interest rates were falling; and (3) the commitment to being fully invested—cash has amounted to less than 1% of assets. He looks for stocks of companies whose earnings he expects to grow by much more than is generally expected, holds them as long as they perform well, but is quick to sell them when something goes wrong.

In contrast to CGM Mutual, which has a high portfolio turnover and is concentrated in few stocks, Dodge & Cox Balanced Fund excelled in the last decade with annual turnover rates of only 10% or so and tended to hold 70 equity positions. Selected on the basis of prices being lower than their perceived values, stocks may be kept for as long as 10 years. It has owned some of its IBM shares for 30.

The fund began the bull market of the 1980s with about 70% of its assets in stocks and the balance mostly in long-term bonds. As its committee-managed bond and stock segments beat their benchmark indexes in the ensuing period, equities were permitted to drift lower as a share of the portfolio, constituting 57% by the end of 1994.

Robert Haber, who has managed Fidelity Balanced Fund and Fidelity Advisor Income & Growth Portfolio since 1986 and 1987, respectively, has pursued slightly different strategies in running the two. For one thing, Balanced can own only investment-grade bonds, while Income & Growth can own junk (up to 35% of assets). Although he has said that his "normal" stock/bond ratios for the two are 60/40 for Balanced and 70/30 for Income & Growth, he has invested more in bonds and less than 30% in stocks in recent years because of his concerns about high equity valuations in the United States. He has given shareholders additional equity exposure via convertibles, however, while moderating risk by building up cash positions. Foreign issues have made up important portions of both the bond and stock portfolios.

Bonds and preferred stocks convertible into common stocks offer opportunities for both capital appreciation and income, albeit less appreciation than common stocks and less income than bonds. With average annual returns of 9.5%, the funds that are primarily invested in convertible securities beat both the S&P 500's 8.7% and Salomon Brothers BIG Index's 7.8% for the five years ended in 1994.

They have performed unevenly, however, as Table 5.20 illustrates, because of differences in the credit quality and maturities of their securities, the length of time until they can be called, the characteristics of the companies

Table 5.20   *Convertible Securities Funds*

| Fund (Maximum sales load) | Total Return | | | 12- Month Yield* | Operating Expense Ratio*** |
	1990– 1994 (Annual Rate)	1992– 1994	1994		
MainStay Convertible (5%R)	14.0%	11.6%	(1.3)%	4.0%	1.99%[b]
Fidelity Convertible Securities (NL)	13.7	12.2	(1.8)	5.2	0.85[a]
Pacific Horizon Capital Income (4.5%)	13.1	11.9	(5.9)	4.4	0.46[a]
Bond Fund for Growth[d] (3.25%)	13.1	16.3	(1.2)	5.5	1.65[b]
Franklin Convertible Securities (4.5%)	11.7	11.3	(1.6)	4.9	1.11[a,b]
Putnam Convertible Income-Growth A (5.75%)	10.1	11.6	(1.9)	5.3	1.11[b]
Vanguard Convertible Securities (NL)	9.5	8.4	(5.7)	4.8	0.73
Value Line Convertible (NL)	8.9	7.4	(5.3)	6.6	1.08
Gabelli Convertible Securities (NL X)	8.8	8.4	(0.2)	5.2	1.38
SBSF Convertible Securities (NL)	8.7	7.7	(6.5)	5.6	1.33[b]
Group average	9.5	8.4	(3.8)	4.3	

X Closed to new investors.
[d]Formerly Rochester Convertible Fund.
See Table 5.1 for other footnotes.

into whose stocks their securities can be converted, the extent to which they own common stocks directly, and the levels of their cash reserves.

James H. Behrmann, who has managed American Capital Harbor Fund, the oldest convertible fund, since 1984, favors investment-grade securities—an emphasis that causes the fund to drop in rank in years, such as 1994, when quality issues lag junk. He tries to be diversified among economic sectors in line with their weightings in the S&P 500 and invests in common stocks of sectors for which no convertibles are available. "I make no sector bets," he says.

William S. Hensel, who has managed Bank of America's Pacific Horizon Capital Income Fund since 1987, attributes his record to doing just that: making sector bets—that is, investing in sectors such as retailing and technology more than their index weightings would indicate. He also is not reluctant to buy convertibles of less than investment grade, provided they are rated at least B.

Michael S. Rosen, portfolio manager of The Bond Fund for Growth since its inception in 1986, is not reluctant to invest in bonds rated even lower than B. He tries to keep his fund close to 100% in convertibles and, being "very opportunistic," says he doesn't care whether the stocks into which they can be converted are growth or value, those of small or large companies.

You may not have noticed it, but none of these three funds has the word "convertible" in its name. They formerly were known as Convertible Securities Fund, Pacific Horizon Convertible Securities Fund, and Rochester Convertible Fund, respectively, but had their names changed largely because marketers have had trouble selling investors on the concept of convertible securities funds.

World Income Funds

The funds invested in debt securities of foreign governments and corporations were formed to provide American investors with vehicles that could offer the advantage of yields and returns that, at any given time, are higher in some foreign markets than in the United States. (And, needless to say, to provide income for those who sponsor, manage, and sell them.)

The securities involve all the basic risks that U.S. debt securities do—interest rate, credit, call—as well as the risks of political instability, renunciation of debt, and so forth. They usually involve higher transaction and management costs, too.

Even more important, as owners of Mexican securities were reminded in December 1994, they also involve the risk that the foreign currencies in which they are denominated would weaken against the U.S. dollar, reducing the dollar equivalents of their income and capital gains and exacerbating any capital losses.

Most world income funds fall into two categories based on their average maturities—short world multi-market income and general world income, as Lipper calls them.

Knowing that short-term debt securities are usually less volatile than long-term ones, you would expect that short world multi-market income funds would involve relatively little risk.

If you invested in one, you would have been surprised. You might even have begun to wonder whether the short-term world bond fund concept is viable.

The Class A shares of the first, Alliance Short-Term Multi-Market Trust, which was offered in May 1989 to "investors seeking high yields and low volatility" and "retired people seeking higher income," did have a 12.2% total return in 1990, its first full year, and a 9.5% return in 1991. In each year, it beat money market funds by around 4%.

By the end of 1991, the number of short world multi-market funds tracked by Lipper was up to 44 (including multiple share classes), six of which were offered by Alliance. The group's assets exceeded $22.1 billion, of which the original Alliance fund alone accounted for $6.2 billion; other Alliance funds, another $2 billion, and Merrill Lynch Short-Term Global Income Fund, which had been launched in August 1990, $6.3 billion.

A key element of Robert M. Sinche's strategy in running the big Alliance fund—and of the strategies of managers of competing funds that followed him—was cross-hedging its exposure to European currencies "to attempt to neutralize fluctuation of principal." It complemented efforts to select the right high-quality securities in the right currencies and to reduce currency risk by conventional hedging of currencies against the U.S. dollar and allocation of a portion of the portfolio to U.S. bonds.

As described in Chapter 3, cross-hedging involves owning bonds of countries whose yields are high, while using forward exchange contracts to sell equivalent amounts of foreign currencies of countries with lower yields. Since it requires currencies that move in tandem versus the dollar, its effectiveness depends on the maintenance of stable relationships among them.

". . . a cross-hedge cannot ensure protection against exchange rate risks," said the 1992 prospectus for Kemper Short-Term Global Income Fund, "and if the Fund's Adviser misjudges future exchange rate relationships, the Fund could be in a less advantageous position than if such a hedge had not been established." (The fund was merged into Kemper Global Income Fund in spring 1994.)

What neither Sinche nor others who used cross-hedging had foreseen was that the European Exchange Rate Mechanism would come unglued in fall 1992 and some major currencies would be devalued.

In his April 30, 1992, report to shareholders, following some turbulence in currency markets, Sinche had described himself as "very positive about the remainder of 1992." And he added: "We feel that the markets have settled down. . . ."

It was not to be. The rupturing of the band within which European currencies were supposed to move made cross-hedging ineffective, and funds suffered a decline in the U.S. dollar values of bonds denominated in currencies that fell against the dollar.

Instead of continuing to beat money market funds' returns, which averaged 3.3% for 1992, the big Alliance fund had a return of only 0.3%. The group as a whole had a return of a *negative* 0.7%, and shareholders began their net redemption. By the end of 1992, the original Alliance fund was down one-third to $4.1 billion; the Merrill Lynch fund had shrunk by more than one-half to $2.8 billion, and the group as a whole was down over one-fourth to $16 billion.

After returns improved in 1993, the group's average return turned down again in 1994, as Table 5.21 shows. Many investors continued to cash in their chips, presumably suspecting that other short-term bond funds or money market funds, concentrated in U.S. securities, made more sense if they wanted low volatility. By December 31, 1994, the group's total net assets were below $6 billion. Alliance Short-Term Multi-Market was down to $1.3 billion; the Merrill Lynch fund, below $700 million.

Use of cross-hedging, whose theoretical risks had become real, had been reduced but not abandoned. Greater use was made of straight hedging against a rising dollar. When the dollar fell against a currency, those who didn't hedge were likely to perform better than those who did—and who, thus, insulated themselves against currency gains and incurred hedging costs besides. Concerned about uncertainty in Europe, some managers increased the percentages of assets invested in the United States, so-called dollar bloc countries—Canada, Australia, and New Zealand—and other regions.

In sum, the 18 funds in operation for all of the three eventful years ended in 1994 had an annual average total return of only 1.4%—a net loss when adjusted for inflation, taxes, and loads. Only seven beat the average. The leaders, Franklin/Templeton Hard Currency and Global Currency Funds, invest in money market instruments but are not money market funds and are not managed to maintain stable NAVs.

Scudder Short Term Global Income Fund, the group's leading no-load fund, which has been managed since November 1991 by Margaret Craddock, has had large positions in the United States and the dollar bloc countries. She also has gone in for short-term securities in developing markets from Greece to Thailand.

General world income funds, primarily invested in intermediate- and long-term foreign bonds, have performed better on the average (Table 5.22). While their weighted average maturities (or durations) have varied, they typically have been considerably longer, subjecting them to greater interest rate risk but also increasing their returns when interest rates were falling.

Table 5.21 *Short World Multi–Market Income Funds (ranked by 3–year performance)*

Fund (Maximum sales load)	Total Return		12- Month Yield*	30- Day Yield**	Operating Expense Ratio***
	1992– 1994 (Annual Rate)	1994			
Franklin/Temple. Hard Curr. (3%)	7.2%[d]	15.1%	12.6%	4.5%	1.38%[b]
Franklin/Temple. Gl. Curr. (3%)	5.9[d]	8.1	8.7	4.2	1.37[b]
Scudder Short Term Global Income (NL)	3.7	(1.1)	8.2	8.3	1.00[a]
Fidelity Short-Term World Income (NL)	3.6	(5.9)	7.9	8.9	1.07
Dean Witter Global Short- Term Income (3% R)	2.8	0.2	6.3	6.8	1.63[b]
Blanchard Short-Term Global Income (NL)	2.4	(4.4)	6.5	7.4	1.44[b]
Van Kampen Merritt Short- Term Global Income A (3%)	1.5	(7.4)	8.3	NA	1.13[b]
Prudential Global Assets A (0.99%)[e]	1.4	(1.3)	5.0	3.9	1.48[b]
EV Marathon Short Term Strategic Income (3%R) Fund[f]	1.4	(5.3)	7.6	8.0	2.00[b]
Prudential Short-Term Global Income A (3%)	1.0	(4.7)	6.9	7.5	1.17[b]
Group average	1.4	(4.3)	7.1	6.5	

[d]Formerly a Huntington Funds portfolio. Franklin Advisers became investment manager and Templeton Investment Counsel, subadviser, in November 1993.
[e]An unusual sales charge, it's 0.99% of the public offering price and 1% of amounts invested that are less than $1 million.
[f]Formerly Eaton Vance Short-Term Global Income Fund.
See Table 5.1 for other footnotes.

Table 5.22   *General World Income Funds*

Fund (Maximum sales load)	Total Return 1990–1994 (Annual Rate)	1992–1994	1994	12-Month Yield*	30-Day Yield**	Operating Expense Ratio***
Scudder Intl. Bond (NL)	11.0%	4.4%	(8.6)%	8.7%	8.9%	1.28%
T. Rowe Price Intl. Bond (NL)	10.5	6.5	(1.8)	6.3	6.0	0.99
Merrill Lynch World Income A (4%)	9.4[d]	5.1	(4.1)	8.7	9.3	0.78
IDS Global Bond (5%)	9.3	6.2	(4.9)	4.9	6.8	1.26
Merrill Lynch Global Bond Fund for Investment and Retirement A (4%)	9.2	5.0	(5.3)	6.1	6.7	0.82
MFS World Governments A (4.75%)	8.4	3.9	(6.6)	1.4	6.5	1.34[a,b]
Merrill Lynch Global Bond Fund for Investment and Retirement B (4%R)	8.4	4.2	(6.0)	5.3	6.1	1.58[b]
(Am.) Capital World Bond (4.75%)	8.4	5.1	(1.4)	6.4	7.1	1.11[b]
Lord Abbett Global Inc. (4.75%)	7.8	4.4	(3.4)	9.1	6.5	1.04[b]
Kemper Global Income A (4.5%)	7.8	2.1	(1.5)	7.0	6.5	1.31
Group average	7.5	3.8	(6.5)	6.5	7.3	

[d]A closed-end fund until November 1991.
See Table 5.1 for other footnotes.

Their managers also employed hedges to mitigate the currency risk inherent in their non-U.S. holdings—with varying degrees of success and at varying costs. Their relatively greater emphasis on total return than on income may have resulted in different geographic/currency mixes among short- and longer-term funds offered by the same fund families. So did the differences in the characteristics of bonds available in attractive markets.

Investors seem to have recognized the differences in their risk/reward characteristics. While engaged in net redemption of short-term funds, they have been buying the longer-term funds on balance, accounting for most of the tripling in these funds' assets from $7 billion at the end of 1991 to $18.7 billion at the end of 1994.

While most of the more than 100 funds in the group (including multiple classes) are well diversified around the world, a few are concentrated in certain groups of countries.

Funds such as Alliance North American Government Income Trust, Benham European Government Bond Fund, and Merrill Lynch Americas Income Fund are concentrated on the basis of geography. Others, such as Fidelity New Markets Income Fund and Scudder Emerging Markets Income Fund, are concentrated in bonds issued in emerging markets in the expectation of greater returns—at higher risks.

Neither group has been in existence long enough to establish 5-year performance records, but early results confirm the volatility expected to be associated with investing in emerging markets' bonds, which are more likely to be characterized by lower quality and currency risk.

An event such as the December 1994 devaluation of the Mexican peso, of course, would affect funds in both groups.

Fidelity New Markets Income, launched in May 1993 and mainly invested in U.S. dollar-denominated Latin American bonds, ranked 106th of 106 funds (or share classes) for the first half of 1994 with a total return of a *negative* 24.5%, first in the year's third quarter with a scorching *positive* return of 19.7%, and 126th of 140 with a *negative* return of 7.5% in the fourth quarter, resulting in a decline for the year of 16.6%. All this may have been sobering to shareholders who had read former manager Robert Citrone, in his June 30, 1993, semiannual report, describe his goal of a double-digit return as "reasonable."

Shareholders of Alliance North American, whose shares brought up the rear in the category in 1994, also will have been sobered by a 30% drop.

Launched in 1992, it had been managed, as the 1993 prospectus said, to seek "the highest level of current income, consistent with what the Fund's Adviser considers to be prudent investment risk, that is available from a portfolio of debt securities issued or guaranteed by the governments of the United States, Canada, and Mexico, their political subdivisions, . . . agencies, instrumentalities, or authorities."

The fund expected to maintain at least 25% of its assets in U.S. dollar securities, the prospectus continued, and that "under the conditions appertaining at the date of this Prospectus, not more than approximately 25% of ... assets ... in securities denominated in the Mexican Peso."

As things turned out, 1994's increase in interest rates cut across national borders, hitting bonds regardless of denomination. And as if a 25% limit on Mexican Peso-denominated securities would not have provided room for damage with the currency's devaluation, Alliance had as much as 40% of the fund's assets in Mexican securities when its fiscal year ended November 30, 1994—just before the Mexican crisis erupted. The 25% limit—an informal, not fundamental, policy—had been omitted from the 1994 prospectus.

Nor was this all. The fund had exercised its ability to seek to produce higher yields by taking the additional risk of borrowing money from a bank to buy more securities than shareholders' capital would provide for. In pursuit of this technique, which Alliance noted on the prospectus cover "is usually considered speculative," the fund had a loan payable on its November 30, 1994 balance sheet of $250 million—equal to 10.8% of the fund's $2.3 billion net assets.

For what makes a more typical, less volatile world income fund tick, consider MFS Worldwide Governments Fund, the oldest, which had a 13.4% average annual total return for the ten years ended in 1994, making it the top-performing bond fund of the decade.

Massachusetts Financial Services launched it in 1981, as you may recall from Chapter 3, to give investors a safe haven from the unattractive U.S. bond market in the form of a mutual fund that could invest in an internationally diversified bond portfolio.

"A fixed-income investor should no more be shut out of opportunities in the U.S. when trends are favorable than he should be locked into the U.S. when the trend of bond prices is unfavorable and the dollar is weak against other currencies or against gold," Richard B. Bailey, then president of MFS, said in announcing the fund.

Ironically, the U.S. bond market turned around dramatically in 1982, and the fund invested 70% to 80% of its assets at home.

Over the years, the U.S. portion was gradually brought down—to as low as 10%—when portfolio manager Leslie J. Nanberg found attractive issues in other major countries: the dollar bloc, Europe, and Japan. He "never felt it appropriate to load up the boat" with emerging markets.

Like managers of competing funds, Nanberg erred in 1994 by expecting the U.S. dollar to appreciate against major foreign currencies, thereby depriving shareholders of gains from the dollar's weakening. He began the year about 20% invested in U.S. dollar securities and hedged most of the remaining portfolio back into dollars, raising his total dollar exposure to around 70%. By year's end he had reduced that to 55% and by March 1995, to 35%.

As a result of his currency bets, duration strategy, and bond selections, the MFS fund had a negative 6.6% total return for 1994, essentially the same as the group's negative 6.5%. These results contrasted sharply with the positive 2.3% total return of Salomon Brothers' World Government Bond Index and the positive 6.0% of its Non-U.S. Government Bond Index, both in U.S. dollar terms.

(Scudder International Bond Fund, the group's No. 1 fund of the last five years, turned in a worse performance in 1994: a negative 8.6%. Its management had been even more optimistic on the dollar, raising its dollar exposure to 90% or more through hedging for most of the year. On the other hand, the management of T. Rowe Price International Bond Fund, bearish on the dollar, began 1994 with a 16% dollar position and slashed that to 4% by year's end. Its total return for the year: negative 1.8%.)

In choosing foreign bonds, Nanberg, who has managed the fund since 1984 after working on it with his predecessor, looks for countries where real (that is, inflation-adjusted) interest rates are high. He is not discouraged by high inflation rates if nominal rates are high enough to give him a cushion when prices decline, he says.

An example of the kind of bonds that helped him to achieve his record is found in New Zealand. In the mid-1980s, he recalls, the country's economy was highly regulated, there had been a long recession, and inflation was high. New Zealand Treasury bills were yielding 19% and government bonds, around 14% to 16%.

But the government was committed to deregulation, giving Nanberg the courage to invest. By 1994, the inflation rate was among the lowest in the world, and the economy was enjoying good growth. Treasury bill yields were down to 6%; bonds, to 8%.

Adhering to his basic guideline, he was able to obtain both high income and considerable price appreciation.

Another case in which he benefited from what he calls "a double whammy" was provided by Ireland. When he began to invest in Irish bonds in 1987, the country's bond market was small and illiquid, and its bonds yielded 3% to 4% more than British bonds of comparable maturities. Following "a dramatic change" in Ireland's economy, in which inflation was brought down, its bond yields dropped to the British level.

Nanberg points out, however, that his strategy doesn't always work. "There are times," he says, "when non-fundamental factors drive the market." One such time: the European currency crisis of 1992.

To deal with interest rate risk, he has adjusted his fund's duration from a low of around 2.5 years to around 6. This compares with the average duration of the world's major bond markets, as measured by Salomon Brothers' index, of about 4.7 years—close to that of the U.S. investment-grade bond market.

He notes that the world average isn't as meaningful as you might suppose because major markets differ considerably. They range from around 5.5 to 6.0 years for Japan, the United Kingdom, and Switzerland, to around 3.0 to 3.5 years for Italy, Spain, and Sweden, according to Salomon Brothers.

CHAPTER 6

How Different Types of Bond Funds Have Performed—and Why: Tax-Exempt Bond Funds

While changes in the supply-demand balances in various sectors of the U.S. bond market may cause the spreads in yields between taxable and tax-exempt securities of comparable quality and maturity to expand or contract for a period, the long-run decline in interest rates has had comparable positive effects on the prices of both. Except for the interest rate spike in 1987, "benign markets have ruled the day," Ian A. MacKinnon, Vanguard senior vice president and head of its fixed income group, wrote his funds' shareholders in March 1994 in comments on the years prior to the Federal Reserve's decision to raise short-term interest rates the month before.

After years in which a steadily increasing number of people in the 28% and 31% federal income tax brackets had taken advantage of the opportunity to earn more interest from municipal bonds and bond funds than they'd have left after taxes on taxable bonds' and bond funds' interest, President Bill Clinton and Congress made tax-exempts even more attractive in 1993.

By creating the 36% and 39.6% federal tax brackets, they made tax-exempt income considerably more enticing to upper-income individuals and couples. Even when tax-exempt yields on short maturities had fallen as low as 3%, they were worthwhile for upper- income investors to pursue. For anyone taxed at 36%, they were the taxable equivalent of 4.7%. For longer maturities that yielded, say, 5.5%, a person in the 36% bracket would have had to find taxable securities yielding 8.6% to have as much money left after paying federal tax. (To keep it simple, I have avoided consideration of state and local income taxes, which may be imposed on dividends from nationally diversified municipal

145

bond funds; they are unlikely to own enough issues from your state to qualify for state and local tax exemption, too.)

With the sea change in interest rates in the first half of 1994, resulting in higher yields for both taxable and tax-exempt bonds, every dollar invested in tax-exempts has produced even more income.

You may have thought that the firming of demand for tax-exempts in 1993 would have resulted in dramatic increases in bond prices, instead of the moderate increases that occurred.

That, of course, would have ignored the supply side of the equation.

With unfilled needs to expand and improve their facilities, the opportunity to reduce their debt service costs, and concerns that their borrowing costs would go up again, state and local governments issued new long-term securities in 1993 at a record $290 billion pace, according to Securities Data Company. About one-third was for new capital; the rest of the proceeds was used to refund issues, sold in earlier years when yields were much higher, as they could be called. (SDC defines *long-term* as an issue maturing in more than 13 months.)

No individual investor or portfolio manager needed to worry that there would be a shortage of tax-exempt paper to invest in.

Fortuitously, state and local government units were in good shape—with some exceptions—to take on debt. After studying their financial conditions, which had improved since the 1990–91 recession, the rating services upgraded more issues than they downgraded.

In this environment, spreads between the highest and lowest investment grades—Aaa/AAA and Baa/BBB—continued to be fairly tight. With only around 0.4% separating the two tiers, even fund managers who aren't usually eager to maintain high credit quality had less incentive to reach for higher yields by stuffing portfolios with medium quality issues.

If any aspect of investing in tax-exempt bond funds caused disappointment to investors in the period prior to the firming of interest rates in 1994, it would have been the taxable distributions of realized net capital gains. They were the inevitable result of the long bull market in bonds. While some municipal bond fund managers may have been more vigorous than others in limiting the realization of gains, a certain amount was unavoidable. Whatever the tax consequences may have been for you, you surely would have been less thrilled with the realization of net capital losses.

The run-up in yields had a major impact on municipal bonds and bond funds in 1994. It also brought opportunity.

As muni bond prices fell—albeit, often less than U.S. Treasury issues of comparable maturities—many municipal bond fund shareholders redeemed their shares. This exacerbated the downward pressure on prices because many fund managers had not maintained sufficient cash reserves to accommodate possible redemptions; they had to sell bonds from their portfolios in a declining market with inevitable adverse consequences for their shareholders. However large the tax-exempt market may be, it is less liquid than the Treasury market. (For one thing, it attracts fewer categories of investors.)

Although the higher yields may not have been enough to offset the year's drops in bond prices, they did make municipal bonds and bond funds more attractive. At the end of 1993, for example, yields on long tax-exempts had averaged 5.25%. For someone in the 28% federal bracket, that meant an equivalent taxable yield of 7.29%, compared with 6.47% for 20-year Treasury bonds. By the end of 1994, long municipals yielded an average of around 6.70%, for an equivalent taxable yield of 9.31%. But 20-year Treasuries yielded only 7.99%. For investors in higher tax brackets, the equivalent taxable yields were even higher.

At the same time that such changes in yield relationships reinforced the demand side of the municipal market, the supply/demand balance was further strengthened by a sharp drop in new issues: down 44% to $161 billion, SDC reported. In contrast to 1993, refundings accounted for less than one-third of the total volume and new financing, over two-thirds.

Short Municipal Bond Funds

Short-term municipal funds have more than filled the bill for investors who wanted tax-exempt income that would be slightly higher than that of tax-exempt money market funds and who agreed to accept slight risk to earn it.

The 5.3% average total return of the funds that were in operation for the five years that ended in 1994 (Table 6.1) exceeded the 3.3% average of tax-exempt money market funds by about 200 basis points, or around 60%, according to Lipper. As more people recognized the risk/reward characteristics of this type of investment vehicle, and more fund sponsors recognized the potential market, it was not surprising that the number of funds had tripled by early 1994.

The differences in fund performance, such as those shown in Table 6.1, were due largely to differences in maturities. Funds that were managed to have maturities of five years—top for the group, as defined by Lipper—benefited from the steep yield curve and falling rates more than those that kept maturities shorter. They also were hurt more when rates rose.

The two Vanguard funds—the largest in the Lipper group, together accounting for 30% of its $10.5 billion assets—serve to illustrate the difference that maturities can make because they have the same low (0.20%) annual operating expenses and have been run by the same manager, Christopher M. Ryon (since 1988), using the same criteria.

He kept the average maturity of Vanguard Municipal Bond Fund's Limited-Term Portfolio at around 3 years—closer to the bottom of the 2-to-

Table 6.1 *Short–Term Municipal Bond Funds*

| | Total Return | | | | | |
Fund (Maximum sales load)	1990–1994 (Annual Rate)	1992–1994	1994	12-Month Yield*	30-Day Yield**	Operating Expense Ratio***
Flagship Tax-Exempt Limited Term A (2.5%)	6.4%	5.2%	(1.9)%	4.9%	4.9%	0.70%[a,b]
Thornburg Limited Term Muni. National A (2.5%)	6.0	4.9	(1.5)	4.9	4.7	0.96[b]
Vanguard Municipal Ltd.-Term (NL)	5.8	4.2	0.1	4.4	4.9	0.20
(Fidelity) Spartan Short-Intermediate Municipal (NL)[d]	5.7	4.4	(0.1)	4.6	4.8	0.55
Dreyfus Short-Intermediate Municipal Bond (NL)	5.6	4.3	(0.3)	4.5	4.5	0.74[b]
Babson Tax-Free Income Portfolio S (NL)	5.4	3.7	(1.7)	4.4	NA	1.02
T. Rowe Price Tax-Free Short-Intermediate (NL)	5.3	4.2	0.3	4.2	4.7	0.60
USAA Tax Exempt Short-Term (NL)	5.2	4.1	0.8	4.4	4.8	0.43
Merrill Lynch Municipal Bond— Ltd. Maturity A (1%)	4.9	3.7	1.3	3.8	3.9	0.40
Calvert Tax Free Reserves Limited Term A (2%)	4.9	3.8	2.4	3.6	4.4	0.67
Group average	5.3	4.1	(0.3)	4.1	4.5	

[d]Minimum initial investment: $10,000.
See Table 5.1 for other footnotes.

5-year range that he is expected to maintain while he kept the average maturity of Short-Term Portfolio, as expected, between 1 and 2 years.

It's no wonder, then, that Limited-Term outperformed Short-Term during this period of falling rates, averaging a total return of 5.8% versus 4.8% annually over the last 5 years while Short-Term led in 1994 with a return of 1.7% versus 0.1% for Limited-Term.

Competing funds that exceeded or approached Vanguard Limited-Term, such as Flagship National Tax Exempt Limited Term and Thornburg Limited Term Municipal Fund, did so apparently because their average maturities were significantly longer: close to 5 years. (The Flagship fund even slightly topped 5 at times.)

Of course, 1994 provided a limited example of the slight risk inherent in longer maturities, even among short-term funds, as three top-performing funds—Babson Tax-Free Income Fund's Portfolio S, the Flagship, and Thornburg funds—posted returns of negative 1.5–2.0%.

Intermediate Municipal Bond Funds

What was true of short-term funds was also true of intermediate-term funds. By accepting longer maturities—between 5 and 10 years—investors were able to pick up higher yields and total returns at the risk of slightly greater volatility (see Table 6.2). As many did so, additional fund sponsors launched offerings in this segment of the maturity spectrum, too—from Baltimore's Legg Mason to Los Angeles' American Funds.

Vanguard's $4.6 billion Intermediate-Term Portfolio, the company's largest tax-exempt fund and second largest bond fund (after Vanguard GNMA Portfolio), set the pace for the intermediate group with an average annual return of 7.4% for the five years ended in 1994—mostly under the direction of Ryon, who took over this fund from Jerome J. Jacobs in 1991. For the latest 10 years, its return was slightly over 9%—also enough to lead the group for that period.

To what is its performance attributable? For one thing, its relatively long average maturity during the time of falling yields and Ryon's timely downward adjustment of the maturity as the end of the long bull market in bonds approached. Expected to maintain an average of 7 to 12 years, he remained around 9 to 10 years for quite some time, earning high income while benefiting from higher bond prices. In early 1993, he pulled the average below 8 years and, by the end of February 1994, to just below 7, putting the fund in an even better position for the higher yields ahead.

Other factors were Vanguard's consistently low annual operating expenses and two of the major policy guidelines, established by MacKinnon, which apply to this fund and its siblings: high credit quality and call protection.

Table 6.2   *Intermediate–Term Municipal Bond Funds*

Fund (Maximum sales load)	Total Return			12- Month Yield*	30- Day Yield**	Operating Expense Ratio***
	1990– 1994	1992– 1994	1994			
	(Annual Rate)					
Vanguard Municipal Intermediate-Term (NL)	7.4%	5.9%	(2.1)%	5.5%	5.7%	0.20%
Scudder Medium Term Tax Free (NL)	6.8ᵈ	5.3	(3.5)	5.3	5.3	0.70ᵃ
Prairie Intermediate Municipal Bond (3%)ᵉ	6.8	4.9	(2.4)	4.8	5.3	0.90ᵃ
USAA Tax Exempt Intermediate-Term (NL)	6.6	5.1	(4.0)	5.7	5.9	0.40
Fidelity Limited Term Municipals (NL)	6.6	5.0	(4.8)	5.7	5.9	0.54
SteinRoe Intermediate Municipals (NL)	6.6	4.9	(3.4)	5.0	5.1	0.71
Dreyfus Intermediate Municipal Bond (NL)	6.6	5.0	(4.6)	5.7	5.6	0.70
Smith Barney Muni Funds-Limited Term Portfolio Ltd. A (2%)	6.5	5.3	(1.4)	5.8	NA	0.68ᵇ
Oppenheimer Intermediate Tax-Exempt Bond A (3.5%)	6.4	4.7	(4.4)	5.4	4.9	1.07ᵇ
Benham Natl. Tax-Free Intermediate Term (NL)	6.3	4.5	(3.5)	4.9	5.1	0.66ᵃ
AIM Tax-Free Intermediate (1%)	6.3	5.1	(1.4)	4.6	4.6	0.61
Group average	6.2	4.7	(3.5)	4.8	5.0	

ᵈCurrent investment objective and name were adopted in November 1990.
ᵉFormerly First Prairie Municipal Bond Fund—Intermediate Series.
See Table 5.1 for other footnotes.

While a number of competing funds had comparable average maturities, others held theirs a little shorter or longer. There was a tendency among them to own bonds rated A or better, but some invested as much as 20% in Baa/BBB's to enhance yields. Call protection to prolong income streams was also a high priority with several managers; to others it mattered less.

General Municipal Bond Funds

With assets exceeding $60 billion, the more than 200 funds (including multiple share classes) that constitute this group make it by far the largest of the nationally diversified municipal bond fund categories tracked by Lipper—and much larger, too, than any of the taxable bond fund categories.

The men and women who manage these funds have more latitude than those who manage the other tax-exempt funds. If they promise you in their shareholder reports or prospectuses that they will invest at least 80% of their assets in securities whose interest, when passed through to you in income dividends, is exempt from federal income tax, they are not exercising discretion. Nor are they offering you something that competitors won't.

They are merely complying with fundamental policies that their funds must adopt—and follow—to satisfy a 1977 SEC requirement if their names imply that their distributions will be federally tax-exempt. (An alternative SEC requirement is that the fund will be invested so that at least 80% of its income will be tax-exempt.) As a practical matter, they shoot for close to 100%.

Beyond this stipulation, however, they are free to make choices, in accordance with their investment objectives and policies, among maturities/durations, premium and discount bonds, callable and noncallable bonds, higher and lower credit quality bonds, insured and uninsured bonds, general obligation and revenue bonds, sectors and states, rated bonds and unrated ones of comparable quality, traditional derivatives such as futures contracts and options and newer ones such as inverse floaters—to name a few.

How well their funds perform depends on the choices they make and the skills with which they implement their strategies.

Their most critical choices probably have to do with maturities or durations because of the impact of interest rate risk on principal (or funds' NAVs). Yet they receive far too little attention in shareholder reports.

This being the principal category for nationally diversified portfolios of investment-grade long-term municipal bonds, many tend to have weighted average maturities of 20 years or more—not hard to achieve since municipal bonds can run 30 years or more. Quite a few of them will significantly reduce their maturities and durations to moderate the drops in their NAVs when they anticipate higher interest rates. Others will be less aggressive in doing so, intending to mitigate the drop in their dividend streams. (When lower rates are expected, many would lengthen maturities and durations.)

Some managers, such as Donald C. Carleton of Scudder Managed Municipal Bonds, invest in securities that will keep their average maturities closer to 10 years—too long for Lipper to classify their funds as intermediate-term—on grounds that such bonds have yields close to those of longer ones but involve less interest rate risk.

When rates are falling and the yield curve is as steep as it has been in recent years, those who stayed around 20 years—such as Pamela Hunter of Chase Manhattan Bank's Vista Tax Free Income Fund, Joseph P. Deane of Smith Barney Managed Municipals Fund, and John M. Holliday of United Municipal Bond Fund—tended to excel. Jacobs could reduce the average of Vanguard Long-Term from over 20 years, when he took it over in 1988, to much lower average maturities by 1993 and still perform well in comparison with other leaders, as you see in Table 6.3, in part because of his fund's lower expenses.

Funds whose prospectuses permit them to invest as much as 25% or 35% of assets in bonds of less than investment grade—municipal junk—tended not to avail themselves of the opportunity to earn higher yields to the maximum because of the tight yield spreads.

Concentrations of 85% to 95% or more in investment-grade bonds were not unusual. In fact, some funds had 85% of their assets in bonds in only the top two of the four investment grades (Aaa/AAA and Aa/AA).

On the other hand, managers such as Prudential National Municipals Fund's Patricia Dolan and Richard J. Moynihan of Dreyfus' General Municipal Bond Fund invested as much as 30% in Baa/BBB, the fourth and lowest. "We felt this strategy-tack was a more prudent way to add yield instead of buying longer maturity bonds that have more interest rate volatility," Ms. Dolan wrote shareholders. (Moynihan also credited derivatives with "abetting the Fund's performance.")

Quite a few enhanced the credit quality—and dampened the volatility—of their portfolios by buying so-called prerefunded bonds. They're old high-coupon bonds whose issuers plan to refund them as soon as the call features of the bonds permit or at maturity. When interest rates are low enough, their issuers sell new bonds to raise the money but park it until it's needed in escrow accounts in which they buy Treasury securities. With the Treasuries serving as collateral until the refunding, the old securities are rated higher (and may be regarded as shorter-term and, thus, less volatile bonds).

A way in which fund policies differ is in whether they emphasize yield or total return. Managers emphasizing yield are likely to buy more high-coupon bonds, even at the risk that the bonds may be called, thereby reducing the funds' income and perhaps resulting in capital losses if the bonds had been bought at higher premium prices. Explaining their strategies to shareholders, those buying premium bonds also emphasize their more stable prices and greater downside protection.

Table 6.3   *General Municipal Bond Funds*

Fund (Maximum sales load)	Total Return			12- Month Yield*	30- Day Yield**	Operating Expense Ratio***
	1985– 1994 (Annual Rate)	1990– 1994	1994			
Vista Tax Free Income A (4.5%)	c	8.0%	(7.6)%	5.2%	5.5%	0.75%[a,b]
Smith Barney Mgd. Municipals A (4%)	9.9%	7.8	(4.5)	6.4	6.3	0.72[b]
UST Master Long- Term Tax Exempt (4.5%)	c	7.6	(5.8)	4.8	6.3	0.85[a]
Flagship Tax-Exempt All-American A (4.2%)	c	7.6	(5.9)	6.3	5.9	0.90[a,b]
(Dreyfus) Premier Municipal Bond A (4.5%)	c	7.6	(6.4)	6.4	6.1	0.85[a]
Smith Barney Muni Funds—Natl. Portfolio A (4%)	c	7.3	(5.8)	6.7	NA	0.67[b]
(Dreyfus) General Municipal Bond (NL)	9.1	7.3	(7.3)	6.3	6.3	0.82[a,b]
Strong Municipal Bond (NL)	c	7.3	(4.6)	6.1	6.2	0.70[a]
Vanguard Municipal Long-Term (NL)	9.7	7.2	(5.8)	6.1	6.3	0.20
Benham Natl. Tax- Free Long Term (NL)	8.5	7.1	(6.2)	5.7	5.8	0.66[a]
Group average	9.0	6.3	(6.5)	5.6	5.5	

See Table 5.1 for footnotes.

Those emphasizing total return may buy more bonds that bear lower coupons, sell at discounts, and are, therefore, unlikely to be called. Given identical maturities, they would have longer durations; therefore, they would rise more during a period of falling interest rates but also fall more when rates rise.

Total return maximizers, naturally, don't rely on discounts alone to guard their funds against bonds being called by their issuers. They also deliberately look for bonds whose terms eliminate the risk of calls for eight to ten years.

Stephen C. Bauer, portfolio manager of SAFECO Municipal Bond Fund since 1981, summed up, in a 1993 report to his shareholders, why he invests in both premium and discount bonds but has leaned more to discount bonds in recent years:

"In general, the best performing bonds were those least likely to be called. They were the bonds with the longest maturities and the deepest discounts from par. . . . Priced well below their redemption value, discount bonds have room to appreciate. . . .

"A bond trading at, or above, its face value and paying more than current interest rates is extremely likely to be called. And its price changes to reflect that vulnerability. . . . Such bonds . . . bring high income and liquidity to the portfolio, but lack upside potential. . . . "

One category of bonds offering higher yields are those sold to finance what are called "private activities"—ranging from airports to student loans—and whose interest payments may be subject to the alternative minimum tax (AMT) for some taxpayers.

Although some managers avoid them to spare their shareholders a federal tax on tax-exempt funds' dividends, others invest up to 20% or so of assets in them. Susan Keenan, however, grabs all she can for her Alliance Municipal Income Fund National Portfolio. She's willing to let AMT-subject bonds make up 90% or more of her fund's assets, as previously noted, because she believes few shareholders might be affected. She does it "for the benefit of all the others who don't pay the tax."

Managers generally prefer revenue bonds, whose debt service is met out of the fees and other receipts of the governmental units that issued them, over general obligation bonds, which are supported by the taxing authority of the governments that sold them. They do so for one simple reason: Revenue bonds have higher yields.

Among revenue bonds, they may pick on the basis of whether a sector provides essential services and, therefore, is less likely to be adversely affected in a recession—services such as water and sewers. Or they may act on the basis of whether a sector is out of favor for a period, such as hospitals. One manager, concerned about their credit quality and perhaps lacking the resources to analyze them properly, may avoid them while another may accumulate them after analysis indicates they may be undervalued and capable of appreciation.

Managers also analyze the supply/demand balances by states to get an inkling of whose issues are a better value at any given time. Several focus on states with high income tax rates at times when supplies of new issues are temporarily flooding the market and driving prices down. Sooner or later, their residents are expected to bid prices up again to earn interest exempt from state and local as well as federal income taxes.

Managers may disagree on whether any particular securities are under-priced or overpriced at any given time, but they agree that there are always some of each. Commenting on the market's being an "imperfect" price-setting mechanism, they try to buy the former and sell the latter. Some manage their portfolios more actively than others in hopes of sweetening their returns.

Holliday, who has run the United fund since 1980, is one of the more active ones. (His portfolio turnover rate exceeds 100% and has even topped 300% in the past.) He maintains a "least attractive" list containing the names of those of his 150 bonds that he wouldn't miss but is in no hurry to sell. When he spots bonds that he believes to have greater potential, he replaces them.

"You can't be a top performer unless you're willing to take advantage of opportunities to take gains," he declares.

Insured Municipal Bond Funds

Given normal relationships in the bond market, a municipal bond whose debt service (but not price!) is assured by insurance policies—and whose credit ratings, therefore, should be high—could be expected to provide lower returns than bonds whose debt service depends on the government units that issue them.

The same would apply to the mutual funds that are primarily invested in insured bonds. For one thing, yields have to reflect the 0.2% to 0.4% insurance premiums paid by the bonds' issuers or owners.

But this isn't always the case. There are times when insured bonds and bond funds have higher returns.

As a consequence, over a longer period the average total returns of leading insured municipal bond funds have been close to those of leading general municipal bond funds, which, you'll recall, invest in investment-grade bonds.

Maturities of the insured bond fund group's portfolios tend to run as long as those of the general municipal bond fund group: 20 years or more. Thus, insured municipal bond funds' returns can be just as volatile unless managers act to mitigate volatility.

The closeness of the performance data for the group's leaders, shown in Table 6.4, indicates a similarity in their maturities.

Table 6.4 *Insured Municipal Bond Funds*

Fund (Maximum sales load)	1990–1994	1992–1994	1994	12-Month Yield*	30-Day Yield**	Operating Expense Ratio***
	Total Return					
	(Annual Rate)					
Nuveen Insured Municipal Bond R (NL)[d]	7.0%	5.2%	(6.4)%	5.9%	6.2%	0.65%
Vanguard Municipal Insured Long-Term (NL)	7.0	5.2	(5.6)	6.1	6.2	0.20
Franklin Insured Tax-Free Income (4.25%)	6.9	5.6	(3.6)	6.2	5.5	0.62[b]
Merrill Lynch Municipal Bond Ins. Portfolio A (4%)	6.6	4.7	(6.7)	6.0	5.9	0.42
IDS Insured Tax-Exempt (5%)	6.6	5.1	(6.1)	5.8	5.6	0.65[b]
AARP Insured Tax Free General Bond (NL)	6.5	4.7	(6.2)	5.2	5.4	0.68
Van Kampen Merritt Insured Tax-Free Income A (4.65%)	6.4	4.8	(6.3)	6.0	NA	0.84[b]
Fidelity Insured Tax Free (NL)	6.3	4.3	(7.7)	5.9	6.0	0.61
Delaware Tax-Free Insured A (4.75%)	6.2	4.5	(3.0)	5.8	5.1	0.98[b]
Oppenheimer Insured Tax-Exempt Bond A (4.75%)	6.1[e]	4.4	(8.1)	5.6	5.3	1.18[b]
Alliance Municipal Insured National Portfolio A (4.25%)	6.1	3.9	(9.2)	6.0	5.5	0.73[a,b]
Group average	6.2	4.6	(6.5)	5.4	5.5	

[d]Class R shares not offered to new investors. Other share classes with different costs are available.
[e]Formerly First Trust Tax-Free Bond Fund—Insured Series. Oppenheimer Management became investment adviser in April 1990.
See Table 5.1 for other footnotes.

Differences in performance may result from the extent to which they invest in insured bonds beyond the 65% of assets required for a fund to be called an insured municipal bond fund—and how they invest the remaining percentages in uninsured bonds. They also may differ in how much they keep in cash equivalents.

Additional ways in which strategies vary include their choices of premium, current coupon, or discount bonds; of callable and noncallable bonds; of prerefunded and zero-coupon bonds; and of the bonds from various geographic areas and sectors.

Several—including AARP Insured Tax Free General Bond Fund, Fidelity Insured Tax-Free Portfolio, and Merrill Lynch Municipal Bond Fund's Insured Portfolio—have bought inverse floater securities. These derivatives, which can increase a portfolio's volatility, may have helped returns when interest rates were dropping but may have hurt when rates were rising.

If municipal bond insurance—whether bought by the bonds' issuers, previous owners, or the funds themselves—only covers timely payment of interest and principal on the insured bonds and does nothing for share prices, why should a fund bother with insurance?

At least in part, to provide an investment vehicle for those who are greatly concerned about credit quality. (For funds concentrated in issues of a single state, this, of course, is an even more important consideration.) When insurance is obtained from one of the major providers of these policies, bonds automatically acquire the top Aaa/AAA rating. Fund managements have to monitor the insurance companies to make sure they themselves stay triple-A.

Fund managers emphasize that insurance is no substitute for proper credit research and that they don't rely only on insurance—even from the top companies—when choosing which bonds to buy.

"Insurance is an extra layer of protection," says David E. Hamlin, who has managed Vanguard Municipal Bond Fund's Insured Long-Term Portfolio since 1986. "We look through the insurance to the underlying credit quality of the issuers."

High–Yield Municipal Bond Funds

A comparison of Tables 6.3 and 6.5 will tell you at a glance that high-yield municipal bond funds, which may be significantly—but not primarily—invested in lower-rated or junk bonds, have not performed better than general municipal bond funds. In fact, in recent years, the group concentrated in investment-grade municipal securities did slightly better. (For the ten years ended in 1994, Lipper figured they had about the same average annual total return: 9.0% for general funds, 8.8% for high-yield funds.)

The major difference among them was in how the return was divided between income and capital. High-yield funds, generally having high current

Table 6.5   *High Yield Muncipal Bond Funds*

Fund (Maximum sales load)	Total Return 1990–1994 (Annual Rate)	1992–1994	1994	12-Month Yield*	30-Day Yield**	Operating Expense Ratio***
United Municipal High Income (4.25%)	7.7%	6.5%	(3.1)%	6.9%	NA	0.76%[b]
Fidelity Advisor High Income Municipal A (4.75%)	7.5	5.2	(8.1)	6.3	6.5%	0.92[b]
Vanguard Municipal High-Yield (NL)	7.4	5.5	(5.1)	6.4	6.7	0.20
Franklin High Yield Tax-Free Income (4.25%)	7.3	6.3	(2.6)	7.2	6.9	0.63[b]
T. Rowe Price Tax-Free High Yield (NL)	7.2	5.8	(4.4)	6.5	6.5	0.79
Great Hall National Tax-Exempt (4.5%)	7.2[d]	6.1[d]	(2.6)	6.5	6.4	0.91[b]
American Capital High Yield Municipal A (4.75%)	7.1	6.4	0.2	7.2	6.5	1.03[b]
Fidelity Aggressive Tax-Free (NL)[e]	7.0	5.3	(5.8)	7.1	7.2	0.64
Scudder High Yield Tax Free (NL)	6.9	5.0	(8.4)	6.1	6.5	0.80[a]
Venture Muni (+) Plus B (4% R)	6.7	6.3	2.3	6.6	6.3	2.10[b]
Group average	6.2	4.8	(5.0)	6.7	6.5	

[d]Formerly Carnegie National Tax Exempt Fund. Insight Investment Management, which had been sub-advisor, became investment adviser in June 1992.
[e]1% redemption fee for shares held less than 180 days.
See Table 5.1 for other footnotes.

income as their objective, paid out higher federally tax-exempt dividends. In 1994, their distribution rates averaged 6.7% versus 5.6% for general municipal funds.

If their yields weren't higher by a wider margin, it was because the funds tended to be rooted, so to speak, in both the investment-grade and the sub-investment-grade camps.

Like general and insured municipal bond funds, high-yield municipal funds usually have long average maturities to benefit from the higher income available toward the top of a steep 30-year yield curve. Thus, they exposed their shareholders to similar degrees of interest rate risk.

Like general municipal bond funds, they tend to be invested in municipal bonds rated across the range of investment grades.

But unlike general municipal bond funds, their mix tended to be more heavily weighted toward the bottom two grades, A/A and Baa/BBB, to pick up additional income.

Also unlike general municipal bond funds, they own bonds rated Ba/BB or lower—municipal junk—to boost income further.

It would be convenient—and surely logical—to suppose that taking greater risks would be rewarded with higher returns and that, therefore, the group's more aggressive funds would have been its top performers in recent years.

That, however, hasn't been the case. The groups listed in Table 6.5 vary in aggressiveness.

United Municipal High Income Fund, the leader, has been about one-half in investment grade and one-half in non-rated issues. Of the latter, manager Holliday says, the credit quality of about one-half, or 25% of the fund's assets, can be regarded as below investment-grade—issues such as those of nursing homes and life-care centers.

Guy Wickwire, who managed Fidelity Advisor High Income Municipal Fund from inception in 1987 to 1992 and resumed the reins in 1994, has been more aggressively invested: about 50% rated investment grade, a small percentage of non-rated issues of equivalent quality, and nearly half either rated below investment grade or non-rated issues of lower quality. Its sibling, Fidelity Aggressive Tax-Free Portfolio, which also has about 50% of its assets in bonds rated of investment grade, is one of the funds able to invest up to 10% in bonds whose issuers are in default.

Among more conservative funds, Vanguard Municipal Bond Fund's High-Yield Portfolio is required by prospectus to be at least 80% in investment-grade bonds and has been in fact close to 90% invested in them.

Scudder High Yield Tax Free Fund, which had been limited to investment-grade bonds until January 1993, when its board agreed to let it allocate up to 35% of assets to junk rated Ba/BB or B/B, has remained close to 90% invested in investment-grade securities—nearly one-half of them rated Baa/BBB.

Clearly, other factors have mattered, too, including fund expenses. Some managers have gone for the yields of AMT-subject bonds—commonly, up to 20% of a portfolio. Others looked for bonds that could be expected to be prerefunded—and, thereby, upgraded from junk.

Kurt Larson, manager of the $5.8 billion IDS High Yield Tax-Exempt Fund, the group's largest, who's 80% or more invested in investment-grade bonds, favors those of providers of essential services: electricity, water, and sewer facilities.

T. Rowe Price Tax-Free High Yield Fund, which has around 65% of its assets in investment-grade issues, has been high on hospitals, having invested 25% to 35% in such securities. William T. Reynolds, head of Price's fixed income group, says he has looked especially for small hospitals in rural settings, where they are the sole providers. He has monitored them closely in view of concerns about hospitals' financial conditions.

"These are situations where the hospitals have to exist," he explains.

CHAPTER 7

Should You Own Bond Funds?

By now, you're probably wondering whether you should buy shares in a bond fund or two. If you already own such shares, you may be wondering whether you ought to hold them, add to them, or switch to other funds.

Before you can answer such questions, you really need to ask yourself whether any type of debt securities is appropriate for you. Since bond funds are simply an indirect—and usually desirable—way of owning marketable debt securities, it's critical to determine whether you should be buying interests in these instruments in the first place.

As you've seen in earlier chapters, marketable debt instruments—whether those of the U.S. Treasury, a multibillion-dollar corporation, or your city or school district—have basic elements in common. They're all essentially IOU notes, promising to pay a stated rate of interest (known as the coupon rate) at regular intervals and to repay the principal on a stated maturity date, and can be bought or sold at any time.

They have fixed face values, called par, but not fixed market values. As their market values fluctuate with interest rates in the period between their issuance and maturity, so do their yields. Their market values can, and do, swing from discount to premium, or vice versa, until they are eventually redeemed at par—unless, of course, they're called before maturity (or prepaid, in cases of mortgage-backed securities).

Marketable debt securities are very different from banks' certificates of deposit (CDs), whose principal value and yields remain fixed, whose safety is insured by the FDIC, and whose redemption before maturity may result in a penalty.

161

Savings: First Things First

Before you think of investing in any marketable securities whose value can fall below your cost, you'll want to be sure that you have enough money in savings—whether in a bank or in a (taxable or tax-exempt) money market fund—and that you need to have *no doubt* about its access and safety.

How much is enough? That's up to you. It should suffice to tide you over an emergency—such as the loss of a job or other income source or a costly illness—by providing for your living expenses for whatever period seems appropriate.

In considering how much of your money should be in savings and where you ought to have it, you'll want to keep at least two points in mind:

1. You pay a price for safety, whether provided by federal deposit insurance or the federal government's promise to pay its own obligations: The types of financial assets that involve the lowest risk are also the ones that offer the lowest interest rates.

2. The safest assets may free you from worry about loss of principal (although the bankruptcy of a commercial bank or savings and loan association in which you have an insured account may cause you inconvenience) but not from worry about inflation. The principal you salt away in a CD or savings account will lose purchasing power (just as will the principal of a marketable security). So will the interest payments: The $550 you get (before income tax) for putting $10,000 in a 5.5% account will not buy in the second year what it will in the first.

There's little you can do about the relatively low yields and inflation concerns other than to choose the highest-yielding but *safe* vehicle(s) for your savings. Even if their rates do fluctuate, taxable or tax-exempt money market mutual funds provide a highly desirable means of earning interest close to market levels—and thus at least slightly higher than inflation.

While they are not *absolutely* risk-free, their record has been respectable. They generally involve so little risk that you may wish to use a prudently managed one, providing high yields and low costs, for a portion of your savings.

(The SEC has tightened the requirements regarding the quality of the paper that money market funds may own. This hasn't kept some funds from suffering losses, notably from derivative instruments. The funds' investment advisers made up the losses in one way or another so that the funds' NAVs would not fall below $1 until September 1994, when the board of a money market fund for institutional investors concluded that its $1 NAV could not be maintained.)

Considering an Investment Strategy

If you have money left over after you've taken care of your savings requirements and/or if you are able to put money aside every month (or other regular period) out of income after providing for living expenses, you can think about investing in securities. When you do, you'll want to have a strategy in mind that's appropriate for you.

If you're still working, you may want to use the money you already have and/or your budgeted monthly surplus to accumulate a lump sum by some future year to (1) enable you to finance a major expenditure, (2) constitute a nest egg to generate additional retirement income to supplement your expected pension and Social Security checks, or (3) satisfy some other goal. You may do so in a tax-deferred account such as an IRA or an employer's 401(k) plan.

If you're in or close to retirement, you may want to invest a sum you already have available or soon will get—such as a sum distributed from an employer's qualified plan and to be rolled over tax-free into an IRA—so that it can produce additional income for you, preferably at a rate that should grow with inflation.

You can achieve either goal—the accumulation of capital or the production of income—by investing in a diversified portfolio of securities. How much of it should consist of debt securities and how much of equities depends on the goal you choose and the time you have to attain it.

In the first case, you'll want to invest in a mix of financial assets whose combined rate of total return (that is, including reinvestment of income) can be expected to provide the growth you require. While you should be able to rely on common stocks to supply most of the growth over time, their short-run volatility makes it prudent not to rely on them exclusively. The stock market could be down when you had planned to use the money.

To reduce your exposure to the risks inherent even in a diversified list of blue chip stocks, portions of your assets should be allocated to debt securities and cash reserves. How you allocate the assets is a function not only of your expected return but also of your ability and willingness to accept risk. The more time—and patience—you have for your money to work for you, the more you should be able to accept the volatility inherent in a growth-oriented portfolio.

If you have any doubt about the desirability of asset allocation, take a look at Tables 7.1 and 7.2, which illustrate the range of annual returns for major asset categories—perhaps surprisingly, as wide for long Treasury bonds as for stocks. They also illustrate the tendency of some to oscillate from being top performers in one year to bottom performers in another (or vice versa).

If you have any doubt about your ability to allocate your assets, you may be interested in knowing that *The Wall Street Journal* periodically runs a table comparing the asset allocation strategies of the nation's largest brokerage firms.

Table 7.1 *High and Low Returns for Principal Financial Assets, 1984–1994*

Asset Category	Highest Total Return		Lowest Total Return	
Common stocks	31.7%	1989	(3.1%)	1990
High-yield corporate bonds	43.3	1991	(8.6)	1990
Long-term IG corporate bonds	29.2	1985	(5.7)	1994
Long-term U.S. Treasury bonds	31.5	1985	(7.6)	1994
Intermediate Treasury bonds	27.0	1985	(5.7)	1994
Intermediate IG corporate bonds	23.0	1985	(4.7)	1994
Mortgage securities	25.7	1985	(1.4)	1994
3-month U.S. Treasury bills	10.0	1984	3.1	1993

IG = investment grade; long-term = 10+ years; intermediate = 7–10 years.
Sources: Bonds and bills, Salomon Brothers; stocks, Standard & Poor's (500 Index).

Or in comparing the allocations of asset allocation funds (which Lipper calls flexible portfolio funds).

They're never identical, and the results they achieve always differ, too.

Seeing how well-known experts disagree—and how poorly some of them have fared—you should feel less reluctant to try your hand. Instead of worrying too much about how to fine-tune your asset allocation for fear of making a mistake, try one formulation for a year. It can be 60% stock funds, 30% bond funds, and 10% money market funds, or 50% stock funds and 50% bond funds, or some other mix.

If necessary or desirable, you're always able to change your allocation—easily—when you're invested in mutual funds.

In the second case—investing for income—you'll want to invest in financial assets that you can rely on to provide you the after-tax income you think you'll need.

In all likelihood, this will mean more bond funds (in your tax bracket, possibly tax-exempt bond funds), but, even if you're retired, it should not necessarily be bond funds alone. Given bonds' vulnerability to inflation's bite and the fluctuation of interest rates, some allocation to equity and money market funds, appropriate to your circumstances, may also be desirable. Since corporate dividends should grow over time with corporate earnings, dividend-paying stocks owned by equity funds should help your portfolio's income to grow.

Whatever your goal—appreciation or income—try to figure out how you can attain it, given your age, employment/income situation, the amount of

Table 7.2   *Leading and Lagging Financial Assets, Annual Total Returns by Years, 1984–1994*

Year	Best Performing Category		Worst Performing Category	
1984	Long-term IG corporate bonds	16.9%	Common stocks	6.1%
1985	Common stocks	31.6	3-month Treasury bills	7.8
1986	Long-term Treasury bonds	24.1	3-month Treasury bills	6.2
1987	3-month Treasury bills	5.9	Long-term Treasury bonds	(2.8)
1988	Common stocks	16.6	3-month Treasury bills	6.8
1989	Common stocks	31.7	Long-term high-yield bonds	(1.1)
1990	Mortgage securities	10.9	Long-term high-yield bonds	(8.6)
1991	Long-term high-yield bonds	43.3	3-month Treasury bills	5.8
1992	Long-term high-yield bonds	19.2	3-month Treasury bills	3.6
1993	Long-term high-yield bonds	20.0	3-month Treasury bills	3.1
1994	3-month Treasury bills	4.2	Long-term Treasury bonds	(7.6)

IG = investment grade; long-term = 10+ years.
Sources: Bonds and bills, Salomon Brothers; stocks, Standard & Poor's (500 Index).

money you have (or will have) for investing, and your ability or willingness to tolerate risks. A pocket calculator or compound interest table may be helpful.

Tables 7.3 through 7.5 may provide some general guidance. They give you an idea of how many years of compounding at various rates it can take to develop a onetime investment or annual investments into $100,000 and how much has to be invested at various rates of return to earn $10,000 annually. Just change the sums to fit your targets.

When you reckon what rate of return or total return (including reinvestment of interest and dividends) it would take to realize your goals, you'll see whether your goals are realistic and, if so, what investment mix may be called for to achieve them.

We know that money market funds have produced an average annual total return of nearly 6% in the latest ten years—exceeding inflation, which

Table 7.3   *How Many Years It Takes to Accumulate $100,000*

	Years of Compounding at				
Investment	5%	7.5%	10%	12.5%	15%
$2,500	75.6	51.0	44.6	31.3	26.4
5,000	61.4	41.4	31.4	25.4	21.4
7,500	53.1	35.8	27.2	22.0	18.5
10,000	47.2	31.8	24.2	19.6	16.5
12,500	42.6	28.8	21.8	17.7	14.9
15,000	38.9	26.2	19.9	16.1	13.6

Note: No provision is made for income taxes.

Table 7.4   *Years of Annual Investments Required to Accumulate $100,000*

	Compounded at				
Annual Amount	5%	7.5%	10%	12.5%	15%
$2,500	22.5	19.2	16.9	15.2	13.9
5,000	14.2	12.7	11.5	10.6	9.9
7,500	10.5	9.6	8.9	8.3	7.9
10,000	8.3	7.7	7.3	6.9	6.6
12,500	6.9	6.5	6.2	5.9	5.6
15,000	5.9	5.6	5.4	5.2	5.0

Note: No provision is made for income taxes.

was slightly over 3.5%—that investment-grade bonds have provided returns of around 10%, and common stocks (as measured by the S&P 500 Index), around 14%.

We also know that in more recent years their returns have been less. So, happily, has been inflation.

If you're at a loss trying to estimate what rates of return these financial assets will provide in the future—during the period you want your money to work for you—don't feel bad. No one else can be sure of his or her prediction either.

Perhaps the most practical thing you can do is formulate a strategy based on what seem to be reasonable rates. If, for example, you can achieve your objective with a long-run, pretax return rate of around 5%, you may want to

Table 7.5 Investment Required to Earn $10,000 Annually

Interest Rate	Investment
4%	$250,000
5%	200,000
6%	166,667
7%	142,857
8%	125,000
9%	111,111
10%	100,000

Note: No provision is made for income taxes.

take little or no risk, and stay primarily with CDs, money market funds, or Treasury bills. For up to 7.5% or so pretax, you'll primarily want debt securities with maturities longer than those of money market instruments. Beyond that, you should consider a larger allocation to common stocks, in addition to debt securities, and plan to reinvest at least a portion of your income so that you can benefit from compounding.

Although average annual total returns of 10% or higher were achieved on stocks and bonds during the last decade, the odds are against earning double-digit returns, on the average over a long period into the future. (Even government bonds bore double-digit yields in the 1980s, you'll recall, but that was because investors such as you had to be compensated for the unusually severe inflation that the nation suffered for a time. You've got to hope that our policymakers won't permit a recurrence.)

Therefore, if your plan calls for an average annual return of more than 10%, you may want to think of moderating your goal, stretching the time to its realization, and/or investing more money. High inflation-adjusted returns are not impossible, but reaching for them could involve securities that require you to take more risk than is prudent.

These are obviously only broad suggestions; you need to adapt them to your situation.

Among other things, you need to take income tax rates into consideration, unless you're planning to invest only in an IRA, 401(k) plan, or other tax-sheltered program. Thus, to actually earn 5% in annual income you may need to think in terms of tax-exempt securities yielding in that range or of taxable securities yielding around 7% (8.28%, if you're in the 39.6% federal bracket and exclude state income tax). To build capital at an average annual rate of 10%, you probably would need a significantly higher pretax rate of total return, reflecting reinvestment of taxable income. That's not easily obtainable.

If your accumulation of a large lump sum depends in part on the realization of capital gains on sales of securities, you must remember your potential capital gains tax liability when projecting the amount you're shooting for.

The Rewards of Owning Debt Securities

If it appears that you should invest mostly or partly in debt securities, you'll want to remember the principal rewards that you should be able to expect from owning them:

Reliable Income Flow

You invest in a debt security—bond, note, debenture, or other—primarily to obtain a predictable flow of income that you can rely on for a certain number of years. Frequency of payments—semiannual, quarterly, monthly—may be important, but reliability is crucial. You obtain this by confining yourself to securities issued by governments or corporations that you can expect to maintain interest payments without fail.

Higher Income

The level of income in relation to the investment—that is, the yield or return on investment—is normally higher for marketable debt securities than for other financial assets and highest for those having (1) longer maturities or (2) lower credit ratings. (I'm excluding foreign bonds, which involve currency risk.) There may be exceptions to the former in periods when the yield curve is not normal. There are *no* exceptions to the latter.

In theory, common stocks, which, after all, are riskier investments, should offer higher yields than bonds. Not many people can remember when they last did. (In the 1950s.)

Tax Exemption

Income from certain governmental bonds is exempt from certain income taxes. Interest on state and local government bonds is usually exempt from federal tax; it also may be exempt from state and local tax. Interest on U.S. Treasury securities is exempt from state and local taxes (but not from federal tax).

Potential for Capital Gains

Because prices of outstanding bonds rise when interest rates fall, it is possible that you could sell bonds for more than you paid for them—that is, to realize capital gains instead of holding them to maturity. Of course, if you still need to generate the same amount of income, you wouldn't be able to do so by replacing what you sold with new bonds of similar quality that bear the same coupon rates. With lower rates prevalent, you'd have to invest more money.

Opportunities to realize sizable capital gains from the sale of bonds do occur from time to time and can be very profitable, but they are not frequent enough to permit you to make long-range plans based on their regular occurrence. With 30-year Treasuries yielding around 7% to 8%, the prospects for rate reductions leading to delicious capital gains are clearly not as high as when the Treasury was printing long bonds with 14% coupons in 1981.

Lower Volatility

Bonds do not consistently fluctuate in step with stocks—at times they move in opposite directions—and they tend to be less volatile than stocks over time. Therefore, the allocation of some assets to bonds should make a growth-oriented portfolio less volatile than if it were invested only in stocks. Of course, bonds also may moderate the portfolio's rate of return during a bull market.

The Risks of Owning Debt Securities

Owning debt securities isn't all reward. It also entails risks, of which these are the main ones:

Interest Rate Risk

The flip side of the potential for capital gains is the potential for capital losses. When interest rates rise, as they did in 1994, bond prices fall—regardless of whether they're backed by the Treasury or not. If you buy a bond at par and intend to hold it until maturity, this shouldn't make any difference; its price will fluctuate, but you should continue to receive the same interest in a timely manner. Eventually, the price will work its way back to par. If you buy a bond at a premium, however, there's no assurance you can avoid a loss by selling before it matures.

Clearly, careful planning is essential. To reduce the risk of loss that could incur if you have to sell before maturity to raise cash, don't buy a bond with a longer maturity or duration than is appropriate to your circumstances and don't buy bonds at premiums.

Credit Risk

You accept the risk that an issuer will default on payment of interest or principal when you buy any domestic debt security other than one backed by the full faith and credit of the U.S. government.

You reduce credit risk when you buy issues of corporations and state and local governments whose expected ability to make payments on schedule has been scrutinized and led to high credit ratings by services such as Moody's and Standard & Poor's, or when you buy issues whose debt service is covered by insurance.

You maximize risk when you buy issues that have been given a low rating or that—with some exceptions—are not rated.

Call/Prepayment Risk

The rights of corporations and state and local governments to call their bonds and of homeowners to prepay their mortgages, when interest rates have dropped, force investors to reinvest unexpected repayments of principal in other securities that yield less. This, of course, means they have to revise their financial plans by reducing their expectation of the income they had hoped to receive until those securities matured.

Inflation Risk

Even if, while fluctuating, the current interest rate for a bond is above the inflation rate—and provides you a real rate of return—the purchasing power of your stream of interest payments will drop over its life. Whether the drop is slow or fast, of course, will depend on future inflation. The purchasing power of your bond's principal will fall, too.

Table 7.6 shows what can happen to the purchasing power of a 10-year bond if you assume an average annual inflation rate of 4% over its life: The $10,000 that you get back would have 33.5% less purchasing power by the end of the tenth year than the $10,000 that you had invested. A 5% inflation rate would have 40.1% less, and so on.

Event Risk

This is the risk that the creditworthiness of an issuer would be jeopardized by an event that raises doubts about its ability to service debt out of earnings.

Table 7.6 *Impact of Constant 4% Inflation Rate on a 10-Year Bond*

End of	Face Value	Constant Dollar Value	Fall in Purchasing Power
Year 1	$10,000	$9,600	(4.0%)
Year 2	10,000	9,216	(7.8)
Year 3	10,000	8,847	(11.5)
Year 4	10,000	8,494	(15.1)
Year 5	10,000	8,154	(18.5)
Year 6	10,000	7,828	(21.7)
Year 7	10,000	7,515	(24.9)
Year 8	10,000	7,214	(27.9)
Year 9	10,000	6,925	(30.8)
Year 10	10,000	6,648	(33.5)

Event risk is usually thought of as something that happens to a corporation, but the financial crisis experienced in 1994 by Orange County, California, illustrates that it can also happen to a governmental unit.

In the case of a corporation—whether due to an acquisition, leveraged buyout (LBO), disastrous accident, loss of a court case involving damages, or some other event—the consequences are similar: Debt expands sharply, earnings are slashed, or both. The company's outstanding bonds are downgraded, causing their prices to fall and perhaps disqualifying them as investments for certain individual or institutional investors, such as investment-grade bond funds.

As their yields rise, of course, they may arouse the attention of junk bond fund managers or others willing and able to take the obvious risks.

Currency Risk

When investing in bonds denominated in foreign currencies, there is the chance that the U.S. dollar will become stronger in comparison with those currencies. As a consequence, the U.S. dollar values of their principal and interest payments will decline.

Direct versus Indirect Ownership of Debt Securities

If, after looking at the pros and cons, you conclude that your investment portfolio ought to include—or even consist primarily of—debt securities, you have to decide whether to own them directly, indirectly, or both. Each approach has advantages and disadvantages.

Indirect ownership is feasible through interests in mutual funds and two other types of investment companies: closed-end funds (sometimes called publicly traded funds) and unit investment trusts (UITs). I've chosen to concentrate on mutual funds. As many people—perhaps you, too—realize, they provide investors benefits that are not duplicated by closed-end funds or UITs, and don't have their drawbacks (such as premium prices in the case of closed-end funds or unmanaged portfolios in the case of UITs).

Advantages of Bond Funds

The advantages of owning debt securities via bond mutual funds may be familiar to you because they're similar to those offered by money market and stock mutual funds, but I'll review them briefly to make sure you're aware of all they offer you.

Diversification

No attribute of mutual funds is more important than the diversification they conveniently—and instantly—afford you, regardless of how much or how little you invest.

Diversification to help reduce the risk of a loss is crucial to anyone who invests in nonguaranteed or noninsured securities. Just because bonds may be safer than stocks doesn't mean that bonds, other than issues backed by the full faith and credit of the U.S. government, are absolutely safe and make diversification unnecessary.

Even when you buy government bonds or notes and don't have to worry about credit risk, it still is desirable—if not essential—to guard against market risk by investing in different maturities. (Unless, of course, you know when you want your money back and are able to select the appropriate maturity in an ordinary Treasury issue or zero-coupon obligation.)

Since most people cannot invest enough money to buy a diversified list of debt securities on their own, mutual funds make a lot of sense. For as little as $1,000 to $3,000, a bond fund provides you as much diversification as you're likely to need. Some funds have even lower minimum initial investment requirements—especially for IRAs. And you usually can make subsequent investments of $100 or less.

Professional Management

If, like most investors, you're occupied with work and other activities, you probably don't have the time it takes to properly manage a diversified portfolio of bonds and deal with the risks just mentioned. Even if you could spare the time, it is unlikely that you would have the requisite knowledge and be able to command the statistical and analytical resources available to portfolio managers of bond funds.

Proper management of a bond portfolio means not only knowing which bonds to buy or sell but also when to buy or sell, how to buy or sell at the most favorable prices, how to adjust a portfolio's weighted average maturity or duration, how to adjust its credit quality, how to hedge prudently against interest rate changes, how to maximize protection against calls and prepayments, and how to perform credit research to check on the suitability of bond ratings or to assess unrated bonds—to name a few of a manager's responsibilities.

Surely there can be little doubt that these requirements indicate the need for competent professionals who can discern opportunities in the undulation of yield curves or the expansion and contraction of yield spreads. You can devote your time and talent to choosing the professionals and monitoring their performance as they manage their (your) portfolios. (The same could be said of closed-end bond funds but not of UITs, which are invested in relatively fixed portfolios that are supervised but not really managed.)

Ease of Entry and Exit

Whether dealing directly with a fund organization through its toll-free 800 telephone number and by mail, or indirectly through a broker or other salesperson, it's easy to obtain the necessary prospectuses, shareholder reports, and other information you need to decide which bond fund(s) to choose.

It's also easy to buy and redeem shares; if you're dealing directly, you can do so by phone, mail, or wire. A number of funds provide plans for automatic investment or withdrawal, in which your money is debited or credited directly to your bank account. Some even offer free checkwriting.

Then, too, bond fund shares are easier to own than bonds. You don't need to worry about their safekeeping or to rent a safe deposit box for them.

No Transaction Costs

There are many bond mutual funds whose shares you can buy directly from the fund organizations without paying anyone a sales charge, or load, at the time of purchase or redemption. These no-load funds put all of your money to work.

On the other hand, when buying individual debt securities, you have to pay a commission or dealer markup—unless you're buying Treasury securities from the Treasury or a Federal Reserve Bank.

Load funds, of course, involve front-end or deferred sales charges as high as 5%. (Closed-ends and UITs involve commissions, too.)

Frequency of Dividends

When you own bonds directly, you usually receive interest payments every six months. Most bond funds, however, distribute income dividends every month or every three months, frequencies that many investors seem to prefer.

Reinvestment of Income

Investors who want to reinvest their income can do so much more easily with bond mutual funds than with bonds. No bond fund dividend is too small to be reinvested.

Unlike bonds, whose $1,000 or $5,000 minimum denominations make reinvestment difficult for all but large holders, bond funds have no minimum for the income distributions that can be reinvested in their shares. Even fractional shares can be purchased—out to three decimal places—and they usually are, inasmuch as income distributions are unlikely to equal multiples of the prices of whole shares.

Constant Maturity

When you buy an individual bond, it has a specific maturity—say, ten years. Every year that you own the bond, the time to its maturity declines, and its price will behave more in line with bonds of a similar number of years to maturity than the years to maturity at the time of its original issue. Thus, a 10-year bond with certain reward/risk characteristics when printed—potential higher return and higher risk than a bond of a shorter maturity—can behave like a money market instrument when its maturity is less than one year away.

Bond funds, whose investment policies require their managers to maintain certain weighted average maturities, will maintain essentially constant maturities. A fund that is supposed to have a weighted average maturity of ten years, say, will still have such an average ten years from now—unless its policies are changed or unless market conditions temporarily call for a different strategy.

Disadvantages of Bond Funds

There are some disadvantages to owning debt securities via bond mutual funds instead of owning them directly, but for many people they are far outweighed by the advantages. Whether they are for you, too, is for you to judge. The main disadvantages follow:

No Specific Maturity

As noted before, bond funds never mature except for a handful of target maturity funds. This means that, in planning your financial strategy, you cannot count on your bond fund investment to return to a certain value by a specific maturity date in some future year.

Knowing this, you invest accordingly, choosing target funds or other bond funds whose weighted average maturities seem to be consistent with your strategy's requirements. As the time approaches for redeeming your fund shares or for lowering the volatility of your portfolio, you can switch from longer maturity to shorter maturity funds or from shorter maturity funds to money market funds.

Transaction Costs

Sales charges on purchases or redemptions of shares in front- or back-end load bond funds may run as high as 5% and, thus, may be higher than the sales commissions imposed on transactions in individual debt securities.

But nobody says that you must buy bond funds with loads. You should be able to find plenty of fine no-load funds that meet your investment objective and other criteria.

Annual Fees

Unless you use an investment adviser, financial planner, or other consultant, you don't pay anyone an annual fee to manage your portfolio when you buy and sell your own securities.

When you buy shares in a mutual fund, however, you have to pay something for the professionals who manage *its* portfolio—the people who are responsible for the performance that attracted you to the fund in the first place.

A fund also incurs other costs for recordkeeping, accountants, lawyers, shareholder communications, and custodians. (You don't actually mail in a check; the amount is subtracted from income prior to the mailing or crediting of income distributions.)

The total annual fee doesn't have to be high, though. For very fine funds, as you may have noted in the last two chapters, it can run from as little as 0.5%, or even less, to 1.0% of average net assets. You simply don't need to consider bond funds whose expenses are high.

Considering what you get for your money, you may conclude that 0.5% to 1.0% is a reasonable price to pay—and less is even better.

CHAPTER 8

How to Find the Most Suitable Fund(s) for You

Now that you know the pros and cons of bonds and bond funds and have concluded that you ought to invest in one or two bond funds to meet your financial goals, how do you decide *which* one or two would be right for you? You'll find out in this chapter.

You *won't* find lists of recommended funds. A fund that's right for you may not be right for another reader with different requirements. And vice versa.

Moreover, a fund that might have been recommendable when this book went to press could have changed its investment objective or policy, investment adviser, or portfolio manager by the time you read this. Such change might have made it an inappropriate investment for you.

Instead of specific fund names, you *will* find the tools to enable you to make your own selection(s) of the fund(s) that should be suitable for you or to confirm the suitability of the fund(s) that a broker, other salesperson, or adviser recommends you should buy.

By becoming familiar with certain major criteria that you can apply on your own, you'll be able to select (1) fund categories and (2) funds within the categories. This need not be difficult. You can do it with a modest amount of effort in your home or public library at little or no cost. Unless your circumstances are unusual, you really don't need to pay anyone a fee or commission to advise you or to sell bond fund shares to you.

I realize that many people—maybe you, too—may feel insecure or nervous when investing for their future or may be impressed by a persuasive broker who bases a sales pitch on high yields or implicit government backing of securities in a fund's portfolio. This may help to explain why as many as 65% of bond and income fund shares sold in 1993, according to the Investment Company Institute, were bought from members of sales forces, of whom most, if not all, presumably earned commissions for their efforts.

That 65% figure, much higher than the 47% for equity fund shares, was due to the high percentages of shares sold by sales forces in GNMA (84%), high-yield (82%), U.S. Government Income (81%), global (77%), and single-state municipal bond funds (77%), the ICI reported. (Compare these, for example, with 60% of the sales of corporate bond funds or 55% of the sales of funds invested in both government and corporate bonds being by sales forces.)

With a bit of research and with confidence in yourself, you can find appropriate no-load funds on your own and save the money that would have gone into commissions. (When yields are 5%, a 5% sales load can offset a year's income!)

To be your own bond fund adviser, you have to understand and remember some simple, fundamental principles. Perhaps the four most important ones are:

1. Whether you plan to take income distributions in cash or to reinvest them, you should *not* choose a bond fund on the basis of its yield. A fund managed to maximize yield may take excessive risks, jeopardizing principal.

2. Rates of total return (reflecting both income and NAV change) for several periods are more meaningful measures of fund performance. But, when studying their levels and variability, bear in mind that past performance doesn't guarantee similar results in the future.

3. Become aware of the types of risk that characterize the fund. They will give you an idea of how it may perform in different market environments.

4. The prospect of your realizing the rate of total return that you expect over time is based on probabilities, not certainty. Bond—and, therefore, bond fund—returns are primarily influenced by levels of and changes in interest rates. *Nobody* can consistently forecast these with accuracy and, therefore, nobody has any business making you any promises of what they are likely to be.

Formulating Your Strategy

Formulating and implementing a bond fund investment strategy, as outlined in the following pages, does not require the precision expected of a surgeon removing your appendix. Nor need a fund choice that turns sour, if caught and corrected in a timely manner, have disastrous consequences. One of the advantages of mutual fund investing is the ease with which you can make changes when necessary or desirable. In no-load funds, you can do so without commissions.

To begin mapping a strategy, you need to decide whether you want to invest in a bond fund because you want to receive income or because you want to diversify a growth-oriented portfolio that is invested mostly in stock funds and/or individual stocks. (When calculating how your assets are divided between stocks, bonds, and bond funds, don't forget to take into consideration your company's stock, including shares you own in a retirement or savings plan.)

If you're planning to invest for income, you need to have an idea of the rate (or yield) that you require and, after comparing it with currently available levels for various savings and investment vehicles, have a sense of whether it's relatively high or low.

If you're planning to invest for diversification, you need to realize that its main purpose is to reduce the volatility of your portfolio. Unless returns from bonds are going to match those from stocks—instead of lagging them, as they have, over the long term—a bond fund is not likely to enhance your portfolio's return.

Should you have any reservations about diversification—about allocating your assets among the major asset classes—you may wish to read the case for diversification as expressed a half century ago by James N. White, president of Scudder, Stevens & Clark Fund (now Scudder Income Fund). His words are as applicable today as when he wrote them in January 1945 in his letter to shareholders for the fund's 1944 annual report:

> The investment of money—as opposed to speculation—is at best a compromise. The ideal security would be one which provided maximum safety, high yield, and opportunity for capital gain. No one security offers all these features. Therefore, we hold high-grade bonds and preferred stocks to provide stability of principal and income as a protection against trouble, in spite of the fact that the yield from such securities is low and there is little chance of appreciation. We include a limited amount of less-than-prime bonds and preferred stocks in the search for a little higher yield and perhaps a moderate capital gain, in spite of risks greater than in highest grade securities. And finally, we own some common stocks to augment income and because of their appreciation possibilities, in spite of the substantially higher risk of loss. The important thing, however, is the conviction that a sound program will include all these types of investments under all except the most unusual circumstances.

(At the time, his fund was 53.8% in bonds and preferreds, 45.6% in stocks.)

Having opted for income or diversification, you need to think about three major aspects of your strategy so that you can make decisions enabling you to choose the fund classification(s) that would seem to be most suitable for you:

1. Your investments' exposure to income taxes.
2. The level of interest rate risk that you are able and willing to assume in your investments.
3. The level of credit risk that you are able and willing to assume in your investments.

After discussing these, I'll also cover other important types of risk that have to be considered in choosing fund categories.

Tax Considerations

The first thing to focus on is whether federal, state, and/or local income taxes are to be a determining factor in your planning.

Accounts in which you own bond fund shares have to fall into one of three categories from a tax standpoint: taxable, tax-deferred, and tax-exempt. They differ in these ways:

- Current income is taxed by the federal government in taxable accounts and may be taxed by state (and local) governments if received in a federally tax-exempt, nationally diversified bond fund that fails to meet your state's requirements for the minimum portion of your state's securities that a fund must own.
- Current income is exempt from federal income tax in a municipal bond fund (unless you are in the minority of taxpayers who are subject to the alternative minimum tax) and also exempt from state (and local) income tax if a municipal bond fund owns the minimum percentage of your state's securities that your state requires.
- Capital gains distributions from both taxable and tax-exempt funds are taxable by federal and state (and local) governments.
- Neither income nor capital gains distributions are subject to current income tax by any level of government when they are credited to you in tax-deferred accounts.

Thus, if you are thinking of a bond fund for an IRA, 401(k), or other tax-deferred account, you'll *only* want a taxable bond fund (such as discussed in Chapter 5) because the yields are higher for funds of comparable credit quality and maturity. (Fund companies usually won't permit you to invest in a tax-exempt fund for a tax-deferred account.) Invested in such an account, you can be indifferent about a fund's absolute level of current income and about its occasional distribution of short- or long-term capital gains. You won't have to worry about paying federal, state, and/or local taxes until you take money out of the account.

If you are investing outside a tax-deferred context, you may need to calculate whether you could earn a higher return on your investment in a taxable fund—after allowing for federal, state, and/or local income taxes—or in a tax-exempt fund (Chapter 6).

Fund marketing executives say that many prospective investors who inquire about bond funds have misconceptions about tax-exempt funds. Some have the impression that tax-exempts are only for wealthier people. Others want to invest in tax-exempts because they have been attracted by ads pushing "double (or triple) tax-free income," when simple analysis would show that they'd be better off in taxable funds.

Since the spreads in yields between taxable and tax-exempt bonds expand and contract because of changes in supply/demand balances in their sectors of the bond market, the advantages may expand and shrink, too. Thus, unless you know what's better for you because you're in the highest or lowest tax brackets, the only way to be sure which is more advantageous is to do the arithmetic.

While the focus in fund selection will be on total return, the calculation to determine the appropriateness of a tax-exempt fund has to be based on yield, which reflects the distribution of the fund's net income from interest-paying securities—regardless of whether the dividends are taken in cash or reinvested. (Capital gains distributions don't enter the calculation because they are taxable either way.)

One approach is to take the average annualized 30-day yield (the one calculated in accordance with the SEC's yield formula) of a taxable fund group that you are interested in. Subtract the income tax you'd have to pay to the federal, state, and local governments to estimate your probable current after-tax rate of return. (You may not have to pay state and local taxes on income distributions attributable to interest from a fund's holdings of certain U.S. government securities.)

Then check whether a tax-exempt fund group of comparable credit quality and maturity would provide an equal, higher, or lower return. Remember that your state and local governments may tax income distributions from nationally diversified municipal bond funds.

To illustrate: Say that taxable General U.S. Government Funds have average yields of 6.5%. This would leave someone in the 15% bracket with a return of 5.5% after federal taxes; 28% bracket, 4.7%, and 31% bracket, 4.5%. If General Municipal Bond Funds had an average yield of 5.5%, anyone in the 15% bracket would really have to do some sharp-pencil work to see which category is preferable and may wind up finding it more profitable to invest in the taxable group and pay the taxes. For anyone in a higher bracket, the choice of a municipal bond fund would seem to be clear.

You'd follow an alternative approach if you are in the 28% federal bracket, see that General Municipal Bond Funds yield an average of 5.5%, and wonder what a taxable fund would have to yield to match that after taxes. You subtract 0.28 from 1.00 to obtain 0.72, then divide the 5.5% by 0.72. The result: 7.6%. For the 15% and 31% brackets, similar calculations would give you 6.5% and 8.0%, respectively.

Table 8.1 provides a range of possible taxable equivalent yields for all federal tax brackets for several tax-exempt yield scenarios.

Such rough calculations or tables only get you started, however, since you can't invest in a fund group average. (You'd also have to figure out the state and local taxes to have a more meaningful comparison.) You eventually will want to repeat the calculation with actual funds that appeal to you; their yields may be higher or lower than their groups' averages. If single-state municipal bond funds are available to you, you may want to include one or more of them in your analysis.

Interest Rate Risk

Given a normal credit market environment in which yields are higher for debt securities of long maturities than for those with short maturities—the relationship depicted by a "normal" yield curve that slopes upward to the right (Figure 3.1)—you invest in long maturities to earn higher current income and, consequently, a higher total return.

Interest rates are continually changing, however, as are the spreads between short-term and long-term yields. The yield curve may be steep at some times, flat at other times.

Because prices of long bonds rise more than short maturities in response to an identical rate change, the longer ones involve greater opportunity for

Table 8.1 *Taxable Equivalent Yields*

	For Tax-Exempt Yields of			
Federal Income Tax Bracket	*5%*	*6%*	*7%*	*8%*
15%	5.88%	7.06%	8.24%	9.41%
28	6.94	8.33	9.72	11.11
31	7.25	8.70	10.14	11.59
36	7.81	9.38	10.94	12.50
39.6	8.28	9.93	11.59	13.25

capital gains when rates fall. (The price of a bond or bond fund with a 6-year duration, for example, will rise twice as much as that of a bond or fund with a 3-year duration when rates fall by 1%.) But because their prices fall more when rates rise, long bonds also involve greater risk of loss.

If you buy an individual bond—any bond—when it's issued and hold it until it matures, interim fluctuations need not worry you.

But they should concern you when you buy shares in a bond fund. Bond fund shares offer you no guarantee that they'll ever return to the prices you paid for them because they don't mature as bonds do.

Since the returns from bond funds whose portfolios have longer weighted average maturities may normally be expected to be more volatile than those of funds having shorter maturities but identical credit quality, it's important to base your choice of each bond fund on your investment horizon: How many years is it likely to be until you'll want to redeem your shares?

Regardless of whether you're taking dividends in cash or reinvesting them, think twice about bond funds whose durations tend to be longer than you're planning to be invested. If you're taking dividends out, there is always the chance that you'll have to invade principal to supplement income—and that you might have to sell some shares at a time when their prices are down. Even if you are reinvesting distributions to accumulate capital, you'll probably want to minimize the chance that prices would be in a cyclical decline just when you want to redeem your holdings.

If you're older—especially if you are retired and rely on investments as a major source of cash—you need to be aware of the risks of long maturities even more than younger persons. Which is not to say that, if you are a young person, you may not also have a short investment horizon because you're saving for the down payment on a house or other not-too-distant goal.

If you are still employed, you are better able to cope with a drop in portfolio values because you can more easily afford to wait for bond prices to recover. Your wage or salary tends to rise over time. And if inflation fears cause interest rates to rise and bond prices to plunge, as you reinvest dividends and/or continue to invest fresh money, you are picking up additional shares at lower prices.

As you saw in earlier chapters, both taxable and tax-exempt fund categories, as classified by Lipper, are primarily divided into three broad groupings on the basis of maturities: (1) short-term funds, which are primarily invested in securities having average maturities of one to five years; (2) intermediate-term funds, whose average maturities range from five to ten years; and (3) funds whose average maturities exceed ten years. (If the groups having flexible or unspecified maturities appeal to you, check on the levels of interest rate risk to which their funds would expose you.)

To start your search for a bond fund—whether taxable or tax-exempt—decide whether to focus on a short-, intermediate-, or long-term group.

(Note: For quite a few funds, the dividing line between short and intermediate maturities is three years, as an SEC guideline defines it, rather than five.)

If you can't decide among the three—because you find short-term funds generate too little income and long-term funds' prices are too volatile—you may find one of the intermediate-term groups an acceptable compromise, at least for your first bond fund investment. Given a normal yield curve, which tends to flatten beyond 10 years (if not earlier)—meaning that you pick up little more income by going out as far as 30—intermediate-term funds may offer nearly as much income as long-term funds but with less volatility.

Of course, if you prefer a fund that will mature in a specific year and want to avoid the risk of reinvesting interest income at lower rates, you could choose a target maturity fund, invested in zero-coupon obligations, whose maturity comes closest to your goal.

Unlike investors in other bond funds, you would know roughly what your shares will be worth upon redemption in a specific future year and, thus, the rate of total return you can expect. Most likely, there will be volatility along the way, but it shouldn't matter; it's the ultimate value that counts. On the other hand, unless the fund is in an IRA or other tax-deferred account, you'd have to pay taxes on credited—but unreceived—income each year until maturity.

Credit Risk

If you know the approximate rate of total return that you expect of your bond fund(s), you may define the level of credit risk—that is, the risk that a bond's issuer will default on interest or principal payments—that you may have to accept to achieve it. Armed with the information, you can aim at a fund category accordingly.

The simple rule of thumb is that taxable bonds that are regarded as safe pay low yields. The safest, U.S. Treasury bonds, pay the lowest of all. The most speculative bonds—those of issuers that may default—pay the most to compensate investors for taking the risk.

Absolute yields will change from time to time and the spreads between yields of the highest and lowest quality bonds will expand and contract, but the relationships among them won't change. The safest securities always will pay you the least.

If your required return is relatively low—that is, only 100 to 200 basis points, or 1% to 2%, higher than (taxable or tax-exempt) money market fund rates—you should be able to concentrate on funds invested in securities having the highest credit quality: U.S. Treasury, GNMA, or other government issues backed by the full faith and credit of the Treasury; high-grade corporate (Aaa-

or Aa-rated, in Moody's ratings), or investment-grade municipal issues. (And you probably can stay with short- or possibly intermediate-term funds.)

If your required return is 200 to 300 basis points (2% to 3%) higher, you should be able to rely on funds that are invested exclusively in investment-grade corporates (Aaa, Aa, A, and Baa), in a mix of governments and investment-grade corporates, or in municipals. (And if you can't find prospects of an adequate return in an intermediate-term fund, you'll probably have to go with one invested in longer—but not necessarily the longest—maturities.) A single-state municipal bond fund may own only investment-grade bonds, but it introduces a different sort of risk: concentration in one geographic area whose economy may be susceptible to the ups and downs of one or two major industries.

If your required return is still higher, you may have to consider the taxable or tax-exempt high-yield fund categories. You may find them acceptable if the economic outlook appears to be favorable and it's likely that issuers of lower quality (Ba or lower) bonds will make their debt service.

Alternatively, if you require a high return and are considering taxable funds, you might look to funds that are linked to the stock market as well as the bond market: flexible income, income, convertible securities, or balanced funds. If you need cash and their yields are too low, you can redeem shares to supplement your dividends. (Should you be investing in a taxable account, be prepared for the work of calculating capital gains for income tax purposes whenever you redeem shares.)

In 1990 and 1991, the years when the most recent recession began and ended, the default rate on speculative corporate bonds rose to around 9%—the highest since 1970—according to Moody's. Prices of high-yield bonds and bond funds slumped accordingly. But by 1993 the default rate had fallen to 3.1%, the lowest in 11 years, and total returns of high-yield bond funds continued to exceed their yields.

Because another recession is likely to occur sooner or later, I urge you to consider high-yield funds only for a portion of your assets. I also recommend that you consider reinvesting dividends to pick up more shares when prices inevitably fall, instead of taking dividends out, if you can afford to do so. But even before checking on high-yield bond funds, be sure to ask yourself whether you are really able, and willing, to assume the default risks inherent in securities of lower credit quality.

You can derive some comfort from the fact that high-yield bond funds epitomize the benefits of the widespread diversification that is synonymous with most mutual funds. One or two issues in a fund's portfolio can go into default, and they, of course, will affect a fund's total return, but the consequences are not necessarily disastrous. If the portfolio is managed by someone proficient in these securities and if it is diverse enough, it probably can absorb the defaults and still provide a higher return than would have been available from a higher-quality bond fund of the same fund family (that is, one with comparable fees).

Other Risks

In addition to interest rate and credit risks, a bond fund may also be subject to other risks that can affect your principal, your income, or both.

Call and prepayment risks—the risk that a corporation or state or local government will call a bond prior to maturity or that homeowners will prepay mortgages that collateralize Ginnie Maes and other mortgage-backed securities—have been widely felt during the years of declining interest rates. They are always likely to be felt when a corporation, government unit, or homeowner has—and wants to take advantage of—an opportunity to cut borrowing costs.

Their impact on you as a bond fund shareholder would usually be a drop in your income as the portfolio manager has to replace holdings with lower-yielding securities.

It's difficult to escape at least some exposure to these risks. The only bond funds that are almost totally immune are those invested in U.S. Treasury securities: Almost all of them are noncallable.

Currency risk is the risk that the dollar will rise in value against one or more foreign currencies, reducing the dollar equivalent of the principal value of, and income from, foreign bonds. Managers of bond funds that are partially or totally invested in foreign securities may engage in transactions to hedge against this risk, but their hedging strategies may turn out to be wrong. And even if they're right, they involve costs, reducing income accordingly.

What you might call yield or return enhancement strategy risk is the risk that a portfolio manager's strategy to enhance yield or return can backfire. Such strategies may involve the use of derivative instruments—common ones, such as futures contracts, or the more exotic ones, such as interest-only and principal-only stripped securities and inverse floaters, that have emerged more recently.

Liquidity risk is the risk that a manager may buy securities for which there is no liquid market—including, but not only, exotic derivatives—and whose daily pricing, therefore, may be difficult.

Stock market risk is attached to funds that are totally or partially invested in securities convertible into common stocks as well as to mixed funds that are directly invested in stocks.

Finally, there is, of course, the risk that a fund may be badly managed by a manager who may be implementing a board's policy and avoiding speculative practices but making poor buy or sell decisions.

Choosing a Category

You're now ready to choose a category (Table 8.2) from which you'll want to pick a fund that, you hope meets your investment goals. You will note that some categories have funds with common characteristics (such as GNMA and U.S. Mortgage, Corporate A-Rated and Corporate BBB-Rated).

The decisions you make that culminate in a category choice—between taxable and tax-exempt, high and low interest rate and credit risks—should depend more on your expected returns and risk tolerance than on current bond market conditions. Your long-term goals and risk tolerance are presumably less likely to change suddenly than the bond market.

While past performance does not guarantee performance in the future— something that you've probably memorized by now—it is at least an indicator of likely results in similar market environments.

The first step in seeing which fund categories' returns may meet your long-run requirements would be to compare historic total return and yield data for the various taxable and tax-exempt categories. You'll find a table of such data, as calculated by Lipper, in the most recent quarterly mutual fund section of *Barron's* (Figure 8.1)—probably in the issue published in the second week of January, April, July, or October.

As you can see, the *Barron's* table provides total return data (reflecting reinvestment of dividends) for the most recent quarter, year, and five years— in this case, for periods ended December 1994—as well as the average 12-month yield. Remember that the average returns for the categories do not reflect sales charges—a point that will be even more important when comparing returns for individual funds—and that the 12-month yields differ from the annualized 30-day yields calculated in accordance with the SEC's formula.

To make the cumulative 5-year data more useful to you, you probably will want to convert them to average annual rates—just as you probably will want to know the annualized return reflected in a fund's ad or promotional material that shows how a $10,000 investment in the fund grew over a certain period.

Table 8.3 gives you a rough idea of the annual rates for several scenarios. To get closer, you'll need a calculator.

Annualized 5-year rates will more quickly indicate how realistic your expectations are for fund groups with certain interest rate and credit risks; along with yields, they also will provide a benchmark against which the most recent year's numbers can be compared.

Since total return represents the sum of reinvested income (indicated by yield) and price change, a lower rate in the most recent year may raise a question as to whether the 5-year rate is sustainable; the latter may reflect an extended decline in interest rates—and increase in bond prices—that has ended. A negative recent rate, such as 1994's, reflects a drop in bond prices, resulting

Table 8.2   *Major Risks of Bond Fund Categories*

Investment Objective*	Interest Rate Risk	Credit Risk	Other Risks
	Taxable		
Short-Term U.S. Treasury	Low	Negligible	
Short-Term U.S. Government	Low	Low	
Short-Term Investment Grade	Low	Low	
Intermediate U.S. Treasury	Moderate	Negligible	
Intermediate U.S. Government	Moderate	Low	Prepayment
Intermediate Investment Grade	Moderate	Low	Call
General U.S. Treasury	High	Negligible	
General U.S. Government	High	Low	Prepayment
Adjustable Rate Mortgage	Low	Low	Prepayment
GNMA	Moderate	Negligible	Prepayment
U.S. Mortgage	Moderate	Low	Prepayment
Corporate A-Rated	High	Low	Call
Corporate BBB-Rated	High	Moderate	Call
General Bond	Varies	Varies	Call
High Current Yield	Varies	High	Call
Target Maturity	High	Negligible	
Convertible Securities	Varies	Varies	Stock Market
Flexible Income	Varies**	Varies**	Stock Market
Income	Varies**	Varies**	Stock Market
Balanced	Varies**	Varies**	Stock Market
Short World Multi-Market	Low	Low	Currency
General World Income	Varies	Low	Currency
	Tax-Exempt		
Short-Term Municipal	Low	Low	
Intermediate Municipal	Moderate	Low	Call
General Municipal	High	Low	Call
Insured Municipal	High	Negligible	Call
High-Yield Municipal	High	Moderate	Call

*As classified by Lipper Analytical Services.
**Risk characterization applies to bond portions of the funds' portfolios.

FOURTH-QUARTER RESULTS BY SECTOR
FIXED-INCOME FUNDS

Type	4th Quarter	1 Year	5 Years	Average Yield
Short Term				
U.S. Treasury Money Market	1.12	3.57	24.76	3.52
U.S. Government Money Market	1.14	3.58	24.53	3.53
Money Market	1.18	3.65	25.15	3.59
Tax-Exempt Money Market	0.75	2.33	17.60	2.30
Taxable				
Adjustable-Rate Mortgage	−1.65	−2.20	26.53	4.94
Short U.S. Treasury	−0.01	−0.22	36.03	4.97
Short U.S. Government	−0.11	−1.65	34.29	5.21
Intermediate U.S. Treasury	−0.01	−3.28	40.29	5.80
Intermediate U.S. Government	−0.09	−3.72	36.88	5.99
Short Investment-Grade Debt	−0.10	−0.37	36.25	5.65
Intermediate Investment-Grade Debt	0.04	−3.36	41.38	6.04
General U.S. Treasury	0.81	−5.77	39.82	6.30
General U.S. Government	0.24	−4.63	37.42	6.54
GNMA	0.25	−2.49	38.80	6.96
U.S. Mortgage	−0.17	−4.17	36.75	7.09
Corporate Debt A-Rated	0.20	−4.64	41.67	6.53
Corporate Debt BBB-Rated	0.01	−4.48	46.53	6.85
General Bond	−1.36	−6.04	46.53	7.58
High Current Yield	−1.34	−3.83	65.62	9.94
Convertible Securities	−2.84	−3.79	57.08	4.32
Flexible Income	−0.95	−3.69	43.76	7.09
Target Maturity	1.68	−8.05	45.91	2.06
Short World Multi-Market	−2.40	−4.25	47.76	7.11
General World Income	−1.52	−6.48	43.77	6.44
Tax-Exempt				
Short Municipal Debt	−0.22	−0.28	29.29	4.08
Intermediate Municipal Debt	−1.19	−3.53	34.92	4.79
General Municipal Debt	−1.64	−6.53	35.96	5.59
Insured Municipal Debt	−1.44	−6.47	34.97	5.44
High-Yield Municipal Debt	−1.50	−4.99	35.19	6.65

FIGURE 8.1 How *Barron's* Presents Quarterly Lipper Performance Data

Reprinted by permission of *Barron's*, © Dow Jones & Company, Inc. (January 9, 1995). All Rights Reserved Worldwide.

Table 8.3 *Five-Year Returns Annualized*

Cumulative 5-Year Total Return	or Value of $10,000 Invested 5 Years Ago	= Average Annual Return
25%	$12,500	4.56%
30	13,000	5.39
35	13,500	6.19
40	14,000	6.96
45	14,500	7.71
50	15,000	8.45
55	15,500	9.16
60	16,000	9.86
65	16,500	10.53
70	17,000	11.20
75	17,500	11.84
80	18,000	12.47
85	18,500	13.09
90	19,000	13.70
95	19,500	14.29
100	20,000	14.87

from an increase in interest rates, that could not be offset by higher income in one year. It need not cause alarm unless we face a period of severe inflation and higher interest rates.

A recent rate of total return that exceeds the 5-year rate, on the other hand, may reflect the year's drop in interest rates (and increase in bond prices that more than offset lower income). It should not lead to unrealistic hopes since it may not continue,

Comparing a 5-year average with a recent year's total return isn't enough, however. Table 8.4 illustrates how similar 5-year averages can fail to indicate the different levels of volatility to which bond funds are subject, underscoring the importance of looking at data for several individual years as well. Annual data remind you that you should consider a bond fund only if you can accept the volatility that you could experience if you stay invested in it for several years. (If you can't, you probably ought to stick with a money market fund.)

And, remember, these are total returns. Principal-only returns, which are especially relevant to you if you plan to take dividends in cash instead of reinvesting them, are even more volatile.

**Table 8.4   The Volatility of Bond Funds
Annual Average Total Returns by Categories—
1990–1994**

Investment Objective	1990	1991	1992	1993	1994	5-Year Annual Average
			Taxable			
Short U.S. Treasury	8.4%	11.7%	5.4%	5.8%	(0.2)%	6.4%
Short U.S. Government	9.0	11.7	5.4	6.0	(1.7)	6.1
Short Investment Grade	8.1	11.9	5.9	6.4	(0.4)	6.4
Intermediate U.S. Treasury	8.4	14.3	6.7	9.8	(3.3)	7.0
Intermediate U.S. Government	8.5	14.4	6.1	8.3	(3.7)	6.5
Intermediate Investment Grade	7.2	15.2	6.9	9.5	(3.4)	7.2
General U.S. Treasury	5.6	16.6	4.7	12.9	(5.8)	6.9
General U.S. Government	7.4	14.5	6.3	9.3	(4.6)	6.6
Corporate A Rated	6.8	16.4	7.2	11.3	(4.6)	7.2
Corporate BBB Rated	6.6	16.8	8.1	12.3	(4.5)	7.9
General Bond	5.4	19.3	8.6	12.9	(6.0)	7.9
Adjustable Rate Mortgage	7.8	10.7	4.7	3.8	(2.2)	4.8
GNMA	9.6	14.5	6.4	6.4	(2.5)	6.8
U.S. Mortgage	9.1	14.2	6.3	7.6	(4.2)	6.5
Target Maturity	2.3	19.7	8.5	19.9	(8.1)	7.9
High Current Yield	(11.1)	36.4	17.7	19.3	(3.8)	10.6
Flexible Income	1.3	19.9	9.4	13.3	(3.7)	7.5
Income	(8.1)	23.0	8.8	12.2	(2.9)	8.0
Balanced	(0.2)	26.0	7.1	10.7	(2.5)	7.9
Convertible Securities	(7.6)	29.7	13.6	15.8	(3.8)	9.5
Short World Multi-Market	18.3	7.4	(0.7)	5.4	(4.3)	8.1
General World Income	12.4	13.9	2.8	17.0	(6.5)	7.5

Table 8.4   *Continued*

Investment Objective	1990	1991	1992	1993	1994	5-Year Annual Average
Tax-Exempt						
Short-Term Municipal	6.4%	8.2%	6.4%	6.3%	(0.3)%	5.3%
Intermediate Term	6.6	10.4	7.7	10.3	(3.5)	6.2
General Municipal	6.0	11.9	8.7	12.4	(6.5)	6.3
Insured Municipal	6.5	11.4	8.7	11.9	(6.5)	6.2
High-Yield Municipal	5.1	11.5	8.6	11.6	(5.0)	6.2

Source: Lipper Analytical Services

As you choose a category on the basis of your estimated future returns and your acceptance of the risks associated with it (Table 8.2), don't be diverted from your emphasis on a long-range strategy by what you hear or read about the near-term outlook for interest rates. Stay focused on your circumstances and your requirements.

As indicated before, your decisions should be based on how you answer such questions as: Should you confine yourself to taxable funds because you're investing in a tax-sheltered account? Is a tax-exempt fund indicated because you're in the 28% (or higher) tax bracket? Are you so risk-averse that you can be content with the relatively low rates associated with short-term funds? Are you able to invest for the higher returns that you expect of long-term or high-yield bond funds?

Screening Funds for Historic Performance

Once you've chosen a category, make your search manageable by screening the group's historic return data to identify the leading performers from which you ultimately may pick one.

Nothing can guarantee that superior past performance will continue. But, if a fund's historic performance data cover enough years to include periods of rising and falling interest rates, they indicate how well it has been managed through both favorable and unfavorable market conditions. They tell you whether a fund has been a consistently above-average performer or had a couple of good years that followed, or were followed by, poor ones.

Thus, whether you're planning to take income distributions in cash or to reinvest them, your next step is to compile a list of ten funds that led the category in total return for the latest five years. (See the next section for pointers on where to get the names.) If that would be too many, take the top five or six, or take all the funds whose rates of return exceeded the group's average for the period.

Five years are widely regarded as sufficient to give you a look at performance over enough years to take in both favorable and unfavorable bond market conditions. That's why data for five years are easily available. If you're looking at a category in which only one or two funds have been in operation for five years, you may want to reduce the period to three years. But, unless there's a compelling reason to do so, don't be tempted to consider funds with shorter records. While you may feel comfortable with an experienced management running a new fund with a conventional investment objective, you don't want to risk your money on inexperienced fund managements or unproved investment concepts.

Given that you've probably based your list on Lipper's or other data services' data, it's likely that you have a mix of no-load funds, front-end load funds, and back-end load funds.

The data may be fine for comparing how well portfolio managers have done their job but not for comparing how well investors have been served. To determine the returns that you would have earned on an investment in them, those for front- and back-end load funds have to be adjusted for sales charges—unless your screen only turned up no-load funds or you limited your search to them. (If you are considering a load fund whose loads are waived for participants in your company's tax-deferred plan, such adjustment would not be necessary, of course.)

Since it's unlikely that you can find adjusted returns in periodicals, you probably will have to get them from the load funds' distributors or salespeople. Fund companies are required by the SEC to reflect sales charges—including any on reinvested dividends—or deferred sales charges in the average annual total returns for 1-, 5-, and 10-year periods that they must include when advertising performance data. Thus, they will have calculated them at least for this purpose. Some of the more enlightened ones, such as The American Funds Group, Merrill Lynch, and Putnam, provide this information voluntarily—and prominently—in their reports to shareholders. (Figure 8.2 shows how Merrill Lynch does it.)

When you've identified the leading performers, you've only begun. You'll next want to determine whether the funds were managed as well as they could have been, given their investment objectives and policies.

For one thing, you'll want to see how well the actively managed fund portfolios performed in comparison with benchmark indexes for the unmanaged pools of bonds in which they were invested—indexes such as those calculated by Lehman Brothers, Merrill Lynch, and Salomon Brothers. Since mid-1993, the SEC has required funds to provide such comparisons in their shareholder reports or prospectuses. If the fund group you're considering is invested in a subset of the market—such as long-term U.S. Treasury securities—

Average Annual Total Return		
	% Return Without Sales Charge	*% Return With Sales Charge***
*Investment Grade Portfolio Class A Shares**		
Year Ended 9/30/94	− 6.03%	− 9.79%
Five Years Ended 9/30/94	+ 8.17	+ 7.29
Ten Years Ended 9/30/94	+10.30	+ 9.85

*Maximum sales charge is 4%.
**Assuming maximum sales charge.

	% Return Without CDSC	*% Return With CDSC***
*Investment Grade Portfolio Class B Shares**		
Year Ended 9/30/94	− 6.73%	−10.07%
Five Years Ended 9/30/94	+ 7.35	+ 7.35
Inception (10/21/88) through 9/30/94	+ 7.77	+ 7.77

*Maximum contingent deferred sales charge is 4% and is reduced to 0% after 4 years.
**Assuming payment of applicable contingent deferred sales charge.

FIGURE 8.2   A Fund's Returns Calculated in Two Ways: with and without Sales Charges
Source: Annual Report, Merrill Lynch Corporate Bond Fund, Inc., September 30, 1994

it would be more appropriate, of course, if the chosen index reflects only that universe, instead of the U.S. bond market as a whole.

In comparing fund returns with index returns, you can expect the index returns to be slightly higher than the funds' because the index data don't reflect annual expenses. (The index results, naturally, don't reflect sales loads either.) But if a fund trails a relevant index by a lot, it could be a clue to high expenses, poor management, or speculative tactics (such as excessive reliance on exotic derivatives) that failed.

You also need to know whether a fund performed with reasonable consistency, year after year, in good markets and bad—and is, therefore, likely to continue to do so—or whether its manager took shareholders for roller-coaster rides.

A simple but quite useful way would be to compare the yearly total returns of each fund that you're analyzing with the average for the Lipper category for each of the five years, such as listed in Table 8.4. If a fund matches or exceeds the group average for four out of five years, it deserves further scrutiny.

You also can check on the variability of returns in more sophisticated ways.

If you're familiar with mathematical concepts, you may wish to study the volatility of a fund's returns by looking at its standard deviation—a measure of the variance in a series of its monthly returns (usually for 36 months) from their mean. The higher the standard deviation, the more volatile a fund's returns.

You also may find reference to a fund's beta—a measure of how the variability of a fund's returns compares with that of a benchmark index. If you do, be sure the beta is calculated to compare the bond fund's performance with that of a relevant bond index—not with the Standard & Poor's 500.

When you compare a fund's historic rate of total return with its volatility, you can judge whether apparently strong performance may have been due more to skillful portfolio management or to excessive risk-taking.

Funds that have had consistently above-average total returns over time while demonstrating moderate volatility are worth a closer look. They are more likely to perform satisfactorily in the future, given the same management and policies, than funds that have had below-average total returns and have performed inconsistently.

If in your going through the data you come across something unusual, such as a fund whose performance has been far ahead of its peers, be sure to look into the situation before you even think of sending any money.

It could be, for example, that the fund has changed its investment objective and been reclassified by Lipper. The total return that drew your attention may have been largely due to performance while aiming at a different objective. You may pass over the fund until it proves itself anew.

It also could be that the fund pursued very risky policies, such as the short-term bond funds whose derivatives strategies backfired in 1994. When a group of funds invest in a universe of homogeneous securities, have similarly skilled managers, similar duration policies, similar expenses, and similar net cash flows, their investment returns are unlikely to be very far apart. If, therefore, an enormous gap exists, a bit of detective work is clearly called for to find out why the gap is there.

Getting Information on Fund Performance

Now you know what to look for. How do you go about getting a list of top fund performers for the category(ies) you're interested in?

You can start, of course, by referring to the appropriate tables in Chapters 5 and 6. But every quarter there may be a change or two in the top ranks of each group, and you'll want to be up to date.

Fortunately, Lipper fund data are disseminated at regular intervals in some publications*, but, unfortunately, they are usually not presented in ways that make it easy to identify the top performers of the last five years in each category.

Other media use data, grouped into fewer categories, from other services. You may find most or all of them in your library or, of course, can always buy them. But their data may make it more difficult for you to identify funds that you want to study.

Some sources provide total returns for five years on an annualized basis while others provide cumulative total returns, necessitating your conversion of the figures to annual rates for your analysis. Or they show how a $10,000 investment in a fund would have grown in five years, which is another way of saying the same thing. You can get an approximate—perhaps sufficient— idea of annual rates by referring to Table 8.3.

Whatever source you use, remember that total return data provided by data services usually are *not* adjusted for sales charges. Their missions are to track fund performance but, in doing so, they may give a misleading comparison of returns on investments experienced by investors in load and no-load funds. A major exception: *Morningstar Mutual Funds*, which provides both adjusted and unadjusted returns for load funds; you have to look for the adjusted returns on the data-filled *Morningstar* pages, though.

Publications Using Quarterly Lipper Data

■ Standard & Poor's/Lipper *Mutual Fund ProFiles*—This quarterly guide, produced jointly by Standard & Poor's and Lipper, is the only publication that conveniently ranks the top performers for 5-year (as well as 1- and 10-year) periods for each Lipper taxable bond fund category (Figure 8.3) but, unfortunately, doesn't do the same for tax-exempt funds as of the February 1995 edition.

ProFiles contains annualized average 5- and 10-year returns, as well as total returns for individual years, for the funds and their Lipper group averages in profiles of over 750 taxable bond and stock funds. The guide also offers 5- and 10-year data (for funds in business that long) in tables

---

*The suggestion here and on the following page(s) that you turn to certain periodicals, annual guides, or other sources for five-year total return data should, of course, not be taken as a guarantee that they will continue to present data as they did at the time this book went to press. Competing fiercely with one another to better serve you, the investor, they do make changes from time to time.

CORPORATE DEBT A-RATED
One Year: 9/30/93 to 9/30/94

Leaders		Laggards	
Fund	% Change	Fund	% Change
Hawthorne Inv:Bond	−0.52	Sm Brny/Shgrsn Inv Gd;B	−11.99
FBL Series:HI Grade Bd	−0.62	Sm Brny/Shrsn Inv Gd;A	−11.56
Crowley:Income	−1.05	Sierra:Corp Income;A	−10.10
Crabbe Huson Income	−2.27	Security Inc:Corp Bond	− 9.72
Arbor:Goldenoak Intmdt;B	−2.29	Advance Cap I:Lg Tm Inc	− 9.27
Arbor:Goldenoak Intmdt;A	−2.40	SEI Instl:Bond;A	− 8.92
Preferred Fxd Inc	−2.44	Nationwide:Bond	− 8.87
Babson Bond:Portfolio L	−2.62	Quest Value:Inv Qual;B	− 8.84
J Hancock Sover Bond;C	−2.77	Quest Value:Inv Qual;C	− 8.76
T Rowe Price New Income	−2.83	Quest Value:Inv Qual;A	− 8.23

Five Years: 9/30/89 to 9/30/94

Leaders		Laggards	
Fund	% Change	Fund	% Change
Vangard Fxd:Lg-Tm Corp	55.59	Keystone B-1	35.54
Bond Fund of America	54.60	Crabbe Huson Income	37.25
Bond Port for Endowments	54.19	AVESTA Tr:Income	38.11
Dodge & Cox Income	51.90	Arch:Govt & Corp;Inv	39.96
Putnam Income;A	50.38	Highmark:Bond	40.49
Sentinel:Bond	49.24	Wright Inc:Total Return	40.74
J Hancock Sover Bond;A	49.18	Nationwide:Bond	41.29
Scudder Income Fund	49.15	Arch:Govt & Corp;Tr	41.43
Dreyfus A Bonds Plus	49.11	Lutheran Bro Income	42.39
Sm Brny/Shrsn Inv Gd;B	49.10	Merrill Corp:Inv Grd;B	42.57

FIGURE 8.3 An Investment Objective's Leaders and Laggards

Ten Years: 9/30/84 to 9/30/94

Leaders		Laggards	
Fund	*% Change*	*Fund*	*% Change*
Bond Fund of America	191.51	Keystone B-1	124.79
Vanguard Fxd:Lg-tm Corp	184.46	Nationwide:Bond	140.44
Bond Port for Endowments	179.61	Security Inc:Corp Bond	142.61
Sm Brny/Shrsn Inv Gd;B	179.06	T Rowe Price New Income	143.25
United:Bond	176.78	Lutheran Bro Income	145.60
J Hancock Sover Bond;A	173.78	Pioneer Bond:A	146.84
Dreyfus A Bonds Plus	169.33	Transam Bd: Inv Qual;A	150.12
Putnam Income;A	168.60	Corp Fund Accum Program	151.16
Scudder Income Fund	168.04	Babson Bond:Portfolio L	159.84
Merrill Corp:Inv Grd;A	166.64	Sentinel:Bond	161.80

FIGURE 8.3 *Continued*

Source: Standard & Poor's/Lipper *Mutual Fund Profiles*, November 1994

listing an additional 1,890 taxable and 750 tax-exempt funds, each one appropriately tagged with its category.

- *Barron's*—Its quarterly survey of mutual fund performance, *"Barron's Lipper Mutual Funds Quarterly,"* presents comprehensive data for *all* the bond and equity funds tracked by Lipper—for 1994's fourth quarter, over 6,100 (including dual and multiple classes of shares): around 4,500 taxable bond and stock funds and over 1,600 tax-exempt funds. They are listed in two alphabetical sequences: taxable (a consolidated sequence of equity and bond funds) and tax-exempt.

Regrettably, the taxable bond funds are not labeled by categories; all simply carry "fixed income" as their investment objective. Thus, you have to know which funds you're looking for in the category you're interested in. If you do, it's easy to find them, ascertain their performance (expressed as returns on a $10,000 investment, which you need to convert to percentages) for the latest 5- and 1-year periods, and compare the figures with the category averages that are in a table of results by sectors in the same issue (Figure 8.1). If you don't have the names, it can be a challenge.

If you're looking for leaders among national or single-state municipal bond funds, you're better off: You can easily find the funds' performance data by classification.

- *The Wall Street Journal*—This newspaper carries performance data for all funds in its Quarterly Review, combining taxable and tax-exempt funds under easily identifiable fund family headings but making it difficult for you to find top-performing funds in individual investment objective categories. The *Journal* labels funds by objective categories but, instead of using Lipper's categories, uses its own, which represent combinations of Lipper's groupings (such as U.S. Treasury, target maturity, and long-term corporate bonds in one). Therefore, they may require you to do more analyzing for your purposes.

  The paper's quarterly offers data for the latest year and annualized data for the latest three and five years, saving you the trouble of annualizing them, and ranks them for performance according to the *Journal's* investment objectives (using letters A through E).

  The paper also offers 5-year performance data between quarterly sections. Every Friday, its daily mutual fund price table gives you annualized returns for the period in addition to daily changes (on other days, the table offers data for other periods) along with the letter grades for performance ranking.

  Occasionally, its daily feature, "Mutual Fund Scorecard," is devoted to one of the major bond fund categories. As illustrated in Figure 8.4, it lists the top 15 (and bottom 10) performers for the category for 1 and 12 months as well as providing their annualized total returns for 5 years, plus the Lipper averages for the group. (The newspaper switched from cumulative to annualized 5-year data in January 1995.) Inasmuch as the funds are ranked according to performance for the most recent 12 months, a table won't include any top performer for the latest 5 years if it failed to be one of the top 15 or bottom 10 for the latest year. Thus, by relying on this table alone, you could be missing out on some quite respectable funds.

- You may be able to find the data you want right in your own daily newspaper. The Associated Press, the leading news wire service, has arranged with Lipper to distribute the firm's mutual fund data to its member papers. If your paper takes the AP service, you should be able to find what you want—depending on what your paper's editors choose to publish from the wealth of data that AP can transmit to them. (If you can't find what you want, don't hesitate to let the business editor know of your interest. Editors usually appreciate feedback from readers.)

Publications Using Other Data

If you are unable to get your hands on the publications using Lipper data or if you already have access to publications using those of others, don't despair.

Mutual Fund Scorecard/Ginnie Mae

INVESTMENT OBJECTIVE: Generally holds at least 65% of assets in Government National Mortgage Association (GNMA) securities

(Ranked by 12-month return)	NET ASSET VALUE[1] DEC. 31	TOTAL RETURN[2] IN PERIOD ENDING DEC. 31				ASSETS SEPT. 30 (In millions)
		1 MONTH	SINCE 12/31	12 MONTHS	5 YEARS*	
TOP 15 PERFORMERS						
USAA Inv Tr:GNMA[3]	$9.57	0.81% −	0.02% −	0.02%	**%	$259.2
Cardinal Govt Obligation[4]	7.82	0.69 −	0.88 −	0.88	6.51	169.7
Vanguard Fxd:GNMA Port[3]	9.58	1.13 −	0.95 −	0.95	7.61	6025.4
Dreyfus Invstrs GNMA Fd[3]	14.15	0.80 −	1.06 −	1.06	7.20	45.3
Sm Barney:Mthly Govt;A[4,5]	11.85	1.24 −	1.47 −	1.47	7.37	45.8
Sm Barney:US Govt;A[4,5]	12.50	1.13 −	1.51 −	1.51	7.47	399.7
Fidelity Spartan GNMA[3]	9.32	1.05 −	1.51 −	1.51	**	387.8
Liberty Finl:US Govt[4]	8.54	0.95 −	1.59 −	1.59	6.83	746.6
Nth Am Fds:Govt Secs;A[5]	9.37	0.60 −	1.59 −	1.59	6.74	104.7
T. Rowe Price GNMA[3]	8.88	1.24 −	1.63 −	1.63	7.06	781.6
SunAmer:Fed Secs;B[3,5]	9.69	1.00 −	1.64 −	1.64	5.65	70.0
Benham Govt:GNMA[3]	9.90	1.02 −	1.67 −	1.67	7.51	1025.1
AARP GNMA[3]	14.56	0.69 −	1.71 −	1.71	6.85	5567.8
Fidelity Inc:GNMA[3]	9.99	1.01 −	2.00 −	2.00	6.84	741.1
Lexington GNMA Income[3]	7.60	1.14 −	2.07 −	2.07	7.07	133.8
AVG. FOR CATEGORY		0.91% −	2.49% −	2.49%	6.77%	
NUMBER OF FUNDS		58	47	47	32	
BOTTOM 10 PERFORMERS						
Princor Govt Sec Income	$10.24	1.55% −	4.89% −	4.89%	7.11%	$254.8
Safeco Tr:GNMA[3]	8.87	0.77 −	4.27 −	4.27	6.41	46.2
Franklin Prt:TX-Ad USG[4]	9.76	1.31 −	4.13 −	4.13	7.07	500.6
P Hzn:US Govt Sec[4]	9.08	0.62 −	3.87 −	3.87	7.01	108.6
Pilgrim GNMA[4]	12.32	0.91 −	3.61 −	3.61	5.57	53.2
MIMLIC Mortgage	9.57	0.85 −	3.59 −	3.59	7.00	27.2
SEI Daily:GNMA;A[3,5,6]	9.03	1.16 −	3.39 −	3.39	7.16	239.0
Wright Inc:Current Inc[3,6]	9.71	1.35 −	3.31 −	3.31	6.85	92.4
First Inv Govt	10.50	0.97 −	3.26 −	3.26	6.14	228.9
Stagecoach:Ginnie Mae[4]	10.18	0.93 −	3.23 −	3.23	**	206.5

[1] Some funds don't qualify for newspaper share price quotation
[2] Change in net asset value with reinvested dividends and capital gains
[3] No initial load
[4] Low initial load of 4.5% or less
[5] Fund has other share classes
[6] Fund may not be open to all investors

**Fund didn't exist in period
N.A.=Not available
* Annualized

Source: Lipper Analytical Services Inc.

FIGURE 8.4   A Daily's Fund Performance Scorecard

Reprinted by permission of *The Wall Street Journal,* © 1995 Dow Jones & Company, Inc. All Rights Reserved Worldwide.

Other sources, using different categories, also may help you to find the bond fund you're looking for. They include:

- Morningstar, whose *Morningstar Mutual Funds* devotes a full-page report—including total returns for various periods—to each of about 500 bond funds (out of a total of about 1,500 mutual funds) but whose data base of nearly 6,000 includes another 2,500. The 500 are classified into eleven categories excluding single-state municipal bond funds and stock market-linked—or "hybrid"—funds. (Morningstar supplies daily data to Tribune Media Services, which feeds them to newspapers—possibly your own—in competition with the AP.)

- Value Line, long-time publisher of *The Value Line Investment Survey*, which deals with stocks, and itself a sponsor of a group of mutual funds, in 1993 introduced *The Value Line Mutual Fund Survey*, which contains full-page reports on about 500 bond funds (out of a total of 1,500 mutual funds) in seven categories excluding stock market-linked and single-state municipal funds.

- CDA Investment Technologies, whose monthly *CDA/Wiesenberger Mutual Funds Report* carries annualized total returns for 10, 5, and 3 years—as well as shorter periods—for over 2,600 bond funds (including multiple classes of shares and single-state municipal funds) in five classifications.

  Since they don't classify bond funds in the way that Lipper does, and you're sold on using Lipper's classification system, you simply will have to try to determine the Morningstar, Value Line, or CDA (or other data services') investment objective category that includes funds that you think will interest you.

  Funds' names should help if they reflect their categories: the XYZ GNMA Fund, Investment Grade Bond Fund, Short-Term Government Securities Fund, and so on. SEC regulations permit fund managements to call their funds more or less what they want. If the names imply specific investment objectives, however, their objectives and policies must conform; fund names may not mislead investors.

- *Money,* in its semiannual roundup of data for around 3,000 mutual funds, provides performance data for 1, 3, and 5 years, as well as yearly percentile rankings, for 762 "major" bond funds and 3-year data for 747 "extra" funds that include multiple classes of shares and single-state municipal funds. Both groups are arranged in alphabetical sequences—not by categories.

  The monthly, which replaced Lipper with Morningstar as a data source when Lipper took on the job of supplying data to daily newspapers via the AP, identifies the major bond funds by six broad investment objective types and six "styles" that reflect maturities and credit ratings. Thus it uses three concepts to characterize each fund. The "extra" funds are identified only by the six types.

Money also carries lists of the top 25 taxable and 25 tax-exempt funds for the latest 3 and 5 years, but their usefulness is limited when one category is dominant, as happened in the August 1994 issue in which high-yield corporate (or junk) bond funds took 20 out of 25 positions for 5-year performance and all 25 for 3-year performance.

- *Forbes*, which has rated mutual funds annually for many years, now carries return data from CDA/Wiesenberger as well as Lipper for over 700 bond funds. They're divided into four groups: taxable, tax-exempt, and global bond funds, for which it gives 5-year annual returns, and junk bond funds, for which the only long-term data are for 9.5 years. (The tax-exempt table includes single-state funds.)

  Forbes also provides letter grades (A through F) for performance in up and down markets. Basing market cycles on different bond market sector indexes for each of the four groups, it has defined as many as 16 up and down markets for municipal bonds in the latest five years (Figure 8.5a), but only one up and down cycle for junk bonds (Figure 8.5b)— illustrating that all bonds do not move up and down in lockstep.

  From the four groups, the magazine culls out "best buys" for ten bond fund maturity and credit quality categories (excluding single-state funds) and gives 5-year returns for peer comparisons.

- *Kiplinger's Personal Finance Magazine*, which obtains data for its annual rankings from Micropal, gives annualized 5- and 3-year total returns in its annual ranking of about 650 taxable bond funds (including multiple classes of shares) that are listed in one alphabetical sequence and identified

Ratio scale (6/30/89 = 100)

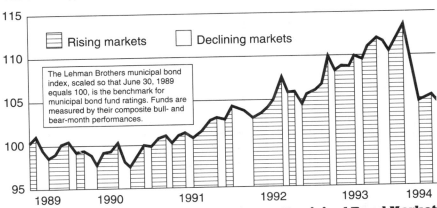

FIGURE 8.5a   **Up and Down Phases in the Municipal Bond Market**
Reprinted by permission of *FORBES Magazine* © Forbes Inc., 1994.

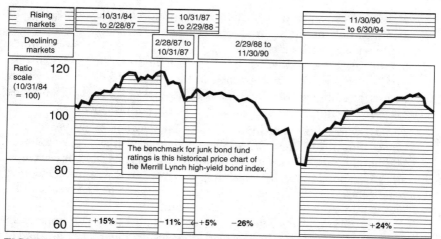

FIGURE 8.5b   Up and Down Phases in the Junk Bond Market
Reprinted by permission of *FORBES Magazine* © Forbes Inc., 1994.

by one of five categories. An additional 235 municipal funds (including multiple classes) are classified by credit quality: higher or lower.

- *Business Week,* which has been using Morningstar data for its annual feature for several years, provides total returns for 5-year and other periods for about 650 bond funds (including single-state municipal). They are arranged alphabetically in four broad groups—corporate, government, municipal, and international—plus convertible.

- Annuals or semiannuals containing performance data for 5-year and other periods (and a lot of other useful information) include *The Individual Investor's Guide to Low-Load Mutual Funds,* published by the American Association of Individual Investors (312–280–0170); *The Handbook For No-Load Fund Investors,* published by *The No-Load Fund Investor,* a newsletter (800–252–2042), *Investor's Guide To Low-Cost Mutual Funds,* published by the Mutual Fund Education Alliance (MFEA) (816–471–1454), and the oldest of all, *Investment Companies Yearbook,* published by CDA/Wiesenberger (800–232–2285).

(Annuals that don't provide performance data but do give you fund phone numbers and addresses and other useful information include the *Directory of Mutual Funds,* published by the Investment Company Institute—202–326–5800—and the *100% No-Load Mutual Fund Investment Guide and Member Fund Directory,* published by the 100% No-Load Mutual Fund Council—212–668–2477. Both cover members of the two organizations. Since ICI is the industry's principal trade association, its directory is much larger. The council's annual is the only one limited to pure no-load funds but does not include those of large complexes such as T. Rowe Price, Scudder, and Vanguard, which belong to MFEA. Some complexes belong to both.)

They are organized differently, as you would imagine.

AAII's *Guide*, whose name was changed in 1994 to reflect the surprising expansion of its coverage to include funds charging a load of 3% or less, classifies over 300 bond funds into seven categories: corporate, corporate high-yield, government, mortgage-backed, general, international, and tax-exempt (including single-state). Funds linked to the stock market are included among growth & income and balanced funds.

The *Handbook* divides about 250 bond funds into six categories according to maturities—long-, intermediate-, and short-term fixed income and short-, intermediate-, and long-term tax-free (including single-state)—and ranks them according to annualized 5-year performance. You have to comb the lists for government, corporate, international bond funds, and so on. The same tables also give you 1-year data as well as 10-year returns where available. (Another table ranks about 80 long-established funds for 10-year performance.) Stock market-linked funds are grouped simply as income funds.

MFEA's *Guide* offers 5-year performance figures and others for bond funds of members (including Benham, Dreyfus, Fidelity, Price, Scudder, and Vanguard) in two sequences: (taxable) fixed income and municipal. It contains a separate listing for single-state funds.

CDA/Wiesenberger's *Yearbook* provides total return data for 5-year and other periods as part of full-page write-ups for about 400 bond funds and returns and other data only for another 1,600 that include single-state municipal funds. It divides bond funds into seven categories (excluding single-state funds) according to their corporate, government, and municipal issuers—not maturities.

Selecting the Funds

Armed with a list of leading funds in the category of your choice from one or more of the suggested performance data sources, you will want to screen them according to a number of criteria to see which one may be the most appropriate for you.

To do this, you will need to do more than see what you can find out about them from the periodicals and other reference sources that you have been studying.

You will need to obtain the current prospectus and most recent annual or semiannual shareholder report for each fund. With all due respect to the people who produce the publications that you have been using, the only information whose accuracy is assured by a fund's board and investment adviser is that which they themselves have issued. Data services can, and do, inadvertently make mistakes. And even though a fund report may be a bit dated by the time you get it, a periodical's or annual's data may be even older.

A fund's directors are liable for what its prospectus contains—a mixed blessing for you as an investor in that, regrettably, the potential liability and the resourcefulness of fund lawyers often result in ambiguity and lack of clarity in prospectus texts. Investors and SEC officials may complain that prospectuses are hard to understand, and some fund companies may work at making them more useful. In the final analysis, though, since fund directors bear the liability for prospectus contents and fund lawyers have the responsibility to protect them, the temptation to be concise usually yields to prudence—and wordiness.

Both the prospectus and the latest shareholder report should be easily available. Just telephone the funds to request them. Since most fund companies have "800" telephone numbers—which you can find in fund annuals, periodicals, or data service listings—the calls shouldn't cost you a cent. (See the Appendix for numbers of a selection of fund complexes.) If you have trouble finding a number, you can dial the information operator at 800-555-1212.

The criteria for which you should screen a bond fund are:

1. Investment objectives/policies.
2. Relative performance.
3. Volatility.
4. Investment adviser.
5. Portfolio manager.
6. Shareholder transaction expenses.
7. Annual fund operating expenses.

Investment Objectives/Policies

First and foremost, you'll want to make sure that a fund's investment objectives and policies are consonant with your own, that they were the same for the entire period for which the performance data impressed you, and that no changes have been proposed.

The investment objective of most bond funds is simply to provide current income. For many, it may be high income. Either way, the sentence containing the objective may include a passage to the effect that the fund aims to achieve it in a way consistent with reasonable risk or prudent risk, whatever that may mean. Sometimes capital appreciation may be given as a secondary objective.

The statement of investment policy deals with the securities in which the fund is permitted to invest to achieve the objective(s).

The Investment Company Act of 1940 requires each mutual fund to state its objectives and policies, concisely and clearly, in the front of its prospectus. A brief statement of the objectives must be on the cover page. Elaboration and description of the policies being followed must be right behind. (For an example of how they're worded, see Figure 8.6, which is excerpted from the prospectus for the American Funds Group's Intermediate Bond Fund of America.)

A prospectus must describe not only the types of securities in which the fund invests, but also any special investment practices and techniques it employs (including their probable effects, such as high portfolio turnover) and the principal risk factors associated with investment in the fund. These may reflect investment in bonds rated Baa/BBB or below investment grade, in securities denominated in foreign currencies, or in other mutual funds. They also may include put and call options and other derivatives, use of borrowed money, and the fact a fund has a short operating history. If its objectives may be changed without a vote of the majority of its shareholders, the prospectus must say so.

If a fund invests in U.S. government securities, the prospectus must not only describe the types of securities but also state whether they are supported by the full faith and credit of the United States, by the ability to borrow from

---

INVESTMENT OBJECTIVE AND POLICIES

The fund's goal is to provide you with current income and preservation of capital.

The fund's investment objective is to seek current income consistent with its stated maturity and quality standards and preservation of capital. The fund will attempt to achieve this objective by investing in a portfolio of bonds with an effective maturity of 3 to 10 years and will not purchase any bonds with an effective maturity of greater than 10 years. See "Maturity" below. The fund will purchase only high-quality bonds (those that are rated with the two highest categories by either Moody's Investors Service, Inc. (Aaa, Aa) or Standard & Poor's Corporation (AAA, AA) or if not rated by either of these rating agencies, determined to be of comparable quality by Capital Research and Management Company, the fund's investment adviser). See the Appendix to the statement of additional information for a further description of these ratings.

FIGURE 8.6   How a Fund States Its Investment Objective and Policies
Source: Prospectus, Intermediate Bond Fund of America, October 25, 1994

the Treasury, only by the credit of the agency or instrumentality, or in some other way.

You will want to determine whether a fund is managed for maximum total return consistent with the level of risk associated with the grade and maturity of securities in which it's principally invested—and which you're prepared to accept. This, you'll recall, implies relatively lower expected total returns for funds taking relatively low risks and higher expected returns for those taking higher risks. A fund managed for maximum income may incur more principal risk than you want.

Avoid any fund that states or implies that it is investing for a constant level of distributions, and resist any broker who makes a similar pitch. Since you know that interest rates fluctuate and that income dividends can be expected to fluctuate accordingly, you know that speculative techniques, return of your capital, or both may be required to supplement income dividends to maintain total distributions at a constant level.

Moderate use of certain techniques, such as engaging in futures contracts to hedge against interest rate fluctuations, may be appropriate, but excessive use of others, such as selling options to maintain a flat payout, can result in missed opportunities for capital appreciation or even in capital losses.

A fund that returns your capital on the installment plan to maintain a flat level of distributions is, in effect, buying your loyalty with your own money. (If data services don't pick it up, erroneously treating return of capital as income distributions, they may be overstating what they cite as the fund's yield.) The part of a distribution that's a return of capital is nontaxable, but that isn't the point (even if a fund may try to give it a positive spin); a fund that makes this a policy fails to provide you a return on a part of your investment—after charging you a fee for management.

If you require a flat stream of cash, you can simply plan to redeem some of your shares to supplement any shortfall in income dividends (even if it does require some added work at tax time).

When scanning a prospectus or annual report, be alert to the possibility that a fund may have changed its investment objectives during the five-year (or other) period for which you are examining performance data. Funds may not disclose it in years following the change, and data services and periodicals may fail to indicate it in their tables.

Thus, for example, your attention could be caught by a bond fund with an impressive historic total return, which, on examination, could turn out to reflect performance of earlier years when the fund was partially or primarily invested in equities. Such discovery probably should lead you to scratch the fund from your list until it has been managed for a few years to achieve its current objective. (It's also possible, of course, that a fund had an inferior record when aiming at a previous investment objective and is doing better now; in that case, I would recommend watching and waiting, too.)

If, however, a fund achieved a high return while in pursuit of the objective you want and you've verified that it still has the objective, you will want to keep it on your list.

Relative Performance

The performance figures that presumably attracted certain funds to your attention were the funds' historic total returns—probably for 1, 5, and 10 years—and their relative positions versus other funds in the same classification. You also may have compared the returns with the averages of the particular peer group, as calculated by a firm such as Lipper.

That's enough to warrant your further study but not enough to warrant your investment of a dime.

You also need to compare the performance with that of a benchmark index, which measures the performance of a relevant sector of the broad, diverse bond market.

If this sounds difficult, it shouldn't be, thanks to the requirement that the SEC imposed on funds, effective July 1993, to provide line graphs in prospectuses or annual reports that would compare the performance of each with that of "an appropriate broad-based securities market index"—any index that fund management deemed appropriate (Figure 8.7). For this purpose, fund expenses, sales loads, and any other fees would have to be reflected.

When this was proposed, some fund managements objected on grounds that it would be unfair to compare an actively managed fund with an index that does not incur costs, but the SEC stuck to its guns.

Thus, when you see a fund's performance close to—or even consistently ahead of—the benchmark index, you may suppose the fund is well managed. On the other hand, when you see a fund's performance lagging an index by a lot—by much more than its annual fees—you may have reason to suspect that the fund may not be worthy of your investment.

As you can imagine, the SEC requires fund managements to stick with the benchmarks of their choice. They can't just switch from one to another if a different index will make a fund look better.

Since the chart may be updated only annually and a particular chart that you're looking at may be dated by the time you see it, you may want to compare a fund's performance with the index by looking up the latter in *Morningstar* or other reference source.

If you're considering a plain vanilla short-, intermediate-, or long-term investment-grade bond fund, you may want to compare its performance with that of Vanguard's Short-Term, Intermediate-Term, or Long-Term Bond Portfolio, each of which is managed to track the relevant Lehman Brothers index. Since these funds weren't started until March 1994, you won't be able to use them for long-term comparisons for a few more years.

Total Return Based on a $10,000 Investment

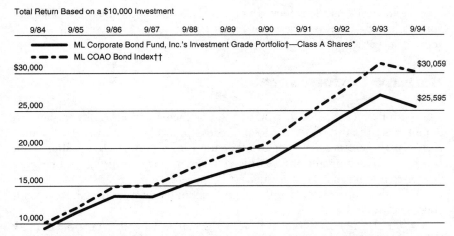

FIGURE 8.7   **Comparing a Fund's Performance with That of a Benchmark Index**

*Assuming maximum sales charge, transaction costs and other operating expenses, including advisory fees.

†The Portfolio invests primarily in long-term corporate bonds rated A or better by Moody's Investors Service, Inc. or Standard & Poor's Corp.

††This unmanaged Index is comprised of all industrial bonds rated BBB3 or higher, of all maturities.

Past performance is not predictive of future performance.

Source: Annual Report, Merrill Lynch Corporate Bond Fund, Inc., September 30, 1994

Alternatively, you may want to compare a fund with Vanguard's Total Bond Market Portfolio, which has tracked the broad investment-grade bond market since 1986 and, therefore, can be used for meaningful long-run comparisons. (Since it's an index fund, instead of an index, its performance data also reflect annual expenses, albeit the traditional low Vanguard ratio of 0.2%.)

Volatility

Knowing how volatile a bond fund has been in the past won't tell you how volatile it may be in the future, but it may give you a pretty good idea.

It's always important to know how volatile a mutual fund may be because of the likelihood that its share price could be less than your cost when you want—or have—to redeem, not to mention the possibility that a volatile fund could cause you to lose sleep before that time. It's especially important if you take your dividends in cash and, therefore, are unable to take advantage of lower prices at which you could reinvest the distributions when a fund is down.

How do you find out about a bond fund's volatility?

There are a few ways, ranging from simple to complicated. There is no agreement that any one of them is superior to all the others. The SEC has been brooding for some time about which, if any, measure it should require funds to publish.

Perhaps the simplest is to look at a fund's total returns over a period of years and see how they fluctuate. Or to look at a fund's NAVs at regular intervals, such as the end of each year. You can do either by looking at the financial highlights table in a fund report or prospectus (Figure 8.8).

The widely used statistical measure of volatility, standard deviation, measures by how much a series of numbers varies from their mean. In the case of funds, it's usually used to see how much variability there is in a series of 36 monthly returns. You may not find standard deviations in fund literature, but you will find them in reference sources such as those of CDA/Wiesenberger, Morningstar, and Value Line. By relating the average returns of several funds for the latest 36-month period to their standard deviations for the same period, you can see which have higher ratios of returns.

Some reference sources may provide betas that compare the volatility of a fund to that of a benchmark securities price index. If a beta doesn't relate a fund to a relevant bond price index—or if you're not sure whether it does—ignore it.

Since interest rate risk is likely to be a fund's dominant source of volatility, it is important to check on the range of weighted average maturities that you may expect of a fund. The longer the maturity, the greater the likely decline when interest rates rise (or the increase when interest rates fall). It should be stated clearly in the prospectus, and the latest shareholder report should state what the average was at the end of the period for which the report was issued.

Even more significant is the portfolio's duration, which, you'll recall, is a measure of the sensitivity of its bonds' prices to changes in interest rates. The longer the duration, the greater the rise or fall when interest rates change.

BENHAM TREASURY NOTE FUND
Years Ended March 31

	1994	1993	1992	1991	1990	1989	1988	1987	1986	1985
Net Asset Value at End of Period	$10.18	10.73	10.52	10.23	9.87	9.63	10.11	10.91	11.97	10.35
TOTAL RETURN*	1.85%	12.36	9.92	11.59	10.61	2.78	1.60	6.60	26.67	12.40

FIGURE 8.8 Prospectus Shows Volatility of NAVs and Returns
*Total return figures assume reinvestment of dividends and capital gain distributions and are not annualized.
Source: Prospectus, Benham U.S. Treasury & Government Funds, June 1, 1994

Because average investors are perceived to have some difficulty in understanding the concept of duration, it may be some time before you'll find a fund's duration cited prominently in its reports, although portfolio managers may refer to it in their discussions of fund performance.

Even Vanguard, which has been a leader in forthright and comprehensive reporting to shareholders, has refrained from volunteering durations. It, however, has provided the next best thing: a table (Figure 8.9) that indicates how much prices would rise or fall given a certain change in interest rates—while avoiding use of the word "duration." (On the other hand, Vanguard did offer an explanation of durations in a shareholder newsletter. It was accompanied by a drawing, from which Figure 8.10 is adapted.)

Whether you find average maturities and/or durations in fund literature, in Morningstar's and Value Line's publications, or elsewhere, you have to remember that those figures were appropriate for the dates indicated. They could have changed by the time you read them, and, while you could bring yourself up to date with a phone call, they presumably will continue to change during the period you would own the fund(s) you choose.

Instead of relying on the precise number, it would be more useful to get a sense of a fund's likely volatility by determining the range of maturities or durations within which a manager is permitted (or likely) to run the fund. If this doesn't come across clearly in the fund's literature, phone calls to the fund are definitely in order.

Percent Change in the Price of a Par Bond Yielding 5.5%		
Stated Maturity	*1 Percentage Point Increase in Interest Rates*	*1 Percentage Point Decrease in Interest Rates*
Short-Term (2.5 years)	− 2.3%	+ 2.3%
Intermediate-Term (10 years)	− 7.3%	+ 8.0%
Long-Term (20 years)	−11.1%	+13.1%
Stated Maturity	*2 Percentage Point Increase in Interest Rates*	*2 Percentage Point Decrease in Interest Rates*
Short-Term (2.5 years)	− 4.5%	+ 4.7%
Intermediate-Term (10 years)	−13.9%	+16.7%
Long-Term (20 years)	−20.5%	+28.6%

FIGURE 8.9   An Illustration of Interest Rate Risk
Source: Prospectus, Vanguard Fixed Income Securities Fund, May 25, 1994

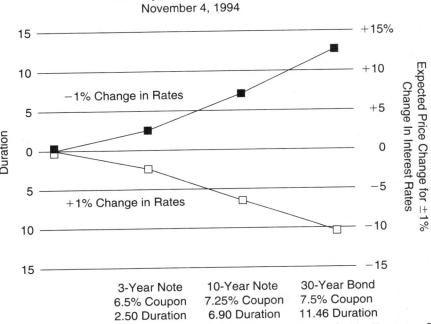

FIGURE 8.10 **How Securities of Different Durations Respond Differently to a 1% Change in Rates**
Source: Adapted from *In the Vanguard,* The Vanguard Group

If a prospectus indicates that a manager doesn't have to operate within a range—or if he/she is permitted to operate anywhere across a wide spectrum—you can't really know how much volatility you could be exposed to and might want to avoid the fund.

Investment Adviser

The investment adviser, whose name appears in the prospectus, is the firm that is responsible for managing a fund's portfolio. It also may be—and often is—the firm sponsoring the fund.

Under the 1940 act, all investment advisory services must be provided pursuant to a written contract, approved by a fund's shareholders. Renewals or changes must be voted on by a fund's shareholders or board of directors (trustees). They can be terminated at any time.

You'll want to be sure that the fund's current investment adviser is the same one it had for all of the period for which you have the performance data that led you to consider it. While a fund should indicate any change in a footnote to the 10-year table of financial information at the front of the prospectus (as I've tried to indicate in the tables in this book), it may have overlooked doing so. Fund data services may not show the change either.

Therefore, it's a good idea to ask the fund the question. If there has been a change, you may want to disregard the fund unless you know something of the new investment adviser's record with another bond fund having comparable objectives and policies. If an adviser only has had experience managing equity funds, why not skip the fund? There are plenty with experience at running bond funds.

If you have the time, read what the prospectus says about the investment adviser. It must describe the adviser's experience, state who controls the firm and the nature of the business of the controlling company or individual(s). While a large number are primarily engaged in investment counseling or fund management, many others are affiliated with broker-dealers, insurance companies, and banks.

Portfolio Manager

Check whether the performance record that attracted you is that of the portfolio manager—an employee or senior executive of the investment adviser or perhaps its sole shareholder—who is still in the job.

This is easy to do now that the SEC requires mutual fund prospectuses to disclose the name and title of the person or persons "who are primarily responsible for the day-to-day management of the fund's portfolio." You should not have to search for the names anymore.

The requirement, which became effective in 1993, stipulates that funds must disclose the length of time that each person has been "primarily responsible" as well as each one's business experience during the past five years.

Although the SEC also now requires funds to advise investors of portfolio manager changes between prospectus printings by means of a prospectus sticker, you still should check by phone to see whether the portfolio manager listed in the prospectus or shareholder report remains in the position or whether there has been a change. Production of a sticker may still be under way.

If you learn that the manager has had the job for over five years—ideally, during both good and bad bond markets—and still has the job, you probably have a good prospect.

If, on the other hand, you learn a manager has been in the job fewer than five years, you know that he (she) is not responsible for the entire five years' performance for which you have data. Find out what you can about the person's record and relevant experience, and regard the fund with skepticism. If the bond market environment has only been favorable during the years of his or her service, the manager will not have been adequately tested.

If he (she) managed a portfolio in 1994, it would be useful to know how well it performed.

Shareholder Transaction Expenses

Do you have to pay charges (or commissions) to buy or redeem a fund's shares? Only if you choose a fund that imposes them.

At the front of a prospectus, a fund is required by the SEC to disclose clearly in a table captioned "Shareholder Transaction Expenses" whether it imposes a sales load on the purchase of shares and on the reinvestment of dividends, a deferred sales load, a redemption fee, and/or an exchange fee—and, if so, how much they are (Figure 8.11a).

If a fund is a no-load fund, it will have the word "none" on each line of the table, as you can see in Figure 8.11b.

The oldest of the sales loads is the front-end load. The maximum rate permitted under a rule of the National Association of Securities Dealers is 8.5%. If imposed on a bond fund when yields are relatively low, it would wipe out more than a year's income. Understandably, most front-end load bond funds charge less.

	Class A Shares	*Class B Shares*	*Class M Shares*
Shareholder Transaction Expenses			
Maximum Sales Charge Imposed on Purchases (as a percentage of offering price)	4.75%	NONE*	3.25%
Deferred Sales Charge (as a percentage of the lower of original purchase price or redemption proceeds)	NONE**	5.0% in the first year, declining to 1.0% in the sixth year, and eliminated thereafter	NONE

*The higher 12b-1 fees borne by Class B and Class M shares may cause long-term shareholders to pay more than the economic equivalent of the maximum permitted front-end sales charge on Class A shares.

**A deferred sales charge of up to 1.00% is assessed on certain redemptions of Class A shares that were purchased without an initial sales charge as part of an investment of $1 million or more. See "How to buy shares—Class A shares."

FIGURE 8.11a   How a Load Fund Discloses Its Sales Charges
Source: Prospectus, Putnam Income Fund, March 1, 1994

Shareholder Transaction Expenses	Short-Term U.S. Treasury Portfolio	Short-Term Federal Portfolio	Short-Term Corporate Portfolio	Intermediate-Term U.S. Treasury Portfolio
Sales Load Imposed on Purchases	None	None	None	None
Sales Load Imposed on Reinvested Dividends	None	None	None	None
Redemption Fees	None	None	None	None
Exchange Fees	None	None	None	None

FIGURE 8.11b   How the Shareholder Transaction Expenses Table Appears in the Prospectus of No-Load Funds
Source: Prospectus, Vanguard Fixed Income Securities Fund, May 25, 1994

It is easy to understand why a broker-dealer, bank, insurance company, or other organization and their sales personnel would *want* a commission for selling mutual fund shares, just as they (or others) would want a commission for selling anything else.

It is also easy to understand why many funds are structured to *charge* sales loads, front-end or deferred: to give an incentive to salespeople to sell the shares, thereby helping the funds' assets to grow and the investment advisers to earn larger management fees, inasmuch as they are based on net assets.

But it is not easy to understand why many investors, capable of doing their own research, of dialing an 800 telephone number to get information, of making decisions, and of doing business by mail, would want to *pay* a load instead of having all of their money working for them.

Anyone paying a load to a broker or other salesperson—even if no more than $500 on an investment of $10,000—should expect to receive something for the money. That something has to be investment advice and/or other service.

Anyone agreeing to pay a load on the reinvestment of dividends has got to wonder what possible service could be rendered to justify it, inasmuch as the work is probably done by a computer in a second or two and the fund has managed to sell additional shares at less cost than it takes to sell shares to new investors. (The Franklin group, which imposed such a charge on a good number of its funds for many years, abandoned it in 1994.)

Anyone agreeing to pay a deferred sales load, which is scaled down over five or six years until it is eliminated altogether, has got to avoid being hoodwinked into thinking it's a no-load fund and to consider whether the possibility of such a charge could inhibit his (her) willingness to get out of a fund if that becomes necessary or desirable.

Five or six years are a long time, during which anything can happen. Who needs to handcuff himself or herself by agreeing to have a deterrent to redemptions? (Or, as some investors think, a penalty for redeeming shares, similar to the penalty a bank might charge for an early withdrawal from a certain type of account.) And why absorb the 12b-1 fee that is commonly associated with deferred sales charges?

What do you get for the load of 5% or whatever it may be? Appropriate recommendations? Sound advice when markets are turbulent? Answers to your questions?

Front-end or back-end, a sales load is an incentive for selling a fund's shares—not an incentive to, or reward for, fund performance. It is *not* paid to the portfolio manager(s).

Performance, good or bad, is independent of the presence or absence of a load. And performance is what matters.

It is self-evident that, if the portfolio managers of two funds—one a load fund, the other a no-load—manage identical portfolios with identical strategies and skills, the investor who has all of his or her money at work in the no-load will have a higher return than the one who had a load taken out.

Whether a fund imposes a load of either type is important to you in your screening of prospects. If your list of funds includes both no-load and load funds, check whether the return data make an allowance for loads. Most of the time—unless you get the data from the funds' own literature, and it is clearly stated that allowance has been made—they don't. Thus, data published by the media or data services overstate the actual return on investment that you would have experienced in the fund(s)—unless you had invested in the fund in a 401(k) or other plan for which loads were waived.

If you're comparing a batch of load and no-load funds, be sure to use load-adjusted total return data for the load funds to put them on a comparable basis with the no-load funds. When asking funds companies themselves for the adjusted data, verify that they are for the same periods that the other funds' figures are for.

Of course, you can easily avoid the trouble by simply confining your search to no-load funds that meet your requirements.

You may find it worthwhile to pay a load to someone who will help you to select a superior equity fund, but I can see no reason for paying a load for a bond fund whose returns over time are likely to be lower. When a load is, say, 5%, it is likely to account for a significant share of your expected return. Even if you amortize it over five years and reduce each year's return by 1%, you need to ask yourself: Why?

Annual Fund Operating Expenses

Each mutual fund also is required to disclose its annual expenses at the front of its prospectus.

In a table, captioned "Annual Fund Operating Expenses" (Figure 8.12), it must report them as a percent of average net assets, broken into three categories—management fees, 12b-1 fees, and other expenses—and totaled.

Another table, which appears under a "financial highlights" caption and is excerpted in Figure 8.13, reports operating expenses as a percent of average net assets for the last ten fiscal years (fewer, if a fund has not been in operation that long). A similar table also appears in semiannual and annual reports.

Since funds' total return data reflect their annual operating expenses, you may wonder why you should bother to check the expense ratios of the funds you're considering. After all, funds that are top performers were able to outscore others in total return after operating expenses were taken into account.

You'll understand why when you consider that, given two funds with identical portfolios and identical gross investment income per share, the fund with the lower annual operating expenses should have the higher *net* investment income per share and the higher yield over time. It should be the better performer.

The two line items—management fees and "other" expenses combined should add up to no more than 1% of average net assets, and you can find well-managed funds with expense ratios of 0.75% or less. Vanguard is well-known for expenses of even less than 0.25%.

Annual Fund Operating Expenses
(as a percentage of average net assets)

Management fees	0.40%
12b-1 expenses	0.26%[3]
Other expenses (including audit, legal, shareholder services, transfer agent, and custodian expenses)	0.12%
Total fund operating expenses	0.78%

FIGURE 8.12 How Funds Disclose Annual Operating Expenses

[3]These expenses may not exceed 0.30% of the fund's average net assets annually. (See "Fund Organization and Management—Plan of Distribution.") Long-term shareholders may pay more than the economic equivalent of the maximum front-end sales charge permitted by the National Association of Securities Dealers.

Source: Prospectus, U.S. Government Securities Fund, October 25, 1994

AARP GNMA and U.S. Treasury Fund		
For the Years Ended September 30	Ratio of Operating Expenses to Average Net Assets %	Ratio of Net Investment Income to Average Net Assets %
1993	.70	7.15
1992	.72	7.69
1991	.74	8.23
1990	.79	8.71
1989	.79	8.76
1988	.81	9.09
1987	.88	8.76
1986	.90	9.49
1985(e)	1.03(f)	10.62(f)

(e)Operations for the period of November 30, 1984 (commencement of operations) to September 30, 1985.
(f)Annualized.

FIGURE 8.13   Annual Expenses and Income as a Percent of Net Assets
Source: Prospectus, February 1, 1994. Reprinted with the permission of the AARP Investment Program from Scudder.

You don't need to pay more than 0.75% to 1%. Expenses in this range would seem to provide for an adequate—not to say generous—fee to compensate an investment adviser so it can suitably reward the portfolio manager. They also should be adequate to cover the other costs of serving you and other shareholders, including account maintenance, postage, administration, printing costs, legal fees, custodian's fees, accounting fees, telephone charges (including those for calls to the "800" number), and so on.

In contrast with these outlays, from which you derive benefits, funds would have a hard time proving that you also derive a material benefit from 12b-1 fees, which are collected from shareholders to finance distribution expenses.

A fund may charge them if it has adopted a written 12b-1 plan in accordance with Rule 12b-1, which was adopted by the SEC in 1980 under the Investment Company Act of 1940 "despite long-standing doubts about both the benefits . . . and whether the practice is fair to existing shareholders," as its 1980 annual report said.

Many do charge the fee—including, for example, nearly 500 of about 1,200 taxable bond funds or classes of bond fund shares, according to Lipper.

More than 400 other taxable bond funds and share classes have adopted 12b-1 plans but don't yet impose the fees; only around 250 of this universe of funds have not adopted a plan.

While the average 12b-1 fee of taxable bond funds that levy it is about 0.4% of average annual net assets, quite a few charge about double that but are still in compliance with a 1993 National Association of Securities Dealers (NASD) rule that prohibits NASD members from offering or selling shares of funds whose asset-based sales charges (such as 12b-1 fees) exceed 0.75%. Another 0.25% may be levied as a service fee. (The SEC had not imposed a cap, and some funds charged more than 1%.)

The same NASD rule prohibits any member from describing a fund without a front- or back-end load as a no-load fund if its sales-related 12b-1 fee and/or service fee exceeds 0.25%. In August 1994, Barry P. Barbash, director of the SEC's Division of Investment Management, wrote fund companies a letter expressing the belief that the NASD rule should apply to the description of any fund "regardless of whether (it) is associated with an NASD member."

What do funds do with the 12b-1 money, and what could be objectionable about their gathering it for distribution expenses?

As envisaged by the SEC, Rule 12b-1 would permit them to tap fund assets—the assets owned by existing shareholders—to finance activities that are "primarily intended to result in the sale of shares" to new shareholders.

The money could be used for advertising, compensation of dealers and sales personnel, printing and mailing of prospectuses (to prospective investors) and sales literature.

When fund sponsors seek the necessary approvals of independent directors and existing shareholders, they commonly do so on grounds that existing shareholders would enjoy reduced operating expenses if a fund's fixed costs were spread across a larger asset base. It's a plausible point, theoretically, until you realize that fixed costs tend to be a small share of total operating expenses.

They probably overlook mentioning that the investment advisers' fees, which also are based on fund assets, would grow with fund size, too.

Initially, 12b-1 fees were seen by some sponsors of directly marketed funds as a way to make shareholders absorb the costs of advertising and promotion that they incurred because they had no sales forces selling shares.

Sponsors of funds with deferred sales charges seized on 12b-1 plans as an additional source of money for paying sales commissions.

When multiple classes of shares emerged—including B shares with deferred charges—sponsors jumped at the chance to have investors in B shares compensate brokers continually for years.

Whether shareholders benefit by having money taken out of their funds' income to pay for attracting additional investors has not been convincingly demonstrated through significant, widespread reductions in fund costs. Some reductions may have been achieved by new funds that started out with exceptionally high costs spread across small bases.

Whether you benefit by having your broker, banker, or other salesperson offer you market interpretation or advice throughout the years while you own a bond fund—if that's what he or she provides you for a yearly check of 0.25% to 0.5% (or whatever it may be) of your fund's average assets—you would know better than I. Only you can judge whether you'd be better off by having more income and doing without the hand-holding.

If, when looking at a fund's ratio of total expenses to assets in the multi-year financial information table, you suspect that it is too low to be true—or, if when looking at a fund's yield or return, you suspect that it may be too high to be true—you may be right. You may have run into a case in which the investment adviser has waived part or all of a fee or agreed to reimburse part of a fund's expenses, thereby reducing the expense ratio and raising yield and return, as Figure 8.14 illustrates. The table or a footnote should say so.

You need to look at what the fee would have been before the waiver or reimbursement, which should be indicated, because that could be what you would be paying sooner or later when an adviser's offer expires. If it's not clear, check it out by phone.

No-load funds, usually sold directly by distributors affiliated with their management companies, are caught in a paradox as far as expenses are concerned.

On the one hand, they have the incentive to keep their costs low so that they can strengthen their appeal to investors who do their own research and look with favor on funds having lower costs—and, therefore, higher returns.

If they try too hard to keep costs down, however, they may not do enough to draw attention to themselves and attract new investors—unless their

For the Year Ended October 31,					
	1994	*1993*	*1992*	*1991*	*1990*
Ratios to average daily net assets:					
Operating expenses	.60%	.60%	.60%	.57%	.50%
Net investment income	5.43%	5.34%	6.10%	7.29%	7.78%
Decrease reflected in above expense ratios due to waivers/reimbursements	.42%	.21%	.25%	.30%	.44%

FIGURE 8.14   How Funds Disclose When Waivers or Reimbursements Hold Down Annual Expenses
Source: Annual Report, Warburg Pincus Intermediate Maturity Government Fund, October 31, 1994

performance is so impressive that media coverage would make self-promotion superfluous. Since they don't pay brokers a commission to stimulate sales, they can't expect anyone else to do their selling for them.

Discount brokers such as Charles Schwab & Co. sell funds of a number of no-load companies without charging a commission; they receive a share of the revenue from annual fees from the sponsors. They impose charges for transactions in other no-load funds when they don't have such arrangements.

Other Considerations

Other factors also require consideration, including:

REGISTRATION

Make sure the fund is registered to be able to sell its shares in your state. Most probably are.

FUND SIZE

Whether a bond fund is large or small should not matter very much to you—once it's large enough to be listed in your newspaper—with one exception: high-yield funds. Because of the default risk inherent in low-grade investments, a larger fund would appear to be preferable because its portfolio is more likely to contain more issues, providing greater diversification.

Otherwise, the benefits of size may be felt more in operating expenses and, therefore, in yield and rates of return. As a fund grows and fixed costs—those that are the same regardless of fund size—are spread across a larger base, the expense ratio should decline.

MINIMUM INVESTMENT

Each fund you choose should have a minimum initial investment within your reach. Most funds' requirements range from $250 to $3,000. If you don't have enough to open an account with a fund you want, simply save your money in a money market or savings account until you've got it. If a fund with a huge minimum—$100,000 or more—appeals to you, you may be in luck; it may be available via Schwab or another discount broker for a lot less.

IRAS AND OTHER PLANS

If you're investing in an IRA or other retirement plan, find out whether the fund offers such plans and, if so, what the minimum initial investment is; it may be lower than for a taxable account. There may be a $5 or $10 annual maintenance fee. (Sales loads may be waived if your employer has an arrangement to enable you to invest in load funds via payroll withholding.)

GOOD SERVICE

Mutual fund investing is a long-term proposition. If you're going to live with the fund(s) you choose, you're going to want to make sure that you get good service: prompt response to your requests for information or literature, patient explanations on the telephone, accurate handling of your instructions and of recordkeeping, prompt and clear statements.

EXCHANGE PRIVILEGE

Your first consideration should be to choose a fund that is likely to help you to realize your investment goals. If a bond fund gives you the opportunity to switch to or from a money market or equity fund in the same complex, so much the better. Remember, though, that a switch out of a bond (or equity) fund is a transaction that may result in a taxable capital gain unless you're doing it in a tax-deferred account.

AUTOMATIC INVESTMENT/WITHDRAWAL PLANS

A number of funds make it convenient for investors to invest their money, or take it out, by arranging to debit or credit their bank accounts. These arrangements are especially desirable for people who invest by dollar-cost averaging and those who wish to take cash distributions on a regular basis for living expenses.

Making Your Selection

If one fund survives your screening as the most promising prospect for you—high total return and low volatility over a 5-year period, reasonably stable income, low cost, good service (or whatever your personal preferences may be)—you're ready to invest.

If two seem to be equally attractive on the basis of performance, volatility, and costs, you may want to lean toward the one that appears to provide better service and more candid, informative reports. Possibly—but not necessarily—it could be the fund that's in a family that has an equity fund whose shares you already may own.

If there are too few—or even no—funds with 5-year records in the category you're considering, you can screen the funds with 3-year records to find the one most likely to satisfy you. Alternatively, you might turn to another investment objective category with similar investment objectives.

There are no guarantees about historical performance for any period—whether 3, 5, or X years—as you know. What you try to do is look for superior performance over a period long enough to have embraced both favorable and unfavorable market environments—and then keep your fingers crossed that superior performance will continue as long as you own the shares.

CHAPTER 9

Investing in Bond Funds and Managing Your Investments

Investing in your first bond fund is easy, once you've screened a list of prospects as suggested in Chapter 8 and made a selection on your own or accepted the recommendation of a broker or adviser.

It requires a few decisions and a form or two, regardless of whether you're dealing directly with the fund company or indirectly through a securities dealer. Of course, if you're investing in a fund offered under your employer's 401(k) plan, you may need to make even fewer decisions because you have fewer choices.

While you may prefer to handle the purchase in person in your community—perhaps with someone you know—you may find it more rewarding to do business with a no-load fund company, which may not have an office in your community. The higher returns that you should earn by having more of your money working for you should make it worthwhile over time to overcome any uneasiness about engaging in transactions by mail with strangers miles away. And although the people you speak with when you dial the funds' 800 numbers can't give you investment advice, they should be able to answer any questions that you may have as you go through the forms.

Forms

If you're dealing directly with the fund, be sure to obtain the proper form(s) when you ask for the fund's prospectus and latest report to shareholders. It'll avoid the need to call again and lose time.

If you're opening a regular taxable or tax-exempt account, one form will do. If you're opening an IRA account and want to invest fresh money in it, you'll need an additional form.

If you're transferring money from an existing IRA and want the new fund's sponsor to ask the other trustee for your money, you'll need a different form. If you're moving the money yourself, remember that IRS allows you only 60 days to do so. (If you're rolling over a lump-sum distribution from a qualified retirement plan, you avoid withholding tax complications by having your plan's administrator transfer the distribution directly to an IRA's trustee.)

Decisions
How Much to Invest

If you're making a one-time investment of the minimum initial amount required by the fund, your decision of how much to invest is made for you. Remember that the minimum for an IRA may be lower than that for a taxable or tax-exempt account.

If you want to invest on a regular basis at whatever frequency suits you, and if you only want to invest the minimum amount required for subsequent investments, the decision of how much to invest is made for you, too. (Again, the minimum for an IRA may be lower.) You only need to choose the frequency.

In this case, you may wish to take advantage of the opportunity to have the fund company take care of the investment for you by arranging for a transfer directly from your bank account. Since it earns a fee for managing your money, it'll be glad to save you the chore of making out a check every so often.

If you want to invest more than the minimum, you should consider whether to invest it all at once or gradually.

If it's not really a lot of money, you may want to do it in four or five equal installments—perhaps monthly. But, if a really large sum is involved— from an inheritance, gift, distribution from an employer's plan, or other source—and especially if you're investing in a more volatile fund, it may be prudent to buy shares over time.

Under these circumstances, you may want to follow the practice known as dollar-cost averaging, which involves investing a certain amount at regular intervals over a longer period to avoid the risk of putting down a large sum just before an unpredictable rise in interest rates—and drop in bond prices. (To avoid withholding tax if you want to roll over a lump sum tax-free from an employer's savings or retirement plan to an IRA but not invest it all at once, move the money into an IRA account in a money market mutual fund first, then feed it into bond and equity funds gradually.)

Dollar-cost averaging is a disciplined way to invest in more volatile bond (or stock) funds regardless of whether the bond (or stock) market is up or down. It avoids the possibility of your responding emotionally to current market conditions—or to comments you read or hear about them—or of your being tempted to try to forecast interest rates.

When share prices are higher, you buy fewer shares; when they're lower—and, thus, when you may hear advice that you should get out of the market—you buy more instead. If you've made a good fund choice and we're in a period of strong economic expansion and rising interest rates, dollar-cost averaging may help you to hold down the average cost of your shares in the long run. Thus, it would result in your owning more shares than the same total investment might have bought at the start.

Cash Distributions versus Reinvestment

Two of the boxes you have to check on the application form for a regular taxable or tax-exempt fund enable you to indicate whether you want to take distributions of income dividends and/or any capital gains realized by the fund or to reinvest the money in additional shares.

If you're investing in a bond fund as part of your strategy to build capital, the decision should be easy: You indicate that you want to reinvest.

If you need the cash, you can ask for income dividends to be paid to you at the monthly or quarterly intervals offered by the fund. Be prepared for the dividends to fluctuate as interest rates fluctuate—especially for the possibility that your checks will shrink when interest rates drop, as happened in recent years. It's more likely to happen, you'll recall, with short-term funds than with long-term funds, whose dividend streams tend to hold up better.

While lower dividend checks may be disappointing, remember that lower interest rates are usually a reflection of lower inflation. When inflation is high, interest rates are higher, too, but your *real* (inflation-adjusted) income—your purchasing power—may not be higher at all.

Try to resist asking for capital gains distributions to be paid to you, too. During periods when funds realize net capital gains—perhaps when bond prices rise as interest rates decline—you would deprive yourself of the chance to benefit from the growth of your principal by taking some of the money out.

Steady Cash Plus Growth

If you need steady current income but want to participate in a fund's growth at least to a limited extent, you may want to refrain from requesting dividend distributions in cash and take a different approach.

Assuming that you've not fallen for a fund that tries to stabilize distributions by pursuing risky option techniques and/or returning some of your principal to supplement interest income, you may want to do the following: Ask to have all dividends and any capital gains reinvested when they are distributed, but then sell enough shares to provide the cash you need—at a rate below the fund's distribution rate—and let the rest continue to earn income for you.

This should not be difficult to do. Just determine how much cash you could get regularly if you took an amount a bit less than the fund's recent yield. If, for example, the fund has had a net investment income of 7% and you've invested $10,000, you might decide to take 6%, or $600 a year. You'd ask for monthly checks of $50, and the fund would sell the requisite number of shares to provide the money. When prices are higher, fewer would have to be sold, of course, than when prices are lower.

If the fund's monthly dividend distributions exceed $50, you would have more money from interest income remaining invested in additional shares and earning income for you.

If and when monthly distributions should fall below $50, you might not have to sell more shares than the dividend distribution had just bought. A drop in income indicating that interest rates had fallen would mean that bond prices are higher. Presumably, your fund's NAV would be higher, too.

Using this approach, you should have a stable payout—a bit less than you would have had by receiving all income in cash—but, over time, a growing principal.

Unfortunately, of course, it would involve additional bookkeeping for income tax purposes to keep track of small capital gains or losses resulting from sales, but it may prove to be worthwhile.

Managing Your Investment: Forms and Records
Confirmation Statements

After you have made your first investment, you'll get a confirmation statement advising you of how many shares you bought at what price. Be sure to check it for accuracy and start a file for the important documents pertaining to your account, including photocopies of the forms you filled out when you opened it.

You probably will get similar confirmation statements every time you make additional investments, except for the automatic reinvestment of income and capital gains distributions.

Periodic Statements

Every three months, you should get a statement that recapitulates what you invested (or redeemed) in the period just ended and itemizes the distributions that you have had credited to your account.

It's important to keep *all* of your statements. You'll need them to properly determine the costs of your shares so that you can calculate the taxable short- and long-term capital gains that you may have realized (or capital losses that you may have suffered) when you redeemed some or all of your shares. They also will help you to figure out how well your investment has performed.

Form 1099-DIV

If yours is a regular account, the fund company (or broker or whoever you're dealing with) will send you this IRS form at the end of every January to report the taxable income and capital gains distributions credited to your account so that you, in turn, can report them on your income tax returns. It doesn't matter whether you got the distributions in cash or reinvested them.

Form 1099B

This is the form you are sent that reports the proceeds from sales of shares in regular taxable or tax-exempt accounts. To help you fill out your tax return properly, you'll need to calculate what the shares cost you.

Remember that sales of shares may result in taxable gains or in losses regardless of whether you received a check for the proceeds, exchanged the shares for shares of another fund in the same fund family, or took advantage of the privilege to write a check on your bond fund account.

Average Cost Statement

To help shareholders to fill out their tax forms, some fund companies provide yearly statements giving the average cost of shares redeemed in an account in the previous year. They usually use the average cost single category method, one of four that the IRS permits you to calculate the cost basis of redeemed shares so that you can determine your capital gains or losses.

If you use one of the other three methods, you probably are on your own. (Either way, you ought to get a free copy of Publication 564, "Mutual Fund Distributions," from your nearest IRS office. It tells you all you want to know about the subject.)

Managing Your Investment: Monitoring Performance

You should not need to race for your newspaper each day to see how your bond fund did the day before, although, of course, you might wish to see how your fund was affected if the bond market had an exceptional up or down day. If you've chosen well and are invested for several years, you should not have to worry about the negligible changes in NAV that occur on most days.

Periodic Review

Except in unusual circumstances—whether in your life, in the market, or at the fund—it ought to be sufficient for you to check on its performance every three months, when new Lipper (or other) data are issued. You also will want to study the report to shareholders that you get from the fund itself every three or six months.

By looking up the Lipper total return data soon after the end of a calendar quarter in *Barron's, The Wall Street Journal,* or one of the other sources mentioned in the last chapter, you will see how the fund performed and how its performance compared with the average of funds in its category.

While, naturally, you want to know whether your fund was up or down—and by how much—after reinvested dividends are taken into account, you also need to see whether its performance was an achievement or a disappointment when market conditions are taken into consideration. You do that by comparing it not only with other funds having similar investment objectives but also with bond market indexes.

Try to check on how your fund's performance compared with the total return of a relevant bond price index that can serve as a benchmark, preferably one designated as appropriate for such evaluation by the fund management itself for the SEC-mandated line graph in the prospectus or annual report.

As the SEC commented in making the case for using an index in this way, "The index comparison requirement is designed to show how much value the management of the fund added by showing whether the fund 'out-performed' or 'under-performed' the market, and not so much whether one fund 'out-performed' another. A fund could underperform a relevant market, while nevertheless comparing favorably with its peers."

When you see that line graph in the fund's literature, it will give you a quick impression of whether the fund is doing as well as could be expected—of whether the manager is adding value. (Since the SEC stipulates that the fund line in the graph must reflect all fund expenses, sales loads, and any account fees, you can quickly appreciate the difference such charges can make, if you're in a load fund.)

In between appearances of the line graph in mailings from your fund, you can look up the index data themselves in places such as *Morningstar Mutual Funds,* which carries several for the government, corporate (investment-grade and high-yield), municipal, and world bond markets as well as the Lehman Brothers Aggregate Index for the total U.S. investment-grade bond market.

If you can't get your hands on these sources, you can do the next best thing by looking up the Lipper performance data for a fund that tracks a relevant bond index, if one is available. Vanguard, which has more bond index funds than any other firm, offers not only the Total Bond Market Portfolio, which tries to match the Aggregate Index, but also the Short-Term Bond, Intermediate-Term Bond, and Long-Term Bond Portfolios, which seek to match the investment performance of the corresponding Lehman Government/Corporate Indexes.

If your fund's total return has exceeded the average of its category and at least come close to matching the relevant index—on an annual basis, say, within 0.5% of the index's return to allow for an acceptable fund expense ratio—you might regard its performance as satisfactory for the period, whether the fund was up or down. And you can turn your attention to other things.

If your fund's total return exceeded its category and index by a mile, control your euphoria. It could be that the manager has invested in securities that are too risky for you—although not necessarily beyond the limits indicated in some opaque paragraph in the prospectus—and you may want to phone the fund to find out. Do the unusual: Ask why a fund has been performing so well.

If, however, your fund significantly underperformed—whether lagging when the market is up or dropping more when the market is down—you ought to find out why. You can call the fund company for an explanation or wait for the next fund report to shareholders. You also may want to look up the fund in *Morningstar* or *The Value Line Mutual Fund Survey* to learn whether their analysts commented on the fund recently.

If the explanations seem reasonable, you may not have a need for concern. Just wait to see what the next quarter will bring. If you have the time and interest—and if you have invested a significant share of your assets in the fund—you may want to be alert to how it performs on a monthly basis, calling up the fund company for its total return. (Unless you're taking distributions of your dividends, figuring changes in the NAV isn't enough.)

Should the next quarterly data show that the fund continues to lag the average of its peers, you should contact the fund company again and, if the lag is significant and the explanation inadequate, you may want to start thinking about a switch—including the possible income tax consequences, if you have an unrealized capital gain.

Sooner or later, you'll get your hands on the shareholder report. Reading it is a must. Look for the portfolio manager's explanation as to why the fund performed as it did in the previous quarter or half year and what significant portfolio changes, if any, may have been made or planned.

The manager may offer commentary on the bond market, which may be an interesting and relevant complement to the description of the fund's performance and strategy. But it is no substitute for the latter. While more fund managements may offer useful accounts now than in earlier years, thanks to the SEC's requirement of an annual management discussion of fund performance, some still seem to try to get away with offering too little information about the fund and too much interesting but less helpful commentary on the overall market.

Look at the tables or charts that show the composition of the fund's portfolio according to maturity, credit quality, exposure to prepayment risk (such as Ginnie Maes), and foreign issuers. See what the report says about the portfolio's duration as well as about any other characteristics that give you an insight as to whether the fund is invested as you expected it to be. And glance at the new line graph when it appears.

Unless you're curious—or suspect that the fund may be engaging in speculative investment practices that you are wary of—you probably won't need to take time to study the fund's portfolio. If it is invested only in "plain vanilla" government or corporate securities, you may not be sufficiently familiar with them to be able to second-guess the manager. If he or she has bought other types of securities for the fund in significant volumes, the report should mention them.

News of Changes

In between reports, keep your eyes peeled for announcements of possible significance, such as changes in investment objective, investment policy, investment adviser, portfolio manager, sales load policy, or annual management or other expenses. The news may come to you in the form of letters from the fund, stickers intended to update its current prospectus, or articles in the press or newsletters.

Word also may come in proxy statements in which you are asked to vote for proposed changes approved by the board of directors. Consider these seriously—especially proposals to adopt a 12b-1 plan that would allow the fund to impose a 12b-1 fee that would cut into your yield and total return—and vote as you think would best serve your interest when you have the opportunity.

Deciding When to Redeem

Sooner or later, the time will probably come when you will want or have to redeem your shares in a bond fund and move the money to another fund—in the same fund family or another—or take the money out. Following are some of the possible reasons.

Wrong Category

You're in a fund that's a perfectly well-managed fund but you realize that its investment objective and policy are not in harmony with your own.

It may be that the fund is too risky for you because its duration is too long, its average credit quality is too low, or some other attribute is inappropriate.

It may be that it's a taxable fund and you realize that you'd be better off in one that's tax-exempt. Or vice versa.

Or it may be the fund isn't risky enough and, therefore, not likely to provide you the return you are seeking. This could be because its duration is too short, for example, or because it's concentrated in U.S. Treasury securities when you don't mind the higher—but acceptable—risk of quality corporate issues.

Whatever the case, the sooner you find out that the category is wrong, the better off you should be if you switch to one that is more appropriate.

Underperformance

The first time you notice that your fund's total return has lagged those of its category's average and of a relevant index for a calendar quarter, you may be tempted to switch out of it, unless the notion occurred to you even sooner.

If you had bought it because of above-average performance, it may regain its relative position and patience may be in order.

But how much patience? How long do you give a manager, who presumably remains in charge, the benefit of the doubt?

There are no hard and fast rules. There is no way to predict if or when a fund can recover. Maybe you should wait a couple of quarters. But if the fund continues to lag its group for three or four quarters, determine why. If maturity/duration or credit quality differences or some other understandable factors don't explain the lag, look for an alternative.

Go through the process that led you to choose the fund to see whether another seems a stronger candidate now and move out after you've found one—provided the tax consequences, if any, are tolerable. You don't want to risk falling short of *your* objective.

Changed Circumstances

Even if a fund's performance continues to excel year after year, you may have to start redeeming sooner or later because changes in your circumstances call for redemptions.

As you get older and your investment horizon gets shorter, you probably will want to take less risk than you could afford when you were younger. This would mean switching from a long-term to an intermediate-term fund, from an intermediate-term to a short-term fund, or from a short-term fund to a money market fund.

It also could mean switching from a taxable or tax-exempt fund concentrated in medium or lower credit quality bonds to one that's in higher quality issues, but not necessarily switching from one in high quality corporates to Treasuries.

If you are in a tax-exempt fund, you also may want to consider switching to a taxable fund in case you drop to a lower income tax bracket in retirement.

Changes at the Fund

If there are changes at a fund—such as a long-time portfolio manager being replaced by an unseasoned one who fails to inspire your confidence, expenses and/or loads being increased, investment objectives being changed, investment policies being made too risky—you may have cause to get out.

Investing in Additional Funds

Should you own shares in two or more bond funds?

It's not at all unrealistic to think of the possibility—indeed, the desirability—if you have enough money to invest.

You may want a taxable fund for an IRA, 401(k), or other tax-deferred account and a tax-exempt fund outside the tax-advantaged plan. Or you may want to diversify your bond fund holdings according to maturities (a short- and a long-term fund, say) or credit risk (a Treasury and a high-yield fund). Or you may want some international exposure, adding a world income fund to your domestic bond fund.

Just select the categories that you feel are suitable and apply the criteria, allocating money in proportions that seem right. You can always change them.

If you want to invest in more than one bond fund, it would be convenient, of course, to be in funds that are in the same fund complex. You may be lucky and indeed find the most promising candidates from two categories in the same family. But when you don't and have to choose between performance and convenience, give the nod to performance.

May you find your choices rewarding and may you enjoy your investments in good health!

APPENDIX A

Fund Families

To help you to obtain prospectuses and shareholder reports from fund families whose bond funds interest you, here is a list of the names and telephone numbers for complexes sponsoring one or more funds that have been in operation for at least five years. Virtually all of them have toll-free 800 numbers.

AARP	800–322–2282
AIM	800–347–4246
Advantage	800–523–5903
Alliance	800–227–4618
American Capital	800–421–5666
American Funds	800–421–4120
Babson	800–422–2766
Benham	800–331–8331
Colonial	800–225–2365
Columbia	800–547–1707
Dean Witter	800–869–3863
Delaware	800–523–4640
Dodge & Cox	800–621–3979
Dreyfus	800–782–6620
Eaton Vance	800–225–6265
Federated	800–245–2423
Fidelity	800–544–8888
Flagship	800–227–4648
Flex-Funds	800–325–FLEX

Fortis	800–800–2638
Founders	800–525–2440
Franklin	800–342–5236
G.T. Global	800–824–1580
John Hancock	800–225–5291
Harbor	800–422–1050
Heartland	800–432–7856
INVESCO	800–525–8085
Janus	800–525–8983
Kemper	800–621–1048
Keystone	800–343–2898
Legg Mason	800–368–2558
Lexington	800–526–0057
Loomis Sayles	800–633–3330
Lord Abbett	800–874–3733
Mackenzie	800–456–5111
MainStay	800–522–4202
Managers	800–835–3879
Massachusetts Financial	800–637–2929
Merrill Lynch	800-MER-FUND
MetLife-State Street	800–531–0131
Neuberger & Berman	800–877–9700
New England	800–225–5478
Nicholas	414–272–6133
Northeast Investors	800–225–6704
John Nuveen	800–621–7227
Oppenheimer	800–525–7048
Overland	800–552–9612
PIMCO	800–800–0952
Pacific Horizon	800–332–3863
PaineWebber	800–647–1568
Phoenix	800–243–4361
Pioneer	800–225–6292
Piper Capital	800–866–7778
T. Rowe Price	800–638–5660
Prudential	800–225–1852
Putnam	800–225–1581
Rochester	716–383–1300
Rushmore	800–621–7874
SEI	800-DIAL-SEI
SIT	800–332–5580
SAFECO	800–426–6730
Charles Schwab	800-2NO-LOAD

Scudder	800–225–2470
Seligman	800–221–7844
Smith Barney	800–EARNS–IT
Stagecoach	800–222–8222
State Street	800–531–0131
SteinRoe	800–338–2550
Strong	800–368–1030
Twentieth Century	800–345–2021
USAA	800–382–8722
UST	800–233–1136
United Funds	800–366–5465
Value Line	800–223–0818
Vanguard	800–276–7231
Vista	800–64-VISTA
Voyageur	800–553–2143
Warburg Pincus	800–257–5614
William Penn	800–523–8440
Wright	800–888–9471

APPENDIX B

Useful Addresses

For Complaints about Mutual Funds

Division of Investment Management
U.S. Securities and Exchange Commission
450 Fifth Street, NW
Washington, DC 20549

For Complaints about Sales Practices

Advertising/Investment Companies Regulation Dept.
National Association of Securities Dealers
1735 K Street, NW
Washington, DC 20006

Glossary*

Average Net Assets: The SEC stipulates that average net assets, when used as the divisor for calculating yearly expense and net investment income ratios for a prospectus' 10-year table of condensed financial information, must be computed on the basis of values determined no less frequently than the end of each month.

Balanced Fund: One that has multiple objectives of income, stability of capital, and possible growth of capital. A fund that is called balanced is required by the SEC to maintain at least 25% of the value of its assets in debt securities and/or preferred stock.

Bond: A common term for a debt security (which more properly may be called something else, such as note or debenture) that is issued by a unit of government or a corporation to an investor from whom it borrows money. It obligates the issuer to repay the loan on a stated maturity date, which may be as many as 30 or more years away, and to pay interest at a fixed rate at regular—usually six-month—intervals until then.

Bond Market: The diffuse, electronically connected network of trading rooms, securities exchanges, brokers, and dealers in which new bond issues are bought/sold (primary market) and outstanding issues are traded (secondary market). While a number of bond issues are listed and traded on stock exchanges, by far the larger share of transactions take place in the over-the-counter market. Bond funds buy

---

*Definitions are generally phrased in a mutual fund context, although many of the terms have wider application.

in both the primary and secondary markets, depending on their needs and bonds' availability.

Bond Market Risk: *See* **Interest Rate Risk.**

Bond Rating: The rating of corporate and municipal bonds according to their relative investment qualities, performed by rating services such as Moody's Investors Service and Standard & Poor's Corporation. It is designed to provide investors a simple way of selecting bonds according to their levels of credit risk. The two principal rating firms use similar symbols to indicate gradations of quality: Aaa, Aa, A, Baa, Ba, B, Caa, Ca, and C (Moody's) and AAA, AA, A, BBB, BB, B, CCC, CC, C, and D (Standard & Poor's). When mutual funds state the quality levels of bonds that they seek to buy, or to avoid, their investment objectives or policies often are expressed in terms of the ratings of bonds that are preferred, acceptable, or unacceptable. Unrated bonds, some of which are held by bond funds, do not necessarily lack quality; it could be that the corporations or governmental units that issued them did not apply for ratings for one reason or another. *See also* **High Grade, High Yield,** and **Investment-Grade Bond.**

Broker: A person or firm engaged in the business of effecting purchases and sales of securities for the accounts of others. If a fund uses a broker affiliated with the fund, it must report the amount of brokerage commissions paid to the firm.

Call: The provision in a bond indenture by which the issuer reserves the right to repay the principal of all or part of an issue prior to maturity. Borrowers find it advantageous or necessary to exercise this option when excess cash flow enables them to cut their debt and borrowing costs, when they wish to sell assets pledged as collateral, when sinking fund provisions require gradual retirement of an issue, or when other circumstances warrant. The call clause specifies the price that the issuer will pay holders. Usually the call price exceeds the face value, inasmuch as it includes a call premium—which declines as a bond approaches maturity—to partially compensate bondholders for depriving them of income they had counted on.

Call Protection: The provision of a callable bond assuring purchasers, such as bond fund portfolio managers, that it cannot be called during a specified period, such as the first ten years after it was issued. A portfolio manager may, of course, try to maximize call protection by maximizing ownership of noncallable bonds.

Call Risk: The risk that a callable bond with a high coupon rate will be called when interest rates come down before its maturity, depriving its owner of expected future income.

Capital Gains Distribution: The distribution to a mutual fund's shareholders of net long-term capital gains realized on the sales of its portfolio securities. A 1970 amendment to the Investment Company Act of 1940 prohibits funds from making them more than once a year except by SEC rule.

Certificate of Deposit (CD):   A form of time deposit at a commercial bank or thrift institution, such as a savings bank or savings and loan association, which has a specific maturity that may range from three months to five years. If withdrawn before the maturity date, a CD is subject to an interest penalty. CDs issued in very large denominations may be in a form that permits their sale or transfer prior to maturity. Negotiable CDs are commonly held by money market mutual funds.

Convertible Bond: A corporate debt obligation that may be exchanged for a specified number of shares of a company's common stock. When the market value of the stock rises above the price at which conversion would be advantageous, the bond's price rises accordingly. When the price of the stock falls, the value of the bond is increasingly determined by the interest it pays, and its drop is cushioned by the yield.

Contingent Deferred Sales Load: *See* **Deferred Sales Load.**

Corporate Bond: A bond issued by a corporation. Unlike a share of common stock, which represents ownership in a corporation—and, therefore, a proportionate share of its profits—a bond represents its debt. A corporation must pay interest to its bondholders before paying dividends to its stockholders. In the event of a company's failure, bondholders are accorded preferential status over stockholders in the division of its assets. A corporate bond may be secured by assets (such as a mortgage bond, which is secured by property) or unsecured (known as a debenture). To owners of secured bonds, a corporation's expected earning power matters even more than collateral, assuring them of timely interest and principal payments. To owners of unsecured bonds, of course, earning power is everything.

Coupon Rate: The annual rate of interest that a bond pays (usually in semiannual installments) as specified on the bond.

Credit Quality: The attribute of a bond reflecting the risk that its issuer will default on interest or principal payments, which may or may not be acceptable to a given bond fund or other investor. While a rating assigned by a rating service may correctly indicate a bond's credit quality, the investment adviser of a well-managed bond fund will go beyond the rating and do its own research to ascertain a bond's investment merit—and to assess whether a bond is fairly priced. *See also* **Bond Rating.**

Credit Risk: The risk that a bond's issuer will default.

Current Yield: *See* **Yield.**

Custodian: A company—usually a commercial bank—that is qualified to keep custody of a fund's securities and other assets, as required by the Investment Company Act.

Dealer: A firm or individual engaged in the business of buying or selling securities on its/his/her behalf. In principal transactions, a dealer earns a dealer markup. When a fund has dealings with an affiliated dealer, it must say so.

Default: The failure of a bond's issuer to pay interest or repay principal.

Deferred Sales Load: A sales charge deducted from the proceeds when shareholders of some funds or of Class B shares of multiple class funds redeem their shares within a specific period of years following purchase. It is calculated as a percentage of the original purchase price or of redemption proceeds and declines annually until it is eliminated. Shares to which a deferred sales load is applied usually are encumbered by Rule 12b-1 distribution fees (*See* **12b-1 Fees**) to compensate brokers and to finance other costs. Funds imposing this load must report to the SEC how much they collect and, if they share the revenue with underwriters, dealers, or others, how much they retain.

Derivatives: A term generally applied to an instrument whose value is based on—or derived from—an index, interest rate, currency exchange rate, security, commodity, or other asset. Derivatives may be used by mutual funds or other investors to hedge interest rate and currency risks, to substitute for direct investment in underlying instruments, and to enhance returns. Some, such as put and call options, futures, and currency forward contracts, have been in common use for years. Others, introduced more recently, magnified the exposure to risk of a small minority of funds—notably some money market and short-term government bond funds that were presumed, as a group, to be low-risk vehicles—and caused losses when the funds were caught owning them during the acceleration of interest rates in 1994.

Diversification: The policy of reducing one's vulnerability to loss by investing in a variety of financial and nonfinancial assets having different characteristics and involving different risks. More narrowly, the policy of having one's financial assets divided among different securities types (such as stocks and bonds) and, within securities classes, among issuers, industries, and/or geographic regions to reduce investment risk. For mutual funds, the Investment Company Act has a specific definition: It regards a fund as diversified if no single issuer of securities included among those representing at least 75% of its total assets accounts for over 5% of the total, and if the securities of any single issuer do not account for more than 10% of that issuer's outstanding voting securities. If a fund does not meet this definition, it's "nondiversified" in the eyes of the law. Whichever it is, every fund must state it at the front of its prospectus. In addition, every fund must meet similar diversification requirements under Subchapter M of the Internal Revenue Code to qualify as a regulated investment company so that it won't be subject to income tax.

Dividend: The payment to a fund's shareholders of the net investment income earned from interest and dividends on the money market instruments, bonds, and stocks in its portfolio. It excludes short- and long-term capital gains realized from sales of securities. If a distribution includes money from any source other than net investment income—such as option income or the return of a shareholder's capital—the Investment Company Act requires a fund to disclose it. Although bonds' issuers typically pay interest semiannually, bond funds commonly distribute dividends monthly or quarterly. *See also* **Capital Gains Distribution.**

Dollar-Cost Averaging: The practice of investing a fixed amount of money in a fund at regular intervals (such as monthly or quarterly) regardless of market conditions. It is intended to thwart the temptation to invest too much during the euphoria of a booming market or to sell in panic during a market slide. On the assumption that a fund is well chosen, buying more shares when prices are lower and fewer shares when prices are higher should result in a lower average cost per share if the discipline is maintained over time.

Duration: The most meaningful indicator of a bond fund's (or other bond portfolio's) sensitivity to interest rate changes. It reflects interest and principal payments to bond holders, not principal repayments alone. The duration of a bond is the weighted average of the years that it will take for the discounted present values of its expected interest and principal payments to equal its current market value. The duration of a bond portfolio is the weighted average of the durations of the bonds it holds. For securities such as zero-coupon obligations, which involve no payments of any kind until maturity, duration equals maturity. For all others, duration will always be shorter than maturity. A low-yield bond has a longer duration than a high-yield bond of identical maturity because interest payments account for a smaller percent of the total of its expected cash flows. Prices of bonds of longer duration are more sensitive to changes in interest rates than those of bonds of shorter duration; therefore, they rise and fall more when interest rates fall and rise.

Event Risk: The risk that the issuer of an outstanding bond issue may become unable to pay interest or to repay principal because of an event, such as an acquisition that encumbers a corporation with too much additional debt.

Exchange Fee: A fee imposed by some funds for exercise of the exchange privilege.

Exchange Privilege: The option that mutual fund families accord their share-holders, enabling them to redeem shares of one of their funds and invest the proceeds in another with a different investment objective—a transaction that, except for tax-sheltered accounts, may result in a taxable capital gain or in a capital loss. The privilege may be limited to a stated number per year to prevent excessive trading, which can interfere with portfolio management and add to a fund's ex-penses—and is, of course, inconsistent with the long-term nature of mutual fund investing.

Expense Ratio: A fund's total operating expenses per share—a management fee, possibly a 12b-1 fee, and other expenses—divided by average net assets per share. The figure must be prominently shown in a fund's prospectus and stated in both annual and semiannual reports. For a well-managed fund, it usually need not run higher than 1% and could be as low as 0.5% or lower. Note: A ratio may have been reduced because some fees are being temporarily waived or reim-bursed by the investment adviser. In that case, a footnote should say so to ensure that you would not be misled into thinking that a fund is certain to be a low-cost fund.

FHA-Insured Mortgages: Mortgages insured by the Federal Housing Admin-istration, established in 1934 and now a unit of the Department of Housing and Urban Development.

Face Value: The principal amount an issuer will repay when redeeming a bond at maturity. Also known as par.

Family of Funds: Two or more mutual funds that share the same investment adviser or principal underwriter, and hold themselves out to investors as being related. Also referred to as a fund complex.

Fannie Mae: *See* **Federal National Mortgage Association.**

Federal Agency Securities: The collective term for securities issued by the two broad categories of federal agencies—those owned by the federal government and those sponsored by it but owned privately—to raise capital for specific sectors of the economy such as housing, agriculture, and education in accordance with public policy.

Federal Home Loan Mortgage Corporation (FHLMC, or Freddie Mac): Established by Congress in 1970 to increase the availability of credit for home buyers. It does this by buying mortgages—overwhelmingly conventional mortgages, but also loans insured or guaranteed by the FHA or VA, respectively—from lending institutions so that the lenders can use the funds to make new mortgages. FHLMC replenishes its cash by issuing mortgage-backed securities, called Mortgage Participation Certificates, or PCs, which it guarantees. With approval of the Financial Institutions Reform, Recovery and Enforcement Act of 1989—sometimes called the "thrift industry bailout bill"—Freddie Mac's capital structure was reorganized and a class of voting common stock was created for distribution to the public. The shares are now traded on stock exchanges. *See also* **Mortgage-Backed Securities.**

Federal National Mortgage Association (FNMA, or Fannie Mae):   Chartered by the federal government in 1938 but a stockholder-owned corporation since 1970, it has helped to provide credit for low- and middle-income home buyers by raising funds in securities markets. FNMA buys mortgages, primarily conventional, from mortgage companies, savings and loan associations, commercial banks, credit unions, and other institutions that originate them. To finance the acquisition of those it retains in its portfolio, FNMA borrows money by issuing unsecured bonds. It packages the other mortgages into pools and issues its own mortgage-backed securities, with its guarantee of timely interest and principal payments, to other investors. *See also* **Mortgage-Backed Securities.**

Federal Open Market Committee (FOMC):   The committee that sets the objectives for the Federal Reserve System's conduct of monetary policy, devises strategies, and oversees open market operations (that is, the buying and selling of Treasury securities to influence the level of bank reserves). Its twelve members include the seven members of the System's Board of Governors, the president of the Federal Reserve Bank of New York, and, on a rotating basis, the presidents of four of the remaining eleven FR Banks. *See also* **Monetary Policy.**

Fiscal Policy: Federal government policy regarding taxation and expenditure. The deficits it has produced have led to an increase in borrowing through the sale of federal debt securities to individual and institutional investors—including bond funds—and to foreign purchasers.

Fixed Income Securities: Bonds and preferred stocks. Although the interest and dividends they pay, respectively, are fixed in amounts, their market values are not. They fluctuate and, therefore, so do their yields. Bonds return to their par value at maturity.

Freddie Mac: *See* **Federal Home Loan Mortgage Corporation.**

Front-End Sales Load: *See* **Sales Charge.**

Fundamental Policy: Any investment or other policy of a mutual fund that may not be changed without approval of a majority of the fund's outstanding voting securities.

General Obligation Bond: A class of municipal bonds that is supported by the taxing power of the state or local government that issues them.

Ginnie Mae: *See* **Government National Mortgage Association.**

Government National Mortgage Association (GNMA, or Ginnie Mae): Established in 1968 as a government corporation within the Department of Housing and Urban Development to increase liquidity in the secondary market for government-backed mortgages by attracting new, nontraditional sources of capital for residential loans. Since 1970, when it pioneered the "pass-through" mortgage-backed security, its principal activity has been its MBS guarantee program. Issued by some 1,200 approved private lending institutions, collateralized by FHA-insured and VA-guaranteed mortgages, and given the backing of the full faith and credit of the United States upon receiving Ginnie Mae's approval, its certificates are the most widely held and most widely traded MBS in the world. At times the GNMA program provides more than 90% of all the money going into FHA- and VA-backed home loans. *See also* **Mortgage-Backed Securities.**

High-Grade Bond: A bond receiving one of the two highest ratings: Aaa or Aa from Moody's, AAA or AA from Standard & Poor's.

High-Yield Bond: Common term for a speculative bond, sometimes called a junk bond. Its purchasers demand a *relatively* high rate of interest—sometimes as much as 4% to 5% or more above those of Treasury securities of comparable maturity—to compensate them for the higher probability of default that such a bond entails. (During periods of "tight" money even Treasury securities' yields are *absolutely* high.) The low credit quality of these bonds is indicated in the ratings they are given by rating services: Ba or lower by Moody's, BB or lower by Standard & Poor's. The ratings may be assigned at the time issues are new or, in cases of older issues—including "fallen angels" that once were of high quality—when companies' financial problems or restructuring influence the services to downgrade their securities. Funds invested in high-yield bonds have performed well at times, poorly at other times.

Illiquid Asset: An asset that a mutual fund cannot dispose of in the ordinary course of business within seven days at approximately the value at which the fund has valued the instrument. Because mutual fund portfolios must be highly liquid to enable them always to meet investors' redemption requests within seven days, the SEC limits money market funds' investments in illiquid assets to 10% of assets and other funds' to 15% of assets. Generally, the ultimate determination of whether a particular mutual fund asset is illiquid is up to a fund's board.

Income Fund: A fund that has as its principal objective the production of current income primarily through investment in debt obligations—usually, a bond fund.

Indenture: The contract between the issuer of a bond and its owners. It covers interest and principal payments, maturity, call provisions, and other terms.

Individual Retirement Account (IRA): A vehicle that enables an individual to save or invest a portion of earned income for his or her retirement in an eligible institution (such as a mutual fund) on a tax-deferred basis, supplementing another retirement plan in which he or she may participate. Depending on current law, annual contributions to an IRA may or may not be deductible from currently taxable income. If deductible, they become taxable—along with investment income that is earned while sheltered from current income tax—when distributed.

Interest Rate Risk: The risk that the prices of outstanding bonds or bond fund shares will fall when interest rates rise. It is greater for bonds of long duration than for those of short duration.

Intermediate Term: Definitions vary. Periods of 3 or 5 to 10 years are common.

Investment Adviser: A firm (or person) that (who), pursuant to a written contract mandated by the Investment Company Act of 1940 and approved by a fund's shareholders, regularly furnishes advice to a mutual fund with respect to buying or selling portfolio securities or is empowered to determine what securities should be purchased or sold. A fund's prospectus must identify the adviser, state the basis of compensation (0.5% of average net assets is common), and note any changes. The adviser may be an autonomous corporation or the direct or indirect subsidiary of such a company. If the latter, the prospectus must disclose who controls the adviser.

Investment Advisers Act of 1940: The act of Congress under which investment advisers are regulated by the SEC.

Investment Company: An issuer of securities, organized as a corporation, trust, or partnership, which holds itself out as being primarily in the business of pooling investors' money for the purpose of investing, reinvesting, and trading in corporate and government securities. The Investment Company Act of 1940 divided investment companies into three principal classes: face-amount certificate companies, unit investment trusts, and management companies. It further divided management companies into two types: open-end (also known as mutual funds—the type covered in this book) and closed-end.

Investment Company Act of 1940: The act of Congress that provides for the registration and regulation of investment companies by the SEC. It was intended to correct conditions, illuminated in an SEC study ordered by Congress in 1935, "which adversely affect the national public interest and the interest of investors." They included inadequate or inaccurate information regarding investment companies' securities and policies, management of investment companies in the self-interest of insiders, concentration of control through pyramiding, unsound or misleading accounting methods, excessive borrowing, and inadequate reserves.

Investment-Grade Bond: A bond receiving one of the top four ratings from the rating services: Aaa, Aa, A, or Baa from Moody's; AAA, AA, A, or BBB from Standard & Poor's.

Investment Income: The interest and dividend income received by a fund from issuers of the securities in its portfolio. It does not include gains realized from sales of securities. *See also* **Net Investment Income.**

Investment Objective: The goal that a mutual fund (or individual or other institutional investor) plans to achieve through investing in securities. Examples: current income, growth of income, long-term capital growth, capital preservation. A fund must declare its investment objective(s) at the front of its prospectus and state whether it (they) may be changed without a vote of a majority of its voting securities.

Investment Policy: The policy (policies) pursued to attain an investment objective. Most important: the type(s) of securities that are to be bought, any special investment practices or techniques that are to be employed, and any concentration in an industry or group of industries (or state, in case of a tax-exempt bond fund). A mutual fund must state its policies in its prospectus, including not only the types of securities to be bought but also, if appropriate, the proportions of assets to be invested in each. The prospectus must designate the policies that are fundamental—and, therefore not to be changed without approval of a majority of the fund's voting securities—and those that may be changed by management. Enlightened managements usually report to shareholders what they're doing and explain why.

Issuer: A corporation or government unit that issues bonds or other securities.

Junk Bond: *See* **High-Yield Bond.**

Load: *See* **Deferred Sales Load** and **Sales Load.**

Long Term: Used in the context of the time remaining until a bond matures, definitions vary. A common one: 10 years or more.

Management Fee: The annual fee that a fund pays its investment adviser for investment advice, portfolio management, and any administrative fees not included in "other expenses." Whatever the basis for compensation, to be disclosed in the prospectus, the fee is reported both in dollars and as a percentage of average net assets.

Market Risk: *See* **Interest Rate Risk.**

Market Timing: A technique intended to enable an investor to buy securities before their prices go up and to sell before their prices go down. Market timing services claim they enable investors to earn higher returns than they could by merely buying securities and holding them. Others question such claims, doubting whether anyone can consistently practice market timing successfully.

Maturity: The length of time until the date on which an issuer promises to repay the principal of a bond.

Medium-Grade Bond: Bonds rated A or Baa by Moody's, A or BBB by Standard & Poor's.

Minimum Initial Investment: The lowest amount of money a fund will accept to open an account. It may range from $250 to $25,000 or more. Few funds have no minimum at all. Minimums to open IRAs and other tax-sheltered accounts often are lower than those for taxable accounts.

Monetary Policy: The policy conducted by the Federal Reserve System to influence the availability and cost of money and credit in order to promote economic growth, employment, and price stability. It is implemented through the management of three tools: (1) open market operations (the Fed's purchases and sales of government securities in the open market in accordance with the directive of the Federal Open Market Committee, which can affect the interest rate at which banks lend to each other—known as the federal funds rate), (2) discount policy (the setting of the interest rate at which eligible banks may borrow funds from the 12 Federal Reserve Banks), and (3) reserve requirements (the level of reserves that commercial banks and other depository institutions must hold against deposits).

Money Market Mutual Fund: A fund that invests at least 80% of its assets in money market securities and seeks to maintain a stable share price, typically $1. To limit its exposure to interest rate risk, it is not permitted to have a weighted average maturity that exceeds 90 days.

Mortgage-Backed Securities: Securities that were conceived to tap additional capital resources for residential mortgages by expanding the secondary market for them. A typical MBS represents an interest in a pool of millions of dollars' worth of conventional or government-backed mortgages but is sold in denominations as small as $25,000. MBS investors receive monthly "pass-through" of principal and interest payments, as well as the unscheduled principal payments from homeowners who prepay their mortgages and the principal of foreclosed mortgages. Of greatest interest to bond funds—and bond fund investors—are MBS issued by lending institutions that originated the mortgages and guaranteed by Freddie Mac, Fannie Mae, and Ginnie Mae, and those both issued and guaranteed by Freddie Mac and Fannie Mae. (Ginnie Mae doesn't issue its own.) *See also* **Federal Home Loan Mortgage Corporation, Federal National Mortgage Association, Government National Mortgage Association,** and **Prepayment Risk.**

Municipal Bond: A bond issued by a state or local government (city, county, school district, special district, et al.) or one of its agencies to provide revenues— usually for capital expenditures—supplementing money collected from taxes and other sources. Municipal bonds are classified into two broad categories: general obligation bonds and revenue bonds. With certain exceptions, their interest payments are exempt from federal income tax and also may be exempt from state and local income taxes. *See also* **General Obligation Bond** and **Revenue Bond.**

Municipal Bond Fund: A mutual fund invested in municipal bonds. The exemption from income taxes of the interest payments received from the bonds' issuers is passed through to owners of a fund's shares. To call itself a tax-exempt fund, the SEC stipulates that a fund must have a fundamental policy requiring that at least 80% of its income will be exempt from federal income tax or that at least 80% of its assets will be invested in tax-exempt securities.

Municipal Bond Insurance: A form of insurance, introduced in 1971 and now written by several companies, that guarantees timely payment of principal and interest on municipal bonds in the event that issuers default. Policies may be bought by state and local governments to cover their new issues or by mutual funds to cover outstanding municipal bond issues in their portfolios.

Mutual Fund: The popular designation of an open-end investment company, which provides a medium for public investors to pool their money for investment in a professionally managed portfolio of government and/or corporate securities. A mutual fund may issue an unlimited number of shares and must stand ready to redeem (buy back) any investor's shares at the current NAV per share at any time. *See also* **Investment Company.**

NASD: *See* **National Association of Securities Dealers.**

NASDAQ: NASD's electronic securities quotations system through which eligible mutual funds' NAVs, offering prices, and other data are collected and disseminated daily to news media, quotation vendors such as Dow Jones and

Quotron, and brokers. To qualify for the media list, a fund must have 1,000 shareholders or $25 million in net assets. To stay on the list, a fund must have 750 holders or $15 million in net assets. To limit the space required to print the entire list, individual newspapers may impose higher minimums.

NAV: *See* **Net Asset Value per Share.**

National Association of Securities Dealers (NASD):   A self-regulatory organization, recognized in statute, which has jurisdiction over broker-dealers and may prescribe rules governing their handling of transactions in mutual funds and other securities. One of its rules established the maximums for the sales loads its members may charge when selling mutual fund shares. *See also* **NASDAQ** and **Sales Load.**

Net Asset Value (NAV) per Share: The value of one share of a mutual fund's common stock. It is obtained by subtracting its liabilities from the market value of its assets and dividing the resulting net by the number of its outstanding shares. NAV is the price at which a no-load fund's shares can be bought and at which all funds' shares must be redeemed. Funds imposing a front-end sales load add it to the NAV. Those imposing a deferred sales charge subtract it from the proceeds of share sales.

Net Investment Income: What remains of a fund's investment income after expenses are deducted; it's distributed as dividends to shareholders.

No-Load Fund: A mutual fund that markets its shares directly to the public and does not charge a sales load, whether of the "front-end" or "deferred" type, to compensate salespeople. A fund cannot be promoted as a no-load fund if it imposes a 12b-1 distribution fee, other asset-based sales charge, and/or service fee whose total exceeds 0.25% of average net assets per year, according to an NASD rule.

Nominal Interest Rate: The rate of interest paid on a bond in current dollars. If a $1,000 bond has a coupon promising annual interest payments totaling $75, it is said to have a nominal interest rate of 7.5%. *See also* **Real Interest Rate.**

Open-End Investment Company: *See* **Mutual Fund.**

Par: A bond's face value.

Portfolio: The financial assets—cash, money market instruments, bonds, preferred stocks, and/or common stocks—owned by an individual or an institutional investor such as a mutual fund.

Portfolio Manager: The employee of the investment adviser—or perhaps the principal owner—who handles the day-to-day management of the portfolio. Some funds have two co-managers. Others have committees to manage their portfolios. Since 1993, the SEC has required funds to disclose the names of portfolio managers and to advise shareholders of any changes.

Portfolio Turnover Rate: The rate at which the assets in a portfolio are changed during a year. SEC requires that a fund disclose its rate in the condensed financial information table at the front of its prospectus. For this purpose, the rate must be calculated by dividing the lesser of purchases or sales of portfolio securities for a given year by the monthly average of the value of the portfolio securities owned by the fund during the year.

Prepayment Risk: The risk that the owner of a Ginnie Mae or other mortgage-backed security will receive principal payments ahead of schedule because a drop in interest rates has led mortgagors to prepay their mortgages. Under the circumstances, investors won't realize the income they had expected for as long as they had expected it. Those reinvesting cash flows from MBS will have to invest the unexpected additional cash at the lower interest rates then prevailing.

Principal Underwriter: A mutual fund's principal underwriter is the firm that, pursuant to a written contract, acts as a principal in buying its shares for distribution or acts as agent in selling a fund's shares to dealers and/or to the public.

Promoter: The individual (company) who (which) initiated or directed a mutual fund's formation.

Prospectus: The pamphlet (part of the registration statement) that a mutual fund is required by the Securities Act of 1933 and the Investment Company Act of 1940 to provide investors when offering its securities for sale. Its purpose is to supply them essential financial and other information about a fund in a way that will assist them in making informed decisions about whether to buy the securities. It covers such things as the fund's investment objectives and policies, investment risks, management, costs, and distributions. No single document is more important to you as a fund shareholder. *See also* **Statement of Additional Information.**

Public Offering Price: The price (sometimes called the "asked" price) at which a fund's shares are sold to investors. For no-load funds, it's the net asset value (NAV) per share. For other funds, it's the NAV plus the sales charge.

Real Interest Rate: The rate of interest after adjustment for inflation, which is a more meaningful measure for some investors or borrowers than the nominal interest rate. If, for example, a bond has a 7.5% interest rate at a time when inflation is 3%, its real interest rate is 4.5%. A bond can have a negative real interest rate when inflation exceeds the nominal interest rate.

Redemption: An investor in a registered mutual fund has the right to request redemption of his or her shares—that is, to sell them back to the fund—at the NAV at any time and expect to be paid in seven days, except in an emergency or other unusual circumstances. (This contrasts with closed-end funds, whose investors sell their shares to other investors, via brokers, at their market value.)

Redemption Fee: A charge, other than a deferred sales charge, that is imposed by some funds on the redemption of shares. It is stated as a percentage of the amount redeemed.

Registration Statement: The document that a mutual fund must file with the SEC, in accordance with the Investment Company Act and Securities Act, prior to making a public offering of its shares. It is divided into three parts: (1) the prospectus (which investors must receive), (2) a statement of additional information (which investors may receive on request), and (3) other information (which is primarily for the SEC's scrutiny and retention).

Reinvestment Privilege: In lieu of cash payments, dividend and/or capital gains distributions can be automatically reinvested in additional shares of a fund, when requested by a shareholder. (A few funds that impose sales loads on ordinary share purchases also impose them on shares bought through reinvestment.)

Reinvestment Risk: The risk that the owner of a debt security, reinvesting interest received from its issuer in another security, will not be able to earn as much from the new investment because interest rates are lower. Investors eager to avoid this risk may buy zero-coupon bonds or target maturity funds that invest in them.

Revenue Bond: A class of municipal bonds backed only by the tolls, user fees, rents, and other revenues received from the activity (such as an airport, turnpike, housing project, industrial development, or pollution control project) for which a government entity issued them. They generally are more risky than general obligation bonds.

Sales Charge (Front-End Sales Load):   The difference between the public offering price (POP) at which a fund's shares are sold to the public by brokers, financial planners, or other sales agents (including an underwriter's own sales force) and the portion of the proceeds that is invested by the fund in behalf of an investor (or NAV per share). It's the sales commission that underwriters, dealers, and salespeople share. Under the Securities Exchange Act of 1934 and the Investment Company Act of 1940, the National Association of Securities Dealers has the authority to prohibit its members from selling a mutual fund's shares at a price that includes an excessive sales charge. An amendment to NASD's Rules of Fair Practice, approved by the SEC in October 1975 and effective in June 1976, set the maximum at 8.5% of the POP (or about 9.3% of the NAV) for funds without asset-based sales charges. It stipulated three conditions: (1) dividends could be reinvested at the NAV, (2) quantity discounts recognizing previous purchases had to be offered, and (3) minimum quantity discounts had to be made available. If a charge is imposed on reinvested dividends, the maximum sales charge is reduced to 7.25% of the POP. If none of the conditions is met, the maximum load drops to 6.25% of the POP. *See also* **Deferred Sales Load** and **No-Load Funds.**

Securities and Exchange Commission: An independent agency of the U.S. government, created under the Securities Exchange Act of 1934, which administers the laws covering the issuance and trading of securities. Its Division of Investment Management has responsibility for overseing the regulation of mutual funds, other investment companies, and investment advisers.

Short Term: Used in a mutual fund context, definitions vary. Sometimes the reference is to maturities that coincide with those of money market funds—that is, as short as a year. In a bond fund context, the reference is usually to periods ranging from 1 to 3 or 5 years.

Statement of Additional Information (SAI):   Also known as Part B of the prospectus, the SAI elaborates on information provided in a prospectus. SAIs must be made available to mutual fund investors on request at no charge.

Subchapter M: The portion of the Internal Revenue Code under which mutual funds that qualify as "regulated investment companies" are freed from the obligation to pay income taxes on their otherwise taxable income that is distributed to shareholders. To qualify, they must distribute at least 90% of their ordinary income to their shareholders—to whom the tax liabilities flow through—and meet certain other conditions, including one of adequate diversification.

(It's another provision in the code, Section 4982, that would subject a fund—and, thus, its shareholders—to an excise tax unless the fund distributes 98% of its ordinary income and capital gains annually.)

Tax-Exempt Fund: *See* **Municipal Bond Fund.**

Taxable Equivalent Yield: The yield you'd have to earn on a taxable bond fund to equal that of a tax-exempt bond fund.

Total Return: The growth (or decline) in the value of an investment in a mutual fund, calculated to include the assumed reinvestment in additional shares of income dividends and capital gains distributions. It is the most comprehensive measure of the results obtained by an investor from an investment and the most meaningful one for comparing the performance of various investments. Total returns covering various periods of years are expressed as average annual compounded rates by some, as cumulative rates by others.

An SEC rule, adopted in 1988 to prevent misleading advertising and to standardize performance data for easier comparison by investors, directs any fund using performance data in an advertisement or brochure to include average annual compounded total returns for the most recent 1-, 5-, and 10-year periods. The data, which must reflect sales charges, were mandated for three periods to show investors how returns can vary. They also may be included in a prospectus or statement of additional information. (If a fund has not been in operation for 5 or 10 years, data for the fund's lifetime can be substituted where appropriate.) Funds may add other return data if they wish, provided they are not misleading.

Results calculated for a fund by its management and by data services may differ slightly, depending on when the distributions are assumed to have been reinvested. Funds that charge sales loads also calculate and disseminate total returns adjusted for such charges, enabling you to make more meaningful comparisons with no-load funds.

Treasury Bill: A U.S. Treasury security, issued in minimum denominations of $10,000, maturing in 3, 6, or 12 months. Purchased at a price below its face value, it does not involve interest payments. An investor's return is the difference between the price paid and the proceeds received when a bill is sold or matures.

Treasury Bond: A U.S. Treasury security, issued in minimum denominations of $1,000, maturing in more than 10 years. Interest is paid semiannually.

Treasury Note: A U.S. Treasury security maturing in from 2 to 10 years. Minimum denominations are $5,000 for notes maturing in less than 4 years—that is, 2- and 3-year notes—and $1,000 for those maturing in 4 or more years. Interest is paid semiannually.

Treasury Securities: Interest-bearing obligations of the U.S. government, issued by the Treasury, through which it borrows money to finance expenditures that are not covered by revenues from taxes and other sources. *See also* **Treasury Bill, Bond,** and **Note.**

12b-1 Fees: Certain distribution costs incurred by a bond, stock, or money market fund (such as advertising and compensation for underwriters, brokers, or other sales personnel) that may be passed on annually to its shareholders. To do so, a fund must have a written plan, approved by independent directors and the shareholders in compliance with Rule 12b-1, which the SEC adopted in 1980. If a fund imposes a 12b-1 fee and other asset-based sales charge, it must say so in its prospectus and state the rate, which can run up to 0.75% of average net assets, according to a 1993 NASD rule. (Another 0.25% may be levied as a service fee.) If one owns a fund long enough, the cumulative cost of 12b-1 fees could be significant. Many funds charge both 12b-1 fees and loads; the fees are usually higher for funds with only one class of shares for which deferred sales loads are charged or for Class B shares of multiple class funds that also are subject to deferred loads.

VA-Guaranteed Mortgages: Mortgage loans guaranteed by the Department of Veterans Affairs (formerly the Veterans Administration).

Withdrawal Plan: The option that some funds give shareholders to withdraw a fixed amount of cash at regular intervals, invading principal when income distributions fall short of the requested sum.

Yield: Widely understood as the rate of current income received annually from an investment, expressed as a percentage of its principal or market value, but *inappropriate* as the basis for selecting a bond fund. A year's net investment income dividend distributions per share, divided by a fund's NAV—and more appropriately referred to as the distribution rate—can be misleading. It can be manipulated by a manager who invests in more speculative, higher-yielding securities—or engages in other speculative practices—to inflate the rate but in the process exposes principal to greater risk. Under an SEC rule adopted in 1988 that requires standardized computation of performance data for use in advertising and sales literature, bond funds must calculate their yields in a way that reflects the amortization of premiums for bonds selling above face value or discounts for bonds selling below. These yields, which are expressed as annualized rates for the most recent 30-day period, must also reflect sales loads, if any. So that investors will get a comprehensive picture of a fund's performance, the SEC stipulated that yield can only be advertised when accompanied by average annual total returns for the most recent 1-, 5-, and 10-year periods. *See also* **Net Investment Income, Total Return, and Yield to Maturity.**

Yield Curve: The graphic plotting of yields of debt securities for a range of maturities. The most widely published is the curve showing the yields of Treasury securities ranging from 3 months to 30 years. When the curve slopes up to the right—indicating that yields are higher as maturities become longer—it is said to have a normal shape.

Yield to Maturity: A more meaningful yield figure for a bond than current yield because it not only reflects the present value of all future interest payments at the coupon rate but also provides for the appreciation (depreciation) that will bring a bond selling at a discount (premium) back to par by the time it matures. A variation is yield to first call—a similar calculation reflecting the call price that would be paid prior to maturity for a callable bond on the first call date.

Yield Spread: The difference between yields of bonds having different quality or other attributes (such as the spread between Treasury and top-grade corporate securities of the same maturities).

Zero-Coupon Securities: Debt obligations of the U.S. Treasury and other issuers that are sold at discount from face value—the size of the discount depending on interest rates and maturities. Instead of periodic interest payments and ultimate principal repayment, zeros provide for a single payment of the face value at maturity. The difference between one's cost and the face value is the return that's earned when a zero is held to maturity. Zeros are popular with investors who wish to avoid reinvestment risk and who want specific sums to be available on a certain date in the future. At times they—and the target maturity funds that invest in them—can be extremely volatile, but this should not concern anyone holding them to maturity.

Index